STEPHEN POLIAKOFF

ON STAGE AND SCREEN

Robin Nelson is currently a Visiting Professor at the University of London, Central School, and an Emeritus Professor of Manchester Metropolitan University. He has published widely on the performing arts and media and on 'practice as research'. Professor Nelson is a co-founder of the international journal *Critical Studies in Television*, for which he has recently guest co-edited a special issue on Archiving (5/2, November 2010). His books include (co-edited with S. Bay-Cheng et al.) *Mapping Intermediality in Performance* (Amsterdam University Press, 2010) and *State of Play: Contemporary 'High-End' TV Drama* (Manchester University Press, 2007).

STEPHEN POLIAKOFF

ON STAGE AND SCREEN

Robin Nelson

Methuen Drama

Published by Methuen Drama 2011

Methuen Drama, an imprint of Bloomsbury Publishing Plc

1 3 5 7 9 10 8 6 4 2

Methuen Drama
Bloomsbury Publishing Plc
36 Soho Square
London W1D 3QY
www.methuendrama.com

ISBN 978 1 408 13108 4

Available in the USA from Bloomsbury Academic & Professional,
175 Fifth Avenue / 3rd Floor, New York, NY 10010.
www.BloomsburyAcademicUSA.com

A CIP catalogue record for this book is available from the British Library

Typeset by Mark Heslington Ltd, Scarborough, North Yorkshire
Printed and bound in Great Britain by Martins the Printers, Berwick upon Tweed

CONTENTS

ACKNOWLEDGEMENTS

First, I want to thank Stephen Poliakoff for several illuminating conversations, and producer Emma Lewis (formerly of talkback-thames) for assistance in tracking down films not readily available on DVD. I thank also Mark Dudgeon of Methuen Drama for commissioning the book and for helpful editorial advice. Professor John Bull and Dr Sarah Cardwell read the penultimate draft and gave helpful feedback, while Dr Avril Haworth, in addition to affording valuable insights on various drafts, assisted with editing and preparation of the book for publication. Thanks are due also to Barry Hanson, David Edgar and Richard Pinner for interview input, and the library staff at the British Library, BBC Written Archives, Manchester Metropolitan University and Central School, University of London for help with access to written materials. The BFI Library also facilitated viewings. I thank all for their support. I trust that I have done justice to the subject, that the facts are accurate and my interpretations of the works intelligible and insightful. As ever, some of the best ideas are other people's; the faults are all my own.

ABBREVIATIONS

BBC	British Broadcasting Corporation
BFI	British Film Institute
C4	Channel 4
ITV	Independent Television
NT	National Theatre
RSC	Royal Shakespeare Company

For Avril

and in memory of my father,
Donald Nelson

INTRODUCTION

The aim of this book is to afford an overview, and offer a framework for critical review, of the substantial career to date of writer-director Stephen Poliakoff. It is the first book-length study in English of a major, if quizzical, dramatist who, despite receiving many industry awards, has not always received the recognition – both in the UK and internationally – the book argues he deserves.[1] Whereas there have been book-length studies of several of his peers,[2] Poliakoff has received scant critical attention from academics, and the reasons why this might be so are touched upon in the discussion to come.[3] Following this Introduction, Chapter 1 addresses several senses in which the dramatist is not easy to categorise, working as he does across media. Even though his early plays directly address British culture in the 1970s, a sense of the Russian Jewish outsider drawn from his family history increasingly informs Poliakoff's work. Emerging initially as a theatre playwright, Poliakoff moved progressively into writing television drama and screenplays for feature film, ultimately directing his own scripts. This book takes the view that, while he has found considerable success in all media, Poliakoff's television work between 1999 and 2007 has been the most consistent, and the crowning glory, of his career to date. Chapter 2 defies the traditional chronological approach taken by studies of this kind to foreground this period of exceptionally impressive output for television.

The book otherwise deals with Poliakoff's published plays for the theatre,[4] and his 'films' (his preferred term for both his feature films for initial cinema release and his television dramas ranging from single plays to mini-series).[5] A chronological list of works is provided in Appendix A, while Appendix B lists the casts of the original productions. The availability of much of the film and television work on DVD (or videotape) has made it less necessary to expound those pieces as much as the earlier theatre plays, which are accessible today

1

mainly through scripts published by Methuen.[6] It is not possible in the scope of this book to discuss the many productions of Poliakoff's plays in the UK and internationally, but reference is made to initial productions, drawing upon press reviews – and, later, internet sources – to convey how the plays and 'films' were received at the time of first showing. Chapter 3 sets the context for a dramatist emerging in the early 1970s and further develops a critical framework, culminating in a sketch of the 'Poliakovian' for readers to consider as they explore what follows. Chapter 4 charts the meteoric rise of Poliakoff to become a resident writer at the National Theatre (NT) at just twenty-four years old.

From here the book broadly follows the progressive stages of Poliakoff's career while grouping together works across media which share themes or approaches. Though he is well aware of the opportunities and constraints of different media – both in their technical and industrial dimensions, and in audience and critical response – Poliakoff does not make sharp distinctions between them in his writing process.[7] He writes primarily to explore what he wants to say in a dramatic form. Poliakoff's theatre work has been described by Charles Sturridge as 'putting the cinema into theatre',[8] and at times Poliakoff has reciprocally attempted to restore to the medium of television something of its theatrical heritage, notably in *Shooting the Past* (1999).[9] Accordingly, Chapters 5, 6 and 7 address clusters of texts without sharply differentiating the theatre work from the film and television output, though attention is paid to medium differences. Given more than forty substantial works, it has not been possible to address them all in equal measure. While most works are discussed, a few regrettably receive no more than summary comment. Emphasis is placed upon bringing out common concerns and approaches. At times, the resonances are specific – as in the reworking into the film, *Close My Eyes* (1991) of the early play *Hitting Town* (1975) – but traces, of which Poliakoff himself may not even be consciously aware, will be otherwise identified through readings of both the texts and the intriguing life story of the Poliakoff family. Chapter 8 addresses 'feature films and films for television' leading to Poliakoff's return to features after a decade break with his most recent work, *Glorious 39*

(2009). Chapter 9 revisits the 'Poliakovian', offering a critical summary of Poliakoff's achievements to date.

References to Poliakoff's writings are given in the body of the text; all other references are located in endnotes.

1 POLIAKOFF
A LIFE ON STAGE AND SCREEN

First impressions

Meeting Stephen Poliakoff, as other interviewers have noted, is by turns a disconcerting and engaging experience.[1] You are conscious first of all of an energy emanating from a somewhat boyish figure, from a man small in stature, casually dressed in jeans and a crumpled cotton shirt and jacket. A shock of dark curls and a beard frame bespectacled but intense eyes. It might be a character from Chekhov or Dostoevsky. As like as not, Poliakoff will be pacing, distracted. He will be twiddling a drinking straw in one hand and clutching a cell phone in the other, frequently glancing at it as if a call or text message is urgently awaited. He speaks in nervously energetic bursts, slightly wary, as if he is not sure what you might want him to say. But, once settled and engaged in a conversation, he is remarkably sharp about his own work. He has a powerful memory and responds well to a challenge, refining points put to him. When I note that his work shows a strong historical consciousness, he agrees but stresses that it is never sentimentally nostalgic. When I raise and challenge his observation made two decades ago that his work is a reaction against a Brechtian approach to theatre, he recalls that in his time at the National he worked on a piece based on Brecht's poems and was surprised to find he shared a sensibility with his fellow-playwright. A formidable intelligence is engaged but occasionally leavened by a self-deprecating laugh. When he learns I am consulting the BBC Written Archive, he remembers the library and its staff with enthusiastic affection and wants me to pass on best wishes.[2]

Authorship in context

The primary aim of this book is to chart the career of the dramatist, Stephen Poliakoff, and to afford a framework for its critical assessment. In so doing, however, it is impossible to avoid reference to the dramatist and his biography since the plays, films and TV pieces are shot through with deep personal and familial traits. In the early twenty-first century, it may seem idiosyncratic, if not outmoded, to inform an overview of an author's work with key aspects of his life. According to the poststructuralist theories of Barthes and Foucault, the author has long been dead and the authorial voice silenced. Barthes famously asserted that 'writing is the destruction of every voice, of every point of origin' and Foucault predicted that 'the author function will disappear'.[3] We inhabit an age in which texts are deemed to be open to productive readings in a field of intertextual play. The identity of the individual writer or reader is similarly thought to be multiple and fluid. As Giddens (1987: 88) summarises: 'Just as the primacy accorded to the author is an historical expression of individualism of the Age of Man, so [in poststructuralism] the "I" of the author is a grammatical form rather than a flesh and blood agent.'

I want to propose at the outset that it is possible to delineate authorial signature within and across a writer's works without indulging in the 'intentional fallacy'[4] or, as Barthes puts it, falling in with 'the myth of filiation'.[5] This book will bring out characteristic themes and patterns in Poliakoff's work, noting his view that all his work in television 'has been completely self-generated' and that he is 'proud that [he has] consistently done individual work – in film/television and theatre – work that has been unlike any other work'.[6] But, however much Poliakoff aims to inscribe his vision in original works, he cannot wholly determine the readings of viewers and he cannot entirely avoid established generic forms. This book thus pursues a 'both-and' sense that authors – and indeed audience members – retain some agency, the extent of which is nevertheless bounded by the broader contexts in which they function.

In the arts today, the dominant model of encounter, extending Barthes's notion of the 'writerly text' (see 1977: 155–64), involves the interactive engagement of the experiencer drawn into the co-production of textual significance. But Poliakoff and his *oeuvre* pose a challenge to the ready dismissal by some poststructuralists of the idea of work with an authorial signature. Poliakoff consciously occupies the last bastion of the playwright in a lineage of 'writers' theatre' and 'authored television', his approach and work sustaining a liberal-individualist tradition of free expression through authorship (see Nelson 2006). Indeed, he has emerged as an 'auteur'[7] in a medium which has not typically been associated with authorship since its very early days.[8] By directing his own screenplays in recent years, Poliakoff has brought together the auteurist tradition of the art-film director along with the dominance of the television playwright in former times when the aim of the director and production team was to realise the writer's vision on the stage or small screen.[9]

From an early twenty-first-century standpoint, a time when the industrial process of writing for television in Britain (following a practice, long since dominant in America) is one of teams of writers for seasons of series or serial output, opportunities today for work of substance written by an individual are significantly reduced. Partly because his early success as an NT playwright carries high cultural status, however, Poliakoff now holds a position of relative power when it comes to negotiating working conditions. His contemporary, Trevor Griffiths, famously told Edward Braun in 1979 that he saw writing for the stage 'largely as the necessary means of sustaining a reputation which would enhance his bargaining power when dealing with television'.[10] A very substantial output of successful playscripts realised in prestigious theatre spaces has no doubt enhanced Poliakoff's standing in the film and television industries. In television at least, he can now insist on maximum creative control over his output, demanding, for example, a longer period of rehearsal with actors than is typical of moving-image media. Moreover, besides writing and directing his screen works over the past two decades, he sits in with editors and works very closely with other contributors such as composers. Indeed, one of the reasons he has eschewed offers from Hollywood is that its working methods do not afford anybody such a position. As he has remarked, 'I am much more like Mike Leigh or Ken Loach; I just want to do my own thing ... It's about having complete artistic control.'[11] In itself, this status is a rare achievement, matched only in British television culture perhaps by the legendary Dennis Potter (1935–94) and by the avowedly idiosyncratic Alan Bennett (1934–) whose work also spans stage and screen, but otherwise unparalleled in modern practice.[12]

If, however, the auteurist approach staunchly defended by Poliakoff is redolent of times past, his concerns are typically of the moment and his work might be characterised as a progressive chronicle of the contemporary. In Poliakoff's early plays, located amid shopping malls, greasy spoon cafes, tower blocks and pop radio stations, he documents the brutalist anomie of 1960s architecture and its impact on a dreary, strife-ridden early 1970s culture after the Summer Party of Woodstock and the 1960s liberalism were over. In subsequent theatre plays he addresses the mid-1970s nuclear stand-off and the rise of racism and the National Front. In the 1980s he deals with Cold War suspicion, pop festivals and runaway kids, while his 1990 plays figure the tensions of immigration policy and the popularity, through increased affordability, of video recording technologies. Later television work revisits the 1970s and charts a not unambiguous progress through the Thatcherite 1980s to burgeoning global capitalism in the 1990s.

The plays are by no means historical documentaries, however, since Poliakoff the playwright is interested in affording a fresh, often quirky, perspective on characters confronted by predicaments. His avowed aim is 'to make the audience look at the world slightly differently'.[13] In Chapter 3, the motives and implications of an invitation to what I call 'complex seeing', will be located in the political context of theatre in the late 1960s and early 1970s through which Poliakoff emerged.

Besides broad socio-cultural commentary, there is a strain of more overt historic documentation in specific Poliakoff works. From *Berlin Days* and *Clever Soldiers* in the 1970s, through *Breaking the Silence* in the 1980s and *Talk of the City* and *Shooting the Past* in the 1990s, and, most recently, *The Lost Prince* and *Glorious 39*, Poliakoff reveals his concern with European history, partly through public events and partly through his own family story. As the descendant of Russian émigré Jews, Poliakoff is conscious of a need to be watchful lest

Europe's latent totalitarian tendencies in the first half of the twentieth century erupt again. Historical research informs this strand of plays and films in which specific events are confronted. Since resonances of his family's experience are, however, more or less audible and visible in much of the work, it is helpful at the outset to recount the family story.

Backstory

Stephen Poliakoff was born in Holland Park, west London, in 1952 to an irascible Russian Jewish father, Alexander (born 1910), and a formidable Anglo-Jewish mother, Ina (born 1913). His parents, having met at a tea-dance, were married in 1939 and had children relatively late. Stephen was brought up in material comfort with an older brother and two sisters, and he was educated at Westminster School and Cambridge. Before completing a degree in history, however, Stephen left King's College at the end of his second year to pursue a career in the theatre – and, subsequently, film and television.

A charismatic figure, Joseph, Stephen's paternal grandfather, had been born into a middle-class family but presented himself in the manner of an aristocratic Russian count.[14] An inventor, he was the first person in the East to record sound on film, possibly the first in the world (as recounted in *Breaking the Silence* and MacGowan 1955). Following the Russian Revolution, the family fell on hard times and was close to starvation, holed up at their house 60 kilometres outside Moscow with a diet of tiny amounts of millet. A chance meeting in March 1920, the result of a broken-down vehicle and the need to use a telephone, brought a member of Lenin's government to Joseph's door. Despite being, in Poliakoff's own account (2008), 'an arrogant and snobbish figure', Joseph found favour with the commissar. His summary appointment as telephone inspector of the Northern District, with the assignment of his own special train and a reasonable amount of income and food, almost certainly saved the family from starvation.[15] Later, Joseph assisted in the development of an auto-mated telephone exchange for Moscow. After Lenin's death in 1924, just ahead of Stalin's anti-Semitic pogroms, Joseph escaped to England with his wife and son, the family's wealth distilled into a diamond concealed in the heel of a shoe. If that diamond had been discovered it is highly likely that they would all have been shot. It is thus unsurprising that Stephen Poliakoff's work is haunted by an awareness of the precariousness of Jews in history and their plight under the totalitarian regimes of Stalin and Hitler alike.

Alexander, Stephen's father, inherited something of Joseph's electrical engineering talents and invented the hospital 'bleeper' in the 1950s. Despite this innovation, the electronics business he ran (with his father's support until Joseph's death in 1958), 'teetered on the edge of bankruptcy before it finally flowered in the 1970s'.[16] In Stephen's dramatic works, Jews ambitious in business often encounter setbacks as a result of prejudice (see, for example, *Playing with Trains* and *Century*). Alexander aspired to rub shoulders with the rich and famous and, in the early 1950s, Winston Churchill was a customer for hearing aids which the Poliakoff business developed. In 1953, however, the Churchill contract was summarily terminated; the likely cause transpired only much later: it seems MI5 were keeping the Poliakoff family under surveillance in the light of its long-standing links with the Soviet trade delegation, and feared Churchill was being bugged.[17]

Alexander regarded Russia as his homeland, having spent his formative years there. Aged six, he had witnessed some events of the 1917 October Revolution from his bedroom window in the family apartment opposite the Kremlin in Red Square and, aged nine, he had experienced the hardships noted above.[18] Throughout his life in England he felt an outsider, scarcely suppressing the loss and pain of exile. Though in much less straitened material circumstances, Stephen's own formative years were spent amid an atmosphere of thwarted paternal ambition and a sense of being somewhat foreign, despite the family's relative wealth and success. Bad-tempered and *déraciné*, Alexander cannot have been an easy father. He sustained a strong sense of the past, of Joseph and life in Russia, recounting the past at most family mealtimes (Poliakoff 2008). In the light of his own experience, however, Alexander strongly encouraged his children to be ambitious and to be original.[19] They did not fall short.[20]

The legacy of science and technology on the paternal side is overtly carried through the siblings and manifests itself in Stephen's work in a demonstrable awareness of new technologies and other scientific developments – for example, in *Remember This* and *Playing with Trains*. Stephen's Russian paternal grandmother, the absent subject of the eponymous play, *Granny* (see below), inhabited the attic and 'instilled in him a continuing fascination with the darker and more complex shades of European history' (Gilbert 2006). But it is from the maternal side, perhaps, that Stephen inherits his love of theatre. His mother, Ina, a descendant relative of the wealthy Montagu banking family, was a would-be actress, while her mother, an elegant and glamorous figure in Stephen's memory, wrote plays on Jewish themes.[21] A sense of time, place and heritage are all important in that their traces are visible in Stephen's work. Indeed, his ambition as a writer is no doubt motivated by the drive of his Russian Jewish ancestry but nuanced by what, in his own account, was a 'classic English preparatory and public school education' in London.[22]

Outline career trajectory

Not cut out to be an engineer, young Stephen found himself a slightly awkward teenager at Westminster School with ambitions to be a thespian. When his first attempts at acting in school plays (in productions of *The Tempest* and *Billy Budd*) were derided by teachers, he turned instead to writing. His first play to receive a public showing was initially performed by his fellow-pupils at Westminster, when he was sixteen.[23] *Granny* (1969)

> concerns two teenage couples and in particular David their leader. It is David who decides that they should not turn up for the final performance of their satirical revue, amused by the idea of the audience waiting indefinitely, who tricks the middle-aged housekeeper into thinking that a German friend has come to London to see her, and who persuades Granny's male companion that Granny (who lives in a flat upstairs and is never seen) is dead. (Kerensky 1969)

The play was revived for a series of amateur performances Poliakoff himself set up at the Abbey Community Centre, west London. It was here that Oleg Kerensky reviewed the play for *The Times*, famously reporting (ibid.) that it was 'more dramatic, with greater command of dialogue and psychological insight than many plays by older authors which have been seen, for example, at the Royal Court'. However, any sense that Poliakoff was to embark on a distinguished career as a play-wright was called in question by his mother, who told him when he was seventeen that his career was 'going nowhere'.[24]

Though he continued to write plays, he found himself reluctantly reading history at Cambridge, from his point of view a 'stuffy' way of life to which he never took, and which he summarily abandoned following the professional staging of *A Day with My Sister* at the Edinburgh Traverse (1971).[25] Two further publicly performed but unpublished plays followed: *Bambi Ramm* (Hampstead Theatre Club, 1970), and the aforementioned *A Day with My Sister*, produced by the up-and-coming Michael Rudman and directed by the playwright David Halliwell, with schoolmate Nigel Planer taking the lead.[26] Poliakoff's next theatre contribution was, in his own dismissive view, a few lines in the collaboratively written *Lay-by* (1971, see Chapter 3). The most significant thing to arise from this adventure is what Poliakoff learned from the experience, namely that he was not cut out to be part of a writers' collective such as were fashionable in the late 1960s and that, unlike many of his contemporaries, he would not initially pursue a Brecht-derived dramaturgy (see Chapter 3). As he remarks of *Clever Soldiers*, the play is 'a reaction to the Brechtian approach to theatre, and in this case to history plays in particular' (Poliakoff 1997: ix). A Brechtian influence informs some of Poliakoff's later plays but, at this early stage in his career, he aimed to 'reach an audience through vivid, tactile emotional theatre: a commitment to visceral writing' (ibid.).

Following Kerensky's review, the Royal Court sent its literary manager, Christopher Hampton, to check out the apparent prodigy, and he introduced Poliakoff to the literary agent Peggy Ramsay, who took him on.[27] His career soon gathered momentum and his output became prolific. In the six years between *Lay-by* and *Strawberry Fields*

(1977), the first production in the Cottesloe, the NT's black-box studio space, Poliakoff stormed on to the London stage with nine plays performed at the Bush, the Little Theatre, Hampstead Theatre and the Royal Court (for full list with dates, see Appendix A). Having won one of two Thames TV playwrights' bursaries to become a writer-in-residence at the National Theatre in 1976, the trajectory of Stephen Poliakoff's career can genuinely be described, contrary to his mother's prediction, as meteoric.[28]

Like other dramatists of his day, however, Poliakoff was soon attracted by the scale of potential audiences in television.[29] Still young, he found success in the medium in which he has arguably done his best work, and which gave rise to a 'second starburst' in the late 1990s and early noughties. Poliakoff's break into television came in 1977 with *Stronger than the Sun*, directed by Michael Apted and launched in the legendary 'Play for Today' (BBC1) strand. Poliakoff followed with his first film for television, *Bloody Kids*, directed by Stephen Frears.[30] On its heels, a second TV film, *Caught on a Train*, directed by Peter Duffell, was transmitted in the BBC2 'Playhouse' strand on 31 October 1980, winning an award for 'best single play'. Thus, not yet thirty years of age, Poliakoff had established himself as a playwright literally on the National stage and as a screenwriter for both film and television.

In the early 1980s, Poliakoff continued to write screenplays. A second 'Play for Today', *Soft Targets* (1982), was followed the next year by *Runners* (1983), both directed by Charles Sturridge.[31] *Runners*, Poliakoff's first feature film, premièred at the Gate Cinema, Notting Hill on 4 August 1983, before a limited cinema release and subsequent television transmission in 1984 in Channel 4's 'Film on Four' slot. Throughout the 1980s Poliakoff continued to write also for the theatre, averaging a play every other year mainly in London venues, without ever quite repeating the impact of his youth. While most of his works received at worst 'mixed reviews', there were some which might be regarded as relative failures. *The Summer Party* (1980) was not a great success at Sheffield Crucible. Indeed, according to Robin Thornber, 'it was a complete disaster',[32] and, even more strident, Ned Chaillet claims that 'Mr Poliakoff gets all the details of reality wrong'.

The play centres on Kramer, a self-assured, controlling police chief constable who quells an incipient riot at a pop festival which happens largely off-stage. Chaillet found that 'the whole thing was completely implausible'.[33] Irving Wardle (1981) thought *Favourite Nights*, in which circumstances entrap a young woman to be a language teacher by day and 'escort' by night, 'a feeble piece' at the Lyric, Hammersmith in 1981. In W. W. Demastes's (1996: 331) judgement of this period of his career, Poliakoff 'has yet fully to replace his earlier accepted and understandable aggressive antagonism with a later, expected vision'. Indeed, when in *Capturing Mary*, young Mary remarks, 'When you have success . . . without really thinking about it when you are very young . . . your confidence can go amazingly quickly when things go wrong' (Poliakoff 2007: 176), she might even be echoing a slight frustration on Poliakoff's part that, after its initial meteoric rise, his career – though highly successful in terms of regularly published work in significant venues – was on slow burn rather than flash ignition.

In 1987, however, Poliakoff's career took a significant turn when he directed his own screenplay, *Hidden City* (Channel 4 1988), which was well received when it premièred at the Venice Film Festival. His next film, *Close My Eyes*, made a significant impact, and thereafter, in spite of a couple of feature films (*Food of Love* 1997, and *The Tribe* 1998) which were less successful, Poliakoff has come increasingly to be recognised as a writer-director, the auteur in film and television, indicated above. In his 'second starburst', the subject of the next chapter, Poliakoff wrote and directed a particularly prolific and impressive output for television. Most recently he has returned to feature film with *Glorious 39*, released in the cinema on 20 November 2009.

Poliakoff has realised forty-two substantial works – twenty-three theatre plays and nineteen screenplays for film and television – in a professional career over thirty-nine years to date, throughout which he has won prestigious awards. As early as 1976, he won the *Evening Standard*'s Most Promising Playwright Award for *Hitting Town* and *City Sugar*. He won a BAFTA Award for the Best Single Play for *Caught on a Train* in 1980. In 1992 he won the *Evening Standard*'s Best British Film Award for *Close My Eyes* and, in 1996, *Blinded by the Sun* won the London Critics' Circle Best Play Award, followed, in

1997, with the Laurence Olivier Theatre Award for Best New Play of 1996. In 2001, Poliakoff was awarded the Prix Italia and the Royal Television Society Best Drama Award for *Shooting the Past*. In 2002 he won the Dennis Potter Award at the 2002 BAFTAs for *Perfect Strangers* (2001), and Best Writer and Best Drama at the Royal Television Society Awards. *The Lost Prince* (2003) gained three Emmy Awards in 2005 including Outstanding Mini Series. Poliakoff's most recent work for the BBC includes *Friends and Crocodiles* (2006) and *Gideon's Daughter* (also 2006) which won two Golden Globes and a Peabody Award in 2007.

Poliakoff's achievements in British theatre and television and his European outlook have not afforded the broader exposure in America that many feel he deserves.[34] Despite this constraint, John Patterson has recently remarked that, when introduced to Poliakoff's work, many Americans are hooked by it:

> Whenever my American friends ask me to name a good English director they've not heard of, I always push them towards the work of Stephen Poliakoff . . . And those who take up my recommendation/challenge usually come back about three weeks later, after a bracing immersion in whatever traces of Poliakoff can be found in LA's video stores, filled with gratitude and suddenly obsessed with Poliakoff's recurring themes: ancient family secrets, the power of images and documents to realign our understanding of histories both national and familial, and London as a city of secrets, forever yielding up surprises and shocks from its subterranean depths and farthest-flung outer suburbs; all somehow viewed by Poliakoff with the fresh-peeled eyeballs of a newly landed immigrant.[35]

It would seem, then, to be only a matter of time before Stephen Poliakoff gets the wider international recognition which sparked with *Close My Eyes* in 1991 but has subsequently failed fully to ignite. The Emmy awards for *The Lost Prince* may be a sign of things to come.

Life into work

As remarked, it is not fashionable today to read works in relation to the author's life as manifest in his or her texts. In the case of Stephen Poliakoff, however, the work is so much informed by the life that it would be unwise to overlook repeated tropes and themes which resonate with the dramatist's personal and family history. An obvious example of where personal biography directly informs Poliakoff's writing is the treatment, in *Breaking the Silence*, of his grandfather's experience of trying to complete his work adding soundtrack to image in cine-film technology in straitened circumstances after the Russian Revolution.

Less directly, but none the less resonantly, a successful and wealthy engineer in *Playing with Trains* has made a fortune from a brilliant development in gramophone technology but nevertheless bemoans the lack of support for invention and innovation in British industry. Eccentric in his dress and behaviour, protagonist Bill Galpin resembles Poliakoff's grandfather. Like his father, Galpin is an outsider who has difficult relations with the British establishment and his children alike. At least in Timothy Spall's presentation of him in a radio adaptation of the play (BBC Radio 4 2010), Galpin is genial enough, with admirable ecological concerns and a willingness to back young talent, but his fierce energy, his constant mobility and his conviction that ultimately he knows best, are not endearing. In particular, his relationship with his daughter, Roxanna, is fraught with tension. Echoing Poliakoff's trajectory, she drops out of Cambridge and, though she has the talent to follow her father's footsteps into engineering, chooses a life in the arts. Set over two decades beginning in the late 1960s, *Playing with Trains* carries clear echoes of Poliakoff's tense relationship with his engineer father. But, as ever, the family history is reworked into the needs of the play, in which there is a tension between admiration for innovators with drive and an awareness of the destructive potential of extreme single-mindedness.

Even less direct, but no less telling, are the events at the centre of the narrative of *The Lost Prince*, which resonate with both public and personal aspects of Poliakoff's life and work. They involve a visit to

George V of the King's Russian cousins, the Romanovs, shortly before the latter family is virtually wiped out in an act of slaughter at the crux of the events of the 1917 Russian Revolution. Though in one sense these historical events have nothing to do with Poliakoff's family history, there is a resonance of the, not royal, but established upper-middle-class Russian Poliakoffs being displaced by the impact of world historical events. As producer John Chapman summarises, *The Lost Prince* 'intertwines a familial story with massive tectonic shifts in world politics . . . a cataclysmic period in history when the great powers of Europe represented by one family had a collective nervous breakdown'.[36] Furthermore *The Lost Prince* is made to feel familial, beyond the facts of a mere encounter between two families, by its dominant point of view. This is the perspective of Johnnie, the youngest son of King George V and Queen Mary, who was kept hidden from public view on account of his epilepsy and seemingly autistic learning difficulties. In consequence, Johnnie is afforded only stolen glimpses of the big events of history, often peeping out at them from behind blinds and curtains. On one occasion, Johnnie, wearing striped pyjamas (having crept out of bed along with his elder brother), witnesses through the balustrades of a balcony the grand banquet held by his father for his Romanov cousins and a host of dignitaries.

This viewpoint has both specific and general resonances for Poliakoff. On one level, it directly echoes the experience of his father who, as a young boy in pyjamas, witnessed some of the events of the Russian Revolution from the window of the apartment in Red Square. Poliakoff (2008) has noted that his father was 'an interesting witness, with a child's-eye view of great events'. Secondly, Poliakoff's sympathy with the plight of Johnnie and his perspective on the world rests partly also in his father's and his own experience of being an outsider. The well-documented nervous tic, apparent in Stephen Poliakoff's compulsive twiddling of a drinking straw, is, in his own account, a trait shared by his siblings, though manifest in different ways.[37] Significantly, the equivalent viewpoint of Johnnie – witnessing major historical changes but viewing them from the edge of the arena – features sufficiently often in Poliakoff's work to amount to a dramaturgic strategy combining intimacy and historical grandeur by deploying a perspective on great events from a nearby, but concealed, angle of vision.

Apart from his short time at Cambridge, Poliakoff has lived all his life in London, travelling frequently across the city on public transport to gain inspiration or to visit specific sites.[38] Buses and trains and the architecture of London locations inform his writing. Indeed, another way of characterising some of his work is social change as reflected in the dynamics of England's capital city. A Croydon estate is the location and context of *Shout Across the River*, while Canary Wharf in the process of construction looms large in *Close My Eyes*. The iconic London Routemaster bus nostalgically graces Paul's birthday party picnic in *Friends and Crocodiles*, as well as serving as a signature 'wipe' in several film sequences. The site of Crystal Palace features in *The Tribe*, and the network of tunnels underlying London, now used mainly for government storage, haunts *Sweet Panic* (1996), *Hidden City* (1988), and *Perfect Strangers* (2001). Poliakoff is personally an obsessive who writes repeatedly about obsessions, often set in literal or metaphorical tunnels relating to anxieties about dark pasts. This is not to say that his works are simply biographical, but to observe that distinctive personal and familial preoccupations inform them.

Poliakoff's deep European consciousness, besides being embodied in him through his family history, is grasped cognitively through his continuing study of socio-historical circumstances. When, for example, he remarks of the context of *Glorious 39*, that, if the English upper classes had won the day in respect of appeasement of Hitler, he would not be here, he speaks knowledgeably of Jewish history as well as feelingly (Poliakoff 2009: viii). Indeed, it is Poliakoff's cognitive understanding which prevents the work from lapsing into nostalgia or sentimentality. Seen more from a cultural materialist than a biographical point of view, a social context or major historical event is typically evident in the hinterground of Poliakoff narratives such that the agency of the individual – or the lack of it – is located in a broader socio-historical structure.

Critical review

In spite of many awards and critical acclaim in the British industrial context, Poliakoff has been overlooked in the academy because, from the outset of his career, he has been contentious and difficult to place. The liberal-humanist tradition in which Poliakoff is located unfashionably emphasises the distinctive originality – the genius even – of creative practitioners. It plays down ways in which contexts might speak through the texts and emphasises the prescient vision of the gifted writer – in the Romantic tradition of the *Vates*, the prophets and soothsayers. The title of one journalistic profile constructs Poliakoff in this tradition as an 'obsessive teller of awkward truths' (Butler 2001). As this book unfolds, different perspectives will be afforded on how Poliakoff has extended his father's sense of being something of an outsider.

Though not wishing to undervalue Poliakoff's distinction, my own sense of things is one of 'agency in structure'. Following thinkers such as Zygmunt Bauman, I hold that 'systems make individuals not the other way round'.[39] And, indeed, Poliakoff's setting of characters in predicaments is consistent with this approach. As Matthew Martin has remarked, Poliakoff's

> [c]haracters tend to define themselves not so much in terms of their own independent beliefs and attitudes, nor in terms of other characters, but in terms of their environment . . . Their reactions to these environmental forces reveal not so much how we should judge these individuals, but how we should understand the dynamics of their lives in connection with contemporary urban life. (Martin 1993: 197)

It is precisely Poliakoff's awareness of a socio-historical context that grounds even his most abstract and metaphorical of works, and problems arise when this grounding is not firmly established.

Furthermore, though Poliakoff's work may be more self-generated than most, it functions in a context of generic expectations people might have of theatre, film or television. For example, part of the success of Poliakoff's television work since 1999 rests upon its resonance with the popular genre of period drama, itself enhanced by the capacity of digital television for deeper and denser imagery in comparison with earlier technologies. Poliakoff does not subscribe to the heritage drama nostalgia of 'romance in bonnets', but access to his more complex work is nevertheless afforded by its visual style. All artists function within an industrial context and, though he may be an ambitious individualist, Poliakoff is by no means an unworldly, romantic author. On the contrary, he is a shrewd self-publicist, acutely aware of the need to make himself and his work visible in contemporary media culture to the point where his standard media tag is now 'the award-winning Stephen Poliakoff'.

Another aspect of my notion of 'agency in structure' is that I see the reading of both texts and contexts as relational and dialogic matters. While I have striven in this book to be accurate about the facts of Poliakoff's career, the following accounts of his texts (playscripts, productions, television plays and films) constitute readings informed by my understanding of the writer in the contexts of the industry, of history, of textual genre and of intertextuality. Contextual forces sometimes shape Poliakoff's voice and writing even when he is consciously resisting those forces – as, for example, in his commitment to 'slow television' in developing *Shooting the Past* at a time when it was axiomatic in the television industry that the pace had to be fast to grab and hold an audience (see Chapter 2).

Given that readings are relational, I should acknowledge where I am coming from in respect of what follows. Of a similar age to Poliakoff, I am a straight, white male who, through my profession, have emerged into the middle class from beginnings more humble than his. My political disposition might accordingly be more to the left than Poliakoff's liberal-left (Fabian) socialism (see Chapter 3). Having grown up in north London very close to Jewish and other ethnic immigrant communities, I share both his feel for the city and an awareness of the dislocations of European (and world) history. I have lived through the same socio-cultural changes. My father, like Poliakoff's, is a formidable man who had high expectations of his children, fuelled in part by a sense of thwarted ambition. I have been involved all my life with theatre, film and television as practitioner, researcher and teacher. In my writing about television drama since the 1980s, I have unpacked and championed practices of 'quality television' (see Nelson 1997, 2007), some of which, like Poliakoff's, have resisted commercial drift. Though I endeavour to take account of other viewpoints, I am not primarily coming from a feminist, youth culture, postcolonialist, gay or other positioned epistemological standpoint beyond that acknowledged.

From my point of view, Poliakoff's work is distinctive in that it reveals identifiable patterns of tropes and thematic concerns articulated in a particular voice, but it is also locatable in relation to established contexts and genres. I am not simply aiming to read the man through the work in a liberal-humanist tradition; nor do I attempt to explain away the author by over-emphasising 'determinant' contextual forces. In my reading, history – and, in particular, family history – writes Poliakoff as much as he writes it. Indeed, the individualist position he adopts is significantly influenced by the ambitions of his grandfather and father to make their mark in the world. As Paul Reisner embarks on a medical research career in *Century*, his Eastern European Jewish father exhorts him to 'be the best – (*shouting*) – and why shouldn't you be? (*shouting through the dust*) The absolute best' (1997a: 312). Alexander Poliakoff wanted no less for his children. Though he did not follow the family engineering path, Stephen's choice of a career in the theatre was encouraged as long as he strove to be original.

As I propose to tell it then, the story of *Stephen Poliakoff: On Stage and Screen* is one of agency in structure.[40] It adopts a 'both-and' strategy since Poliakoff's life and work afford an interesting case study of the ways in which an authorial voice might be discerned across a range of texts, which nevertheless relate intertextually to each other and to other texts.

2 A SECOND STARBURST
TV MINI-SERIES 1999–2007

Stephen Poliakoff's work is now better known than it has ever been courtesy of his remarkable output for television, beginning with *Shooting the Past* (1999) and followed in quick succession by *Perfect Strangers* (2001) and *The Lost Prince* (2003). Within three years, another burst of energy produced *Friends and Crocodiles* (January 2006) and *Gideon's Daughter* (February 2006), which were initially commissioned as parts of a trilogy.[1] Another two-parter, *Joe's Palace* and *Capturing Mary*, was followed by a BBC 'Culture Show' commissioned supplement *A Real Summer* (all transmitted in 2007). Since he refers to all his moving image work as 'films', Poliakoff might baulk at my referring to these pieces as 'TV mini-series' and, indeed, some of the above might stand alone as cinema films. But, though not entirely adhering to moulds, the works equate to contemporary television's revival of the long-form series or serial narrative in offering more than three hours of television over two or more episodes. Indeed, *The Lost Prince*, which might also be seen as a two-part film, won an Emmy for 'outstanding mini-series'.[2]

To those familiar with Poliakoff only through his recent output on television, it may even come as a surprise that he is an acclaimed theatre playwright who had an equivalent period of prolific output in the theatre in the early 1970s (see Chapter 4). Hence the more recent success on television is dubbed here 'a second starburst'. Just as he capitalised on the early recognition of his playwright's talent in the 1970s by producing half a dozen plays in quick succession, so, having caught the attention of both industry mandarins and a significant viewing public in the late 1990s, Poliakoff worked intensively in moving picture media, building upon his sporadic successes in film and television in the two decades in between.

The proposition of this book is that the late body of moving picture work marks the height of Poliakoff's career to date, concurring with Sarah Cardwell (2005: 180) that 'the medium of television is the one which has most successfully cultivated Poliakoff's talent as a writer and director'. The argument, exemplifying the idea of 'agency in structure', is that technological and industrial circumstances arose in the mid–late 1990s on to which Poliakoff's distinctive capacities happily mapped. Contemporary 'high-end' television, as I have called it elsewhere, affords a platform for distinctive work, aspiring to be 'cinematic', of the kind Poliakoff has always striven to write.[3] 'High-end' work in contemporary television is typically exemplified by the 'US Quality TV' in the late 1990s, for which *The Sopranos* might serve here as an example.[4] That is to say, in an era which has been dubbed TV3, some dimensions of television drama production (notably HBO Premium) moved away from the formulaic, 'lowest common denominator' approach which characterised 'the network era' and afforded not only significant budgets but imaginative scope for TV mini-series. The development of digital television with wide-screen aspect ratio and much enhanced sound and vision qualities, along with the potential for extended satellite distribution, are technological factors which encourage a 'cinematic' visual treatment in conjunction with honed dialogue, possibly reworking former film and television genres into a new hybrid product.[5]

As an established theatre playwright and film-maker, Poliakoff was well placed by the late 1990s to take advantage of this historical moment. He is a skilled writer of dialogue, but also has a strong sense of visual story-telling evident in his previous feature films (see Chapter 8). However Poliakoff is not a team player in creative production and, as with film, it was less likely in mini-series, where the stakes in terms of budget are high, that any individual might be afforded the total creative control Poliakoff demands. Moreover, Poliakoff had openly criticised the British television industry on the one hand for sustaining formulaic drama demanded by cost-accountant schedulers to serve the needs of ratings, and, on the other, for aping America, the fast pace of whose output precluded, in his view, the development of complex character in particular situations which had become the trademark of his own work.

With what might be seen as typical arrogance, Poliakoff made a wager with the BBC. In an encounter with Mark Thompson, then BBC's Director of Television, he argued that: '[i]f they would stop being frenetic, forget market research and trust the audience, they would not regret it. "Just give me four hours of screen time and I will deliver original quality drama."'[6] As he has since acknowledged, Poliakoff meant what he said, but at the time even he did not expect the success of what became his 'slow television' strategy. In some respects he thought his 'two fingers' gesture to the industry's establishment might mark his swan-song in television, not the beginnings of a new chapter in his career.[7]

Shooting the Past (1999)

Shooting the Past (*StP*) gained 2.5 million viewers on its first showing, but the real significance of this viewing figure is that *StP* was up against *24*, a highly attractive 'American Quality TV' product in this market segment. Furthermore, the consistency of numbers indicated in the audience research suggests viewers who joined the series stayed with it.[8] This is particularly gratifying to Poliakoff in that *StP* is defiant in deliberately transgressing key mainstream television drama codes.

First, he proposes to 'slow television down to the point that it stops . . . [with] scenes so long that they seem ridiculous' and, indeed, there are a number of dialogue-led, long scenes reminiscent of old-fashioned theatre in their requirement of the actors to realise them in a single take.[9] Secondly, where romance is a recognised draw, Poliakoff opts to deny viewers the satisfaction of a sexual relationship between protagonists Marilyn Truman (Lindsay Duncan) and Christopher Anderson (Liam Cunningham). He is shrewd enough, however, to create a chemistry such that an affair is a possibility. Thirdly, Poliakoff rejects contemporary television orthodoxy by opening, not with a fast-cut sequence to a high-energy soundtrack, but a single character, Oswald Bates (Timothy Spall), speaking directly to camera, announcing that he is in the process of committing suicide. Indeed, Poliakoff adapts in *StP* a 'narrator as framing device' tried out in the theatre plays, *Blinded by the Sun* and *Remember This* (see Chapters 6 and 8 respectively) which, though less uncommon today than in the past, is still sufficiently rare in fiction to have a de-familiarising impact.[10] The strategy, in the wake of Brecht (see Chapter 4) sets the desire to know what will happen against an awareness that it has already happened as Oswald presents the drama to come. This double-perspective approach does not undermine interest in the narrative outcome but it disposes the audience both to be caught up in what will happen and simultaneously to reflect on what is happening. Oswald directly and intimately addresses the audience, quietly announcing that he is recording his last moments on an old audio tape recorder and by stills photography. Speaking quietly but deliberately to camera, Oswald challenges the audience as to how 'a chubby man wearing a cardigan, talking into a tape machine – how can that be urgent? Why should we care? Or rather, why should you care?' All this is part of Poliakoff's 'slow television' strategy motivated by an interest 'in how short scenes had become on television' but, in specific, it invites 'complex seeing' by opening up a critical distance on a medium in which viewers are also being invited to immerse themselves.

Poliakoff's critique of the medium of television might appear to be a reactionary gesture, resonating with the strains of his Frankfurt School attitude to popular culture (see Chapter 4). It might, however, be more positively constructed as an extension of the avant-garde trajectory aiming to disrupt expectations, as expounded by Hans Magnus Enzensberger. For, if a medium becomes appropriated to the extent that it loses any critical function, it may, according to Enzensberger, require refunctioning (*Umfunktionierung*) to revivify its capacities.[11] In *StP*, Poliakoff is taking a serious look at the medium of television. The television image historically was considered ephemeral since, prior to recording technologies, the live transmission dissipated. It is now arguably even less substantial in transmission in respect of a very fast cutting tempo. In the extreme, it is no more than the flickering of dislocated signifiers, divorced from any apprehensible referents.[12] The ultimate slowing down of a moving image is the freeze-frame, and *StP* deliberately foregrounds still photography. With this strategy, Poliakoff is seeking to reconnect signifiers with signifieds and restore television's capacity to deal with the weight of experience. Poliakoff believes, as Christopher Hogg summarises: '[in] foregrounding the intrinsic aesthetic and narrative worth of the televisual image, not as an ephemeral byte within a rapid-fire delivery of plot to be instantly forgotten, but as something which deserves the viewer's consideration and appreciation, and which has the potential to linger in the mind' (Hogg 2010: 444). This move does not, however, entail a return to a closed realist text; indeed the foregrounding aims to open up an interpretative space for viewers to negotiate unresolved strands of narrative and the ambiguities in the layering of a densely constructed textual weft.

Moreover, while introducing his 'two fingers' strategy, Poliakoff is also shrewd in respect of grabbing and holding an audience. Spall is an actor well known for his comic roles (notably in *Auf Wiedersehen Pet*) as well as more serious roles (in the films of Mike Leigh, for example), and thus the presentation and situation of the opening are immediately compelling in their ambiguity, drawing viewers in. Oswald intimates that recent events have brought him to this pass and dedicates the account to follow to 'anybody who has suddenly lost their home or business, or been overlooked for promotion', an intriguing proposition designed to make an apparently personal appeal to many people. Subsequently, the device of Oswald talking directly to camera is used intermittently to develop the narrative and comment on the action as well as to extend the intimacy with his persona and predicament.

Over three episodes, *StP* tells the story of the attempt to save from dissolution the Fallon photographic library, located in an eighteenth-century mansion just to the west of London where Oswald Bates is deputy librarian. Illustrating another strategy to grab viewers' attention, the establishing shots feature the grand house surrounded by a deer park. The genre of 'period' drama is thus evoked in *StP* – and, indeed, the location and mysterious interiors are part of its visual attraction. Ultimately, however, it is not the costumes, furniture and fittings that dominate visual interest but still photographs in black and white. The library's photographic collection has developed piece-meal from the days when a philanthropic insurance company founded an educational establishment. It has continued to run on a small-scale commercial basis until the present moment, when the insurance company owner has finally sold the estate. An American foundation has bought the building and plans are in place quickly to convert it into a cutting-edge business school, 'the American School for Business for the Twenty-first Century'.

In one of a number of structural oppositions which shape *Shooting the Past*, conservatism (archaism, even) appears to be pitted against modernity. Christopher Anderson and his humourless assistant Styeman (Andy Serkis) inhabit a dynamic, high-tech word of mobile phones, lap-tops and global communication, whereas the world of Marilyn Truman and her staff is old-fashioned, with secretary Veronica (Billie Whitelaw) operating a typewriter and Oswald relying on an idiosyncratic catalogue system which is largely a matter of his human memory. The librarians live at a measured pace, taking formal meals, whereas Anderson and Styeman waste not a moment. Indeed the driver of the core tension of the plot is Anderson's announcement that they expect the library to be vacated within days, remarking that its contents, if not dispersed, will have to be destroyed. The future, it would seem, is to annihilate the past, in its relentless pursuit of the trajectory of modernity. And that, of course, is one accent of the mini-serial's title; another is the opposite – sustaining the past by the sheer force of the photographic still images.

Indeed, it is the power of the still photographic image which leads ultimately to a narrative resolution but, more significantly, it exercises its magic both within and beyond the diegesis. In each of the three parts, Oswald's extraordinary knowledge of the collection reveals a clue to a mystery. In the first part, while still employed at the library, he produces within seconds an image not just of Anderson's obscure home town in America, but his very street. In part two, illustrating Poliakoff's preoccupation with European history, the fortunes of a young girl refugee from the Nazis are traced through to her survival as a bag lady in London. As Hogg notes, '[t]he story of young Lily Katzman is related by Marilyn to Anderson because it draws upon images from all over the collection, stressing to him the unique value of the archive as a whole' (ibid.: 446). Finally, in part three, at the time of Oswald's suicide attempt, Marilyn slowly reveals to Christopher his own backstory by following Oswald's hints about the unconventional life of Anderson's grandmother.

Equally compelling, however, are the photographs themselves. As Amy Holdsworth (2006) summarises:

> Throughout the drama as a whole, still photographs are presented in two distinct modes: as part of the movement of the drama, often seen from a character's point of view, or inserted into the film, where they take on a different quality and pace, constructed through editing, not camera work. Poliakoff relies heavily upon the aesthetic quality of the photographs themselves, the nuances of light and dark and the stylised set up of lighting and shadow that characterise Hollywood portraiture for example.

The photographs are slowly set before the camera, sometimes in montage sequences, and left a couple of seconds for viewers to ponder, the camera on occasion moving in to the image, literally and metaphorically inviting viewers in. It is a risky strategy but Poliakoff adjudges that 'when a film camera looks at a photo for a split second, it's always interesting'.[13] To underscore the patterning and repetitions of *StP*'s compositional principles, the haunting refrain of Adrian Johnston's music folds back on itself, fading in and out and intensifying appropriately to mark specific moments of narrative insight.

The compulsion of the still is matched by the overall cinematography of *Shooting the Past*, which is beautifully lit and shot by Bruno de Keyser and Ernest Vincze. The internal geography is constructed by library stacks containing boxes of stills which create tunnels for 'staging in depth' shots, a trope distinctive of Poliakoff's directorial work typically affording images of entrapment by way of long-shot viewpoints. Rows of photographs pegged up on strings augment the shadowy interior, against which focused pools of light create an atmospheric chiaroscuro. Any colour – as, for example, in young assistant Spig's (Emilia Fox) costumes, or Marilyn's blonde hair – stands out in relief against the grey-buff backdrop. As the camera quite frequently moves alone through the stacks the focus is less on the characters and more, through a foregrounding of the space which embodies them, on past stories (all those other stories which might have been told). Time is also thus afforded for viewers' critical reflection.

More traditionally, but no less effectively, shot/reverse shots between portrait photographs and the characters lock pairs of eyes in an intense mutual gaze. This feature is particularly effective when Anderson views the rediscovered images of his grandmother, the intercutting appearing to reinstate him in his own history. In the final photograph, Anderson is seen sitting on his mother's knee at a cafe table with his grandmother. It is a startling moment of recognition for him, not just of his grandmother whom he had all but forgotten, but of a bohemian impulse in him which he now realises he has unhappily suppressed. By the use of photographs, and other powerful means, Poliakoff drew a substantial audience in defiance of the doxa that contemporary television drama must be inexorably fast-paced to prevent viewers from channel-hopping.

In *StP*, Poliakoff's visual eye for cinema is harnessed to his playwright's skill. The dialogue is sparse and where exchanges are long and slow, they are calculated to compel by functioning on several levels. Moreover, Poliakoff draws upon a characteristic of his theatre work by again creating complex characters who turn out not to be quite what they at first appear. Oswald may seem unacceptably eccentric and old-fashioned but, in fact, is a modern man *au fait* with new technologies. Marilyn also proves that she has more capacity than she credits herself with, in trying to interest an advertising agency in the collection and finally by deciphering Oswald's cryptic clues to the Anderson mystery. Above all, however, it is Anderson who finds in himself a bohemian artist, a person he has formerly glimpsed but repressed.

The moment of revelation at the end of *StP* is densely layered emotionally and dramatically, since the extraordinary revelations about Anderson's family past coincide with the present moment when Oswald is presumed dead by Marilyn who believes she has overheard it reported in the background of a telephone call to the hospital. It transpires, however, that Oswald Bates has not in fact died but actually shown some improvement. Marilyn's relief in an admixture of elation, sorrow, guilt and pleasure simply brings her finally into an embrace with Anderson but, though there has undoubtedly been a level of sexual attraction between them, Poliakoff eschews a traditional romantic ending, presenting it as one element in a palimpsest of other human feelings which at this moment in the drama have far greater importance. The photographic collection is, however, largely saved, Anderson himself facilitating its purchase. As we shall see in *Friends and Crocodiles*, another aesthetically stunning piece, Poliakoff would seem to infer that friendships might take precedence over sexual liaisons in life as well as in television drama. But first, we turn to Poliakoff's follow-up to *StP*, *Perfect Strangers*.

Perfect Strangers (2001)

Perfect Strangers – though it may not contain *StP*'s critique of television, nor offer *Friends and Crocodiles*' commentary on the spirit of the times – stands, in my judgement, among the highest of Poliakoff's achievements in this phase of his television work. The control of a complex narrative with many strands to its weft over three hour-long episodes, including fifty named characters and many extras, is a majestic writing achievement in itself. But the realisation on screen through an elaborate patterning of images across numerous locations, some grand in scale and others domestic interiors, adds up to that coherent authorial-directorial vision to which Poliakoff has always aspired. *Perfect Strangers* is not a public history like *The Lost Prince* but it nevertheless tells an extended family story spanning three generations which adds up aesthetically and thematically to more than the sum of its parts. Tensions in the narrative are embodied in the interplay of words, images and music to convey not just the feelings of the characters in particular moments but the feel of 'being in time'. The recursive loops of Adrian Johnston's haunting soundtrack, the exploratory – rather than explanatory – dialogue, and the repetition of visual tropes work together, and play against each other, to create a rich texture rarely offered even by 'quality television' in place of the pleasure of narrative closure.[14]

Perfect Strangers focuses on the Symons family, parts of which are well-to-do, while other parts have fared less well financially. Indeed access to a world of grand houses and significant opulence is afforded to everyday television viewers by way of the suburban 'Hillingdon branch'. At the outset, the wealthy patriarch of the family, Ernest Symons (Peter Howell), assisted by his sister Alice (Lindsay Duncan), are hosting a family reunion at a London hotel. The Hillingdon head, Raymond (Michael Gambon) is reluctant to attend, however, partly because his business has failed and he does not want to face his more successful relatives. But he is persuaded to attend by his son Daniel (Matthew Macfadyen), and wife Esther (Jill Baker). On their arrival at the hotel, another feature of attraction to a broad audience is introduced, namely genealogy, the website for which is said to be the most accessed on the entire internet. Stephen (Anton Lesser) is the self-appointed Symons family genealogist, assisted by the obsessively organising Poppy (Kelly Hunter). Knowing little of family connections because his father has kept his distance, Daniel is curious about the chart everybody is given to pin on the wall of their hotel room, and keen to keep the appointment with Irving (Timothy Spall), who is the sole person to ask to meet him. The adventure into the labyrinth of the family secrets unfolds from here.

Each of the three parts delves into the backstory of a family member or group affording a backbone structure to the mini-serial. While the narrative of the Hillingdon branch might be considered central, there are so many strands and interconnections that what Raymond, Esther and Daniel collectively and independently discover remains ultimately part of the broader metaphor of *Perfect Strangers*. Many Poliakovian traits are evident in the composition. For example, several characters turn out not to be what they at first appear. The most striking example, perhaps, is the three grey-permed women, surrounded by boxes of biscuits, who precede the Hillingdons in their meeting with Stephen to receive available evidence of their links to the family uncovered in his researches. In part one, the women appear to have led untroubled, perhaps narrow and self-indulgent, lives. In part two, their extraordinary backstory is revealed. In synopsis, the younger two, Violet and Edith, doted on their older sister, Mary Grace, who cared for them since their parents were ineffectual. In the Second World War, however, the two girls were evacuated to a cold house in north Wales, from which they ran away, making their way on foot back home to Birmingham. There they found a completely dysfunctional family, Mary Grace having declined after a severe shock when her fiancé was reported missing. Again they ran away, living rough in the woods for months, until finally discovered. The unfolding of this backstory requires that the excess of biscuits must be re-evaluated, as indeed must the women's entire being. But it is the sonic and visual treatment which shifts the focus away from the resolution of this narrative strand to the lived experience of its impact. In the dénouement in part three at another family gathering, Edith and Violet are seen to lie down in the grounds under an open sky in spite of wearing their best blue clothes, echoing their earlier attire. Mary Grace is with them but she stands a little apart.

There are four major, and several less developed, revelations of this kind arising from the family reunion and contributing to the patterning of *Perfect Strangers*. In part one, it is the genealogist himself, who explaining to Daniel the significance of a German atlas in his possession – and resonating with a Poliakovian theme – relates the story of Jewish refugee children, a boy and a girl. By being adopted and learning by heart a bogus family tree, the girl, Stephen's mother, survived. The boy, to whom the atlas belonged, did not. To bind this story into the weft of *Perfect Strangers*, the boy is pictured from below – in an imaginary flashback – at the top of a staircase with elaborate wrought-iron railings. The sole image Stephen has for Daniel depicts him from a low angle, dressed in a blue 'little prince' costume, on a staircase with similarly elaborate wrought-iron railings, another piece of the pattern in which the cinematic treatment complements the narrative.

Indeed, throughout *Perfect Strangers*, images appear to characters (and viewers), sometimes explicitly in dreams or overtly marked as flashbacks, but at other times in almost subliminal flashes. Some are prefigurations (Daniel's vision of seducing Rebecca [Claire Skinner] at the Foreign Office). Ultimately, they are all placed in the bigger picture, but not necessarily explained. Still photographs, following *Shooting the Past*, and animated sequences, as if of home movies, serve to: illustrate backstory (Charles [Toby Stephens], Rebecca and Richard [JJ Feild] with Alice); trigger memory (Raymond's father dancing), and to afford chance insights (Daniel's spotting of Richard in a photograph in Alice's suite). They, too, are pieces in the visual puzzle. In this manner, innocuous objects are also discovered to have significance (the guitar found by Rebecca and Charles, and the leather coat they give to Daniel) and free-floating signifiers are anchored (the willow tower structures in Esther's garden). In part one, Raymond eats scrambled eggs with Alice at two in the morning and, in part three, he shares an omelette with Ernest's son, Peter (Tony Maudsley). Once the idea of complex patterning is established, it commands attention because the smallest detail may hold significance. As Sarah Cardwell (2005: 191) has remarked: 'Repetition is a formal quality that permeates the work, delivering a sense of coherence and unity. Music and dialogue [and, one might add, visual tropes], intricate and expressive in themselves, become part of a coherent whole through the way in which they are intimately connected with other elements of narrative, theme and style.' The 'slow television' approach, carried through from *Shooting the Past*, affords time to gaze and reflect in a process of viewing quite different from the 'glance' marked by several commentators as the dominant mode of postmodern television (Caldwell 1995; Nelson 2007). Cardwell also observes (2005a: 191) how, in Poliakoff's dialogue, '[t]he repetitive reshaping of ideas into different words has the effect of stalling the narrative, slowing the pace more generally'.

An added sense of structure is carried by the cinematography (Cinders Forshaw) with its precise lighting and significant framing. Throughout, Daniel is featured framed in doorways and against windows while Rebecca's bare back repeatedly catches the light at the banquet in part one as if reflecting Daniel's gaze. Subsequently a lighting contrast often picks out one side of their faces in the manner of *film noir*. In contrast, though Rebecca accuses her of treachery,

Alice is typically shot full-face and well-lit. Repeated image structures include: staircases shot from below or above to afford striking frames for the characters; corridor 'tunnels' – another Poliakovian trope – ranging from the hotel corridors to the hedges at the final family gathering; face-to-face intimacies, shot from the side in the manner of the famous face/candle *gestalt*. In the colour scheme, Poliakoff's favourite red features in Rebecca's borrowed apartment and, in turn, Rebecca (at the banquet) and Esther (final sequence) wear striking red dresses.

The major narrative strand in part three unpacks some aspects of the visual structure. It concerns a feud between Rebecca (and to a lesser extent Charles) and Alice about the effacement from the family tree of their late brother, Richard. This oversight triggers guilt and anger about the fact that they had all turned their backs on, then avoided, and finally excluded Richard when he changed from a bright and easy-going university student into an obsessive who sought strong vibrations – at locations on picnics, on buses, and in material objects. When the trio's parents had followed their pleasures abroad rather than caring for their children, childless Aunt Alice, who wanted desperately to be a mother, took on the maternal role. They all remained extremely close until the fracture recounted above.

When Richard wandered into the path of a train and was killed, however, each of them found it very hard to bear, and the intensity of their feelings breaks out in the dénouement, the controlled surface persona of each in turn being unsettled by the depth of their grief. Daniel gets caught up in the cross-fire since he has befriended them all at the reunion – or rather, they have sought him out partly for their own ends. Charles and Rebecca see something of Richard in Daniel to the point that Charles gets angry seeing him in the leather coat his brother used to wear. Rebecca, in contrast, though somewhat reluctantly, reciprocates Daniel's strong sexual attraction to his cousin and they embark on a passionate affair (echoing the incest in *Hitting Town* and *Close My Eyes*). Alice, noticing that Daniel is spending time with Charles and Rebecca, makes a conscious effort to get to know him. They all, consciously or otherwise, see his potential as an ameliorating force in their troubled relationships, as if Daniel might serve the bonding function undertaken by Richard in their former mutual love. But when Daniel serves as a go-between and takes the initiative to try and bring them together, the initial result is disastrous.

Though narratives of suffering painfully endured permeate *Perfect Strangers*, there is gentle humour, too, in the parade of family eccentrics. Irving's (Timothy Spall) flamboyant personality, imaged in his idiosyncratic dress sense and pink Mercedes car, is amusing in his restless 'orbiting' with an undisguised eye for the main chance belying his attempts at sophistication. He delights that a surveyor, Daniel, is a relative he might use to his advantage. Sidney (Michael Culkin), more modest in every respect, needs help from Rebecca with his luggage, admitting that he is too mean to use a porter and always regrets it. Poppy's over-enthusiasm raises a smile, as she bristles with red mapping pins and precisely timed schedules as the guests arrive at the hotel, and ultimately barks for guests to come to the marquee for dinner at the final gathering for Martina's (Camilla Power) engagement. The wittier lines are largely reserved for Raymond, whose grouchy temper is frequently expressed in a searing irony and, in his drunken 'karaoke' speech at the family banquet (superbly delivered by Gambon in a mixture of laughter and pain), he resorts to mordant jokes. Poliakoff even indulges in a couple of private jokes: Alice tells the children the story of the crocodile which is to inform the title of *Friends and Crocodiles* and the 'little prince' image of Daniel prefigures *The Lost Prince*, his next project.

It is the solving of Raymond's mystery, however, which directs *Perfect Strangers* towards resolution when, revisiting Ernest's former garden in which his father is photographed dancing, he is assisted by Stephen to make connections. Raymond's father was quite uncharacteristically dancing for his lover, Henrietta, mother to Ernest. The discovery of a painting of a 'little prince', attired entirely as Daniel had been in the photograph Stephen gave him, leads to the insight that Daniel had been used by his then elderly grandfather as a go-between with Henrietta and love token to represent his sustained devotion. The pattern is repeated, of course, with Rebecca's use of him as a go-between. Raymond finds the discoveries cathartic as he can now see in his humourless father a brighter, romantic side and he judges himself less harshly from this newly grasped perspective. Esther, too, has been recovering lost family history by using the internet to trace her roots. To her and Raymond's surprise she is related to William Beckford, who is said to have composed with Mozart. More important, however, for resonances with Esther's penchant is his love of building towers. In a detailed analysis of the sequence bringing this narrative strand, not so much to resolution, but to a complex unravelling, Cardwell (2005a) has brought out (in detail greater than the scope here affords) the intricacy of the patterning of word, image and music in such a way as to afford the *jouissance* of an aesthetic pleasure through a deferral of the more ordinary pleasure of narrative closure.[15]

Though the seniors of the Hillingdon branch appear to be rejuvenated and more relaxed than when they set off for the reunion, Daniel has seriously upset Rebecca in his underhand attempt to bring her to speak with Alice, and she now will not speak to him either. Separately they make their way, as bidden by Poppy, to eat in the marquee. Alice's position in the family requires her to make a speech and she expressly mentions absent friends, naming Richard and revealing the feeling of desperate loss with which his absence has left her permanently scarred. In a final visual patterning, Charles and Daniel raise their glasses in acknowledgement of Alice's toast and, although she does not complete the pattern, Rebecca appears somewhat disposed to be reconciled. Sidney and Daniel remark on the odd and unexpected juxtapositions of Poppy's seating plan, and Sidney suggests they have ironically ended up next to the member of the family with whom they have most in common.

The conclusion without closure of *Perfect Strangers* obliquely manifests a disposition to humanism, evident throughout Poliakoff's work, but articulated more specifically in these television mini-serials where the dynamic canvas afforded by the scope of four hours has allowed him not only to explore individuals in multiple relationships through time, but the very experience of time. It would simply not be possible to make *Perfect Strangers* as a single play for television or, indeed, as a feature film. The long-form serial narrative perfectly complements the weight of the subject matter. In turn, Poliakoff's established playwriting skill is complemented by his cinematic disposition now facilitated by digital technologies, adding layer upon layer to a complex verbal and visual weft. Though humanism may be out of fashion in allegedly 'post-human' times, Poliakoff reminds us that, amid the difficult business of living, the endurance of relationships with those who matter most to us – family members or friends (and not necessarily lovers) – is a bedrock to our lives. Anyone who has lost somebody they loved will recognise the gut-wrenching and enduring pain (superbly conveyed in turn in *Perfect Strangers* by Sheila Burrell as Grace, and by Toby Skinner, Claire Stevens and Lindsay Duncan) and the power of those forces which, failing completely to sever intricate bindings, can nevertheless drive family members to fall out or friends to become 'perfect strangers'. My sense of 'agency in structure' leads me to differ from Daniel when he speaks of a genetic patterning from which we cannot escape. *Perfect Strangers* persuades, however, that iterative patterns inform our lives such that we need to show resolve if we wish to avoid being overpowered by them.

The Lost Prince (2003)

The Lost Prince is the most tightly structured and densely patterned of all Poliakoff's work and sits alongside *Perfect Strangers* at the pinnacle of his achievement, thoroughly deserving the Emmy awards it received. Like *Perfect Strangers*, it is an exploration of an extended family and the interconnections and tensions in their relationships and their histories. It just happens that this family includes not only the monarchs of the British realm, George V and Queen Mary, but the Tsar and Tsarina of Russia (the Romanov family) and the crowned heads of the majority of European countries and states, with the exception of France. *The Lost Prince* is set against the momentous events leading up to the First World War when the different parts of the extended dynasties of Europe were drawn into opposition. It is a family story on several levels, however, as well as multiple in its dimensions, and it is personalised for viewers particularly through the character of Johnnie (Daniel Williams/Matthew Thomas), increasingly effaced (like Richard in *Perfect Strangers*) from the family.

Part of the impact of *The Lost Prince* lies in its unfolding of the almost unknown, but true, story of Prince John, the youngest son of King George (Tom Hollander) and Queen Mary (Miranda Richardson) who, because he was epileptic and autistic, was hidden from public view at a time when such a condition was deemed an embarrassment. Following a clue in his reading as a student of history, Poliakoff's research revealed 'a different boy' from the one caricatured in the few lines of reference to him in official histories.[16] Poliakoff not only redresses a historical effacement by revealing Johnnie's true disposition but, in a bold structural parallel, he sets the narrative of his progressive exclusion against his father's increasing implication in a disastrous war. A comparison is thus invited between the fragmentation of the royal families and the increasing cohesion of Johnnie's 'family' which ultimately includes his devoted nanny, Lalla (Gina McKee), his brother Georgie (Rollo Weeks) when available, and a motley collection of good-hearted rustic servants. The story is told over two ninety-minute episodes first transmitted by BBC1 on consecutive days in January 2003.[17]

The structural paralleling is very elaborate and it is possible in the scope here to illustrate just a few key sequences as part of the pattern. In part one, the Romanovs visit their cousins and a striking visual panorama shows a bevy of young women, the Romanov cousins, accompanying the Tsarina, all beautifully dressed in white with white parasols, to watch their father fishing and swimming in the sea. Johnnie, being unusually sensitive to vibrant sound and colour, is very taken by the aesthetic beauty of his cousins, and amusingly observes of the Tsar, floating on his back in a maroon bathing suit, that he resembles an emperor fish. This last image recurs intermittently throughout *The Lost Prince*, to the moment of the Tsar's bloody death. In part two, exiled to a farm prior to the moment of their execution, the Romanov girls and their parents are shown working in their white garb amid the muck and straw of the animals, the contrast in their fortunes being visually drawn. To take another example, at the heart of part one, King George throws a magnificent banquet inviting all the family. It is a very colourful and grand affair, secretly observed by Georgie and Johnnie (with a coat over his pyjamas) from the gallery.

A note is brought quietly to the Prime Minster, Asquith, which he whispers 'might change everything'. It is the second signifier of the war, the first having been dismissed on the grounds that there will be no fighting 'because they're family'. Johnnie gets over-excited by the bold sound of the musicians when they strike up, leading to the third of six epileptic fits which also punctuate the piece. In part two, King George holds another banquet at Buckingham Palace, but the reduced size of the table, depicted in a wide-angle shot paralleling that which established the magnificence of the first banquet, indicates reduced circumstances. Food is in short supply and the room is cold because George has turned off the heating such that *the atmosphere is sepulchral*' (Poliakoff 2003: 140).

A final example of many in this most tightly structured work is the pair of scenes in which the royal children are required to recite, either musically or verbally, before the King, Queen and extended family. In the first of these scenes, the eldest son, David, offers some lines from Tennyson, and Georgie confidently recites some lines from Victor Hugo in French. Although called the youngest by his grandfather Edward VII (Michael Gambon), Georgie points out that he's 'not the youngest, Johnnie is here . . . you've forgotten him' (ibid.: 10). Johnnie does not perform on this occasion but in the parallel scene towards the end of part two he surprises everybody. Johnnie is evidently a slow learner and his appointed tutor has given up on him, but Lalla, with sustained belief and great patience, has coached Johnnie. His parents are deeply preoccupied with the war and, as usual, have no time for Johnnie. After he has uttered a few hesitant lines of Tennyson and a line from Victor Hugo in French, the King requires him to stop because the war cabinet has arrived early. Johnnie, however, is defiant and refuses to be silenced. He insists they all remain seated and stuns them with a bright and substantial trumpet solo. It is the first time in his life that he has commanded his parents' undivided attention and, given their reactions, their approval. Indeed, it is the moment in this impressive two-part TV mini-series that Johnnie's view of the world takes precedence.

Underscoring the dramatic structure, indeed effecting its cinematic mode of visual story-telling (cinematography by Barry Ackroyd), is an equivalently elaborate visual patterning, revolving predominantly around a colour design of white, black (or dark navy) and red. Again, selected illustrations must suffice. On the beach in the Romanov scene a strip of red carpet transects the shot and offsets the glaring white and navy blue, but it is blood, spattering their costumes, which lends a red hue to the parallel scene in part two. Red carpets blaze across the banquet scenes where some of the military uniforms are also scarlet; red rugs adorn the Romanovs' lakeside picnic spot at the opening of part two, linked visually to Buckingham Palace where a red carpet runs the length of the corridor. There is red edging to the nurses' capes, and the emblem of the Red Cross stands on a white background when Queen Mary visits a war hospital. The bodies of the mutilated war victims, wrapped in white bandages with smears of blood, afford a cruel parody of the Romanov splendour on the beach and a prefiguration of their demise.

There are many shots through chinks in part-opened doors or beneath blinds emphasising the perspective of the outsider looking in. There are also numerous shots of characters, particularly Johnnie, behind bars or in cages as a result of Georgian windows or wrought-iron staircases (as in *Perfect Strangers*). Another distinctive strand in the dense weave involves Poliakovian 'staging in depth' long-shots down tunnels and along corridors. They are in the palaces (above and below stairs) – one memorable example involving the tracking of King George's parrot chased by Johnnie through the warren of kitchen passageways. Similar long corridors, now cast in a cold, blue light, convey the stark, inhospitable regime of the naval training school where Georgie and his fellow-cadets are forced to immerse themselves under cold showers and in a bath of ice. There are pergolas in the gardens and colonnades in courtyards, as well as tunnels in the countryside constructed by over-arching trees. Apart from affording interesting visual frames, collectively these serve to convey a labyrinthine environment in which the protagonists are trapped.

There are numerous sonic echoes, too, not just in another fine Adrian Johnston soundtrack which ranges from a solo trumpet – paralleling both Johnnie's performance and a last post – to a full orchestra with predominant brass which swells to punctuate time-shifts in *The Lost Prince* in place of visual fades to black. Indeed the score fades in and out of the entire work, shifting in register from military drill to lyrical underscore. Russian music brought by the Romanovs in part one is reprised on Johnnie's beloved gramophone in part two. The guns of war in part two echo the rifles at the shooting party in part one.

It will be evident from the brief account above that *The Lost Prince* extends the principles of dramatic and cinematic composition achieved in *Perfect Strangers*, creating a denser web, not just of artistry – though *The Lost Prince* is undoubtedly beautiful to watch – but of visual narration. As part of the structural parallelism, the successive removes of Johnnie demanded by his parents sees his accommodation diminish from a palace to a relatively small house in the grounds to a run-down farm cottage. In contrast, his father, who actually prefers smaller houses with small rooms, is increasingly projected into the palace as the demands of war require his presence in London. The ultimate irony is that Johnnie, supported by Lalla, finds his identity amid a contented family in the artistic environment of his beloved garden, while the King presides over family fragmentation, double-dealing and death, the loss of his identity marked by an enforced change to Windsor of the family name to avoid German associations. Johnnie's natural disposition is to tell it how he sees it when he is constantly being told to be seen and not heard – and ultimately not to be seen at all. When Georgie lies to his father that the game of toy soldiers involved battles between the planets, not European countries, Johnnie blurts out that one side was France. He gauchely repeats to his parents what he has overheard Asquith remark, namely that everybody was laughing at their small home and grounds. To Asquith's face, Johnnie tells him he has a big head. Thus Johnnie's ultimate triumph over an atmosphere of duplicity and repression is a metaphor for Edwardian society and a need for a release of building pressures which the war in Europe both represented and achieved.

The final imagery of *The Lost Prince* affirms the humanism which we can see strengthening through Poliakoff's later works. When Johnnie succumbs to a final fit after playing joyfully with Georgie in the countryside, the funeral is held at the local church. While all the royal family and its entourage are formally dressed in black, the Queen beckons the locals, dressed in their everyday clothes, to come into the churchyard from the hinterground where they have waited at a respectful distance. Particularly following the glimpses of smiles amid tears of joy which marked Johnnie's trumpet performance, a sense is conveyed of rebuilding a family along the principles of Johnnie's free-spirited and aesthetically driven life in place of the instrumental, regimental, buttoned-down Edwardian court. The point is emphasised by Georgie's final remark: 'You know Lalla . . . I was thinking he [Johnnie] was the only one of us who was able to be himself' (ibid.: 179). Although on one level this remark is somewhat romantic, even a little trite, it in fact resonates back through *The Lost Prince* and, indeed, through Poliakoff's work. Though agency can evidently be constrained in structure, Johnnie's tenacity serves as an example of how, with will and the right support, people might resist oppression even to the point where they might change their circumstances.

Friends and Crocodiles (2005)

'This film was absolutely stunning . . . a modern English masterpiece'

'This drama was a huge disappointment. The scenery, the casting, the story were all first class [but] there wasn't enough time to get to know the characters so at the end you didn't care what happened to them'[18]

It has been remarked that Poliakoff's work divides audiences: they either love it or hate it. The above contrasting audience responses represent that binary as reflected on the BBC website at the time of first transmission and, in this section, I use the freely given responses of viewers partly to frame my own sense of the value of Poliakoff's work which, of course, does not appeal to everybody. It is interesting that one respondent calls *Friends and Crocodiles* a 'film' and the other calls the piece a 'drama'. Having argued that this phase of television work marks the high point of Poliakoff's career to date precisely because it brings together his playwright's capacity for character and dialogue with a film-maker's eye for fluid images in motion in a way which is perfectly suited to the digital TV medium, it may be that, in *Friends and Crocodiles*, Poliakoff veers to the cinematic at the expense of clarity of narrative and deep exploration of character which is still required, even of the most successful 'high-end' television drama.

Friends and Crocodiles (*Friends*) is the most ambitious of Poliakoff's projects, aiming to chart key socio-cultural trends over two decades from the early 1980s to the 'dot.com bust' between 2000 and 2002.[19] It is reminiscent of one of his heroes, Charles Dickens, in the effort to meld a core storyline running through a world teeming with characters, accompanied by a commentary on the vagaries of the changing times. He approaches the task in a characteristic way with two central characters who, like Marilyn Truman and Christopher Anderson, are not romantic lovers but are inextricably bound together – in this case as business partners and ultimately the 'friends' of the title. Some viewers complained that there was no 'chemistry' between Paul Reynolds (Damian Lewis) and Lizzie Thomas (Jodhi May), and more traditional viewers may have been disappointed by the lack of a consummation typical of more formulaic television romance.[20] But one respondent perhaps caught the relationship in drawing a comparison with *Close My Eyes* (see Chapter 5) and describing it as 'fractured, not quite sibling' in its intense intertwinings, and indeed towards the end of *Friends and Crocodiles*, Paul quizzically refers to Lizzie as his 'sister' (2005: 93).[21]

There are three key phases in the narrative. In the first phase, Paul, a self-made property multi-millionaire, employs Lizzie, first as his secretary and then as his personal assistant. In the second phase, Lizzie, now advanced to a senior position in a 1990s 'bright ideas' company, employs Paul as a consultant. Both engagements prove disastrous. In the first phase, Lizzie, neat in a pencil skirt and buttoned-up blouse, represents Apollonian order where Paul, despite his avowed wish to bring to fruition his many creative ideas, is distracted by a Dionysian lifestyle of sex and wild parties. In the second phase, Paul, who has squandered much of his wealth on worthless projects, cannot accommodate to the 1990s open-plan, high-tech world of proposed virtual-reality headsets and e-books. He becomes almost reactionary, positing just one idea – hard-copy book-shops with available coffee, before he is sacked. In the third phase, Lizzie gets married at just the point where she has taken a new job with a large established company, AET. She is selected to join the board when the Chief Executive, Anders (Patrick Malahide), deter-mines to sell off AET's hard industrial base and invest entirely in internet and telecom services. Paul, meanwhile, has retreated into the depths of the countryside with his two common-law wives and a bevy of children, smoking dope and luxuriating in a hot-tub. The dot.com company goes spectacularly bust, having cost thousands of the former workers their jobs and the investors their money. Lizzie is distraught, a broken woman, who, though happily married, feels compelled to call again upon Paul. She has repeatedly imagined hearing him saying 'I told you so' as the situation rapidly deteriorates. Paul, however, has recently relocated to an old schoolhouse and resumed work activities, having capitalised upon his one good idea in the 1990s, a chain of bookshops. He is now picking up some of the recuperable industrial business which AET literally threw out. Since it seems they cannot function successfully without each other but cannot work directly together, Paul suggests to Lizzie that they communicate by e-mail.

The situations outlined above afford opportunities for some of Poliakoff's favourite visual moments: summer parties and picnics, travel and the built environment. In the first phase, set largely in the interiors and exteriors of Paul's vast mansion and grounds, there is first a picnic for Paul's salon of 'characters' – a mixture of artists, a poet, a medieval historian, an MP, a de-schooler, and sundry hangers-on – whom Paul has collected because he finds them interesting, in addition to a bevy of beautiful, and mainly half-naked young women, lounging around the garden and sharing Paul's bed. The occasion of the picnic is Paul's birthday and this panoply – perhaps the equivalent of a Dickensian world peopled by idiosyncratics – is invited to take a ride on Paul's present to himself, a Routemaster London bus. Secondly, there is a huge summer party to which all Paul's associates, including lords, bishops and members of parliament, are invited. The two occasions, both organised by Lizzie against her better judgement, are deliberately wrecked by Paul, the first in a minor way by him driving the bus recklessly, against express advice, on to the grass where it gets stuck, the second catastrophically by inviting, beyond the agreed guest-list, a number of unemployed punks to come and wreck the joint, and giving quad bikes to some of his wilder friends to run amok. Most specifically, they dismantle Paul's workroom which Lizzie has transformed from chaos into order under the expectation that she will be supporting Paul in the realisation of some of his ideas which she genuinely finds exciting. In one of a number of explicit contrasting parallels in the structure of *Friends*, Lizzie's wedding is a more ordered re-enactment of the summer party and it is Paul who threatens to be the disruptive force.

These situations afford the opportunity for some large-scale and splendid cinematic visuals (cinematography, Barry Ackroyd) as many of the viewer responses attest. There are wide shots of superb locations, notably the grounds and house occupied by Paul, the similar location for Lizzie's wedding and the fine building destroyed by AET to achieve a new look for a new age. The interiors of Paul's mansion are opulently furnished with warm wood panelling and doors. Paul's party is visually the most colourful. It is dominated by red pavilions and lanterns which pick up on the distinctly red room he used to develop his plans with Lizzie and the red Routemaster bus at the picnic. At the party Lizzie wears a shocking pink dress, a Poliakovian trope not suggesting, as might be conventional, the scarlet woman. Large numbers of extras – beautiful people, beautifully dressed – crowd the space until things go pear-shaped. Boats in the form of swans glide across the lakes at both Paul's party and Lizzie's wedding. The latter is predominantly white in contrast to the red of Paul's party, a white marquee hosting the bride in a white dress with white swans on the water. In contrast the AET building is in more sombre tones of grey and brown such that red visual splendour is bleached and sullied by turns as the piece progresses, only returning to muted red warmth emanating from the bonfire at the end, when Lizzie is again wearing red.

For those viewers disposed to the visual pleasures of cinema, *Friends* offers a feast. But for those more held by the 'followability' of a TV drama narrative, the approach by way of visual metaphors may have proved problematic. Where, in both *StP* and *Perfect Strangers*, the core storyline is clear, indeed compelling, even though complicated by a range of narrative devices and time-shifts, in *Friends* the details of the time-line are not easy to establish. It is clear that there is a broad historical sweep from the 1980s to the early noughties. But the piece expressly opens in 1997 (marked by a subtitle), when an older Paul (from phase three) is haunting Sneath. Following this sequence the action dissolves – through shimmering water from a puddle to a swimming pool – back to 1981 (again marked by a subtitle), progressing forward from there.[22] But phase one of *Friends* is also overtly referenced towards the end as 'the last dregs of seventies-style anarchy' (ibid.: 88). If we assume accordingly that phase one, though marked 1981 (the Toxteth riots of 1981 also feature briefly on a television report), loosely represents trends threading through a period from the late 1970s to the early 1980s, there is then an abrupt jump-cut, marked by '*a jarring sound cut*' (ibid.: 49), to a new location, London, and presumably a new time, since Lizzie is seen, fashionably dressed and shopping with a colleague. This is the height of the age of consumerism, the late 1980s, perhaps 1989, since, though there is no indicative subtitle, there is a passing reference to Margaret Thatcher, Prime Minster since 1979, suggesting that 'she's only done ten years, she wants to do at least twenty' (ibid.: 69). Time has certainly passed, marked by 'a fade to black' (ibid.: 49), as Lizzie, in the interim since she acrimoniously parted company with Paul, has established a successful career in a dynamic 'future visions' firm. Phase three, marked by another 'fade to black' (ibid.: 83), is the dot.com boom and bust era between 1997 and 2002. Lizzie makes passing reference to the election at which, 'after all these years Labour has got in' (ibid.: 92), that is 1997, the inauguration of Tony Blair's government. Thus, though it is not easy, it is possible to deduce that the time-span of *Friends* runs in three phases over eight-year gaps: 1981, 1989, 1997 and culminating around 2002. It thus instances Poliakoff in his role as commentator on the times, charting key currents in the Thatcher years, 1979–90 and on into the early beginnings of 'New Labour'

(1997–2010).[23] Indeed, this period of British history is the object of an oblique political critique in *Friends*. However, almost a quarter-century of time, and lack of clear signposting presented at least the more literal television viewers with a lack of narrative 'followability'.[24]

Furthermore, the character development has been called into question, specifically in respect of a lack of ageing. Paul has shoulder-length hair in the 1997 'retro-hippy' phase (when we meet him at the outset and again at the end of phase two, when he is stalking Sneath), and at the rural commune (when Lizzie visits to find him living with Angela and the disabled Rachel, who are among the numerous women encountered in phase one). Otherwise, neither his nor Lizzie's appearance changes much, beyond the fashion of their clothes, between the ages of twenty-five and nearly fifty. Lizzie certainly looks wasted after the dot.com débâcle, but not particularly aged.

Significant minor characters are also under-developed. Oliver, the child prodigy, features in all phases and, though he is plumper at the end than in his youth, he too does not appear to have overly changed over two decades other than in failing to fulfil his promise and becoming introverted, for reasons we are left to surmise. Key members of the 'salon' alter by way of changing their spots in the late 1980s and early 1990s: the Albert brothers (artists), conventionally suited, claim to be 'creating anarchy in the city now'; and Redfern (the de-schooler) is now Chief Educational Adviser advocating '[c]hecking a child's progress . . . testing and testing' (ibid.: 77 and 78 respectively). Their time-serving marks the contrasting integrity of Paul's character and those of Oliver and Butterworth (the historian) who stick with him. But the minor characters serve more as functionaries rather than living, breathing characters. Particularly since in *StP* and *PS*, Poliakoff had secured his reputation for compelling and convincing characters, the horizon of expectation was such that some television drama viewers were left disappointed by *Friends and Crocodiles*.[25] Finally, in reviewing critical responses, the ending was considered weak. Timbo of London observes that, 'the most cringe-worthy scene was our heroine's tearful phone call to Paul' and Rachel Alban of Darlington reported that, '[t]he ending disappointed me . . . the conclusion was a teenage like email business partnership'.[26]

In contrast with the above criticisms of *Friends and Crocodiles* made, as I see it, from the 'drama' perspective of a more literal concern with plausible character motivation and narrative followability, many plaudits for the 'film' emphasised its visual splendour, many coming from those who read the imagery at the level of metaphor. In one summary *Friends* is a

> very intelligent and haunting drama that reminded me of the hedonistic, greedy and emotionally corrupt days of the eighties into the nineties. At the same time, I felt the magic of the era and the belief that anything was possible. However, with it all came great pain in changing to accommodate it, and that raised the question of whether it was all worth it.[27]

The capacity in this way to read television, a mass domestic medium which typically deals in the everyday, is part of an aesthetic disposition perhaps not shared by all viewers. While Poliakoff's ambition is, as noted, to challenge viewers to develop new ways of seeing, the compositional features of the text must work to this end within the parameters of the medium, though testing its borders. And *Friends* does indeed evidence a number of built-in structural parallels which gravitate in this direction.

There are a number of consciously constructed comparative scenes: destruction characterises all three phases – the break-up of Paul's party, the messing up of the creative projects office and the smashing of the lamps as the final metaphor for AET's ravages; in phase one as noted, Paul employs Lizzie and in phase two reciprocally she employs Paul; Lizzie's wedding uses a similar location and decorations to Paul's party, the swans on the lake explicitly drawing the parallel; the reappearance in new guises of several members of Paul's salon; the chaotic personal workspace of Paul's which Lizzie organises contrasts with the sleek, open-plan office of the 'big ideas' firm which Paul shuns, but only to turn his private office into chaos; in phase one, Paul is discovered by Lizzie in bed with two naked women where, in the rural retreat, he is again discovered with two naked women in the hot-tub but now in a familial, if unorthodox, setting; the bus ride at the picnic is echoed in the bus rides to 'the end of the line' (ibid.: 71) Paul insists Sneath take with him; there are numerous images of characters in 'tunnels', in this case long corridors or colonnades. This detailed structural patterning invites a formal, as distinct from a more literal 'character-in-narrative' reading, but Poliakoff's work is at its best (in *StP*, *Perfect Strangers* and *The Lost Prince*) when it is not a matter of 'either-or' choice between metaphor and grounded narrative but 'both-and'.

In addition to the structural patterning noted, the crocodile of the title appears on several occasions, literally as a baby crocodile in Paul's possession and finally featured on a television item, caught by Lizzie in which its mystery is explained. In his rural retreat Paul tells Lizzie that he contemplated the baby crocodile because this reptile alone survived for two hundred million years after a 'huge bang' (ibid.: 95), caused by an asteroid hitting the earth, wiped out the others. The mystery of how it survived is apparently answered when the television programme reveals that crocodiles 'possess one of the most powerful antibiotics in their system known to science' (ibid.: 101).

In a work which, despite its weaknesses, has patently been carefully structured, the title might be expected to carry specific metaphoric resonance. At the end, through all that has gone between them, Paul and Lizzie have both gained insights. Though they are inexorable antagonists, they also complement each other. Paul's suggestion that, 'now with e-mail we could set up a business and we need never to be in the same room' is intended to mark the value of a future partnership based upon their insights. They are at the core of a band of inextricably bound 'friends' who must work together in spite of their sibling-like antagonisms. The final scene finds most of Paul's 'salon' back together, stacking a huge bonfire to make space for a new start. The hedonistic indulgence of the early 1980s has been left behind and even Butterworth has achieved something, since the final line tells us that he is 'on the last page of his book' (ibid.: 113).

Against the greed of consumer individualism of the 1980s and the postmodern privileging of surface style over substance in the 1990s and the dot.com disaster of the early noughties, Poliakoff appears to be positing the power of deep friendships and the durability of collective human endeavour, emulating the crocodile. This may smack more of a Dickensian sentimentality than sharp political analysis, but it is consonant with that deep strain of humanism running through Poliakoff's work. But it may be that *Friends*, while it offers a visual feast, exemplifies a tendency in Poliakoff's earlier work for the spiralling of metaphor to become a bit detached from its grounding in the actuality on which it riffs.

Gideon's Daughter (2006)

Gideon's Daughter is a sequel to *Friends and Crocodiles* in the literal sense that it was transmitted a month later and that it features, as participant narrator, Sneath (Robert Lindsay), the self-serving politician and socialite from the first part of the intended trilogy. It also extends the reflective commentary on the political times by picking up where *Friends and Crocodiles* left off, in the early years of 'New Labour' following the success of Tony Blair's campaign in May 1997.

The visually striking opening sequence picks up in specific on an event which marked a curious moment in British history, namely an unprecedented public expression of grief over the death on 31 August 1997 of Princess Diana by ordinary people who did not know her personally but who responded as if they did. The flowers strewn all along the Mall at that time are a *leitmotiv* in *Gideon's Daughter* for surface allure without depth, a key trope of postmodernism. They echo an advertising campaign, by protagonist Gideon Warner (Bill Nighy), featuring flowers strewn around London which instigated his rise from an ordinary public relations manager of a group of musicians to a celebrity PR guru. Gideon has come to embody the idea of 'spin' and celebrity which became the hallmarks of New Labour, having indeed been instrumental factors in winning the election.

Gideon's Daughter is narrated by Sneath under the guise of him writing a book which he dictates to a newly arrived secretary Becca (Samantha Whittaker). Wearing only pyjama bottoms, Sneath stands in marked contrast to Becca's neat office attire, the moment echoing Lizzie's arrival for work with Paul in *Friends*. Indeed, Sneath's hints of a

lurid, sexually explicit story resonate with Paul's gratuitous confrontation of Lizzie with his free approach to sexual conduct. But Sneath's
story, though it embraces sex, is a personal narrative of another kind
dealing with deeply felt loss, namely parents' literal and metaphorical
loss of their children. The flowers of the opening sequence are in fact
not lining the Mall but another central London street where a young
boy has been knocked off his bike and killed. As we later learn, they
have been liberated from the Mall by obsessively angry father, Bill
(David Westhead) and placed at this site as part of his campaign to get
a bicycle lane rerouted to avoid the blind corner which led to the death
of his son. The transplanting of the flowers, however, overtly draws the
comparison between a media-manufactured memorial to the 'people's
princess' and the gnawing emptiness of the loss of a close relative, a
child. This narrative grounds *Gideon's Daughter*'s broader contrast
between the worlds. On one hand is the world of the chattering
classes, taken up with high-level meetings in palatial offices; with
movie premières and lavish parties and with focus groups and media
manipulation; on the other hand, there is the everyday world of people
in the London suburbs, working all night in 24/7 convenience stores
because grief over their personal loss deprives them of the capacity to
sleep. The latter situation is specifically that of Stella (Miranda
Richardson), mother of the dead boy and estranged wife of Bill.

It is Gideon's encounter with Stella which is at the core of Sneath's
narrative, which sees Gideon embark on a journey out of the world of
spin, back to his roots and beyond.

As the media world spins Gideon higher and higher to the point
where he is untouchable, 'the toast of Whitehall, the flavour of all
flavours' (ibid.: 190) – and even his lack of interest, inability to listen,
lateness and unreliability are interpreted by clients as signs of genius –
he himself increasingly sees through the hype and comes to reject it.
In parallel with Stella and Bill, he is haunted by the metaphorical loss
of his daughter Natasha (Emily Blunt) who is on the point of leaving
home, either for university in Edinburgh or for the Colombian jungle
to work on a wildlife protection project. As he recognises, however, he
effectively 'lost' Natasha when he was absent from his wife's bedside at
the moment she died of cancer while he was outside making phone

calls to his various girlfriends. The young Natasha feels this to be an act of betrayal of her mother and the conflict between father and daughter reaches a crisis point for Gideon when, at her school-leaving ceremony, Natasha sings a sad song ostensibly about the notorious affairs of Georges Simenon from the point of view of his daughter, who had an obsessive love for him. But entitled 'Papa', the song clearly has resonance for Gideon despite the fact that Natasha tells him, 'It's just a song' (ibid.: 150). Natasha's anger with her father expresses itself rather as a fierce independence and she seems to be courting the dangers of Colombia almost to punish him. For, as Stella later observes, it is Gideon who has an excessive love for his daughter as much as the other way round.

Having spotted Stella from his office window arguing with a man who turns out to be her estranged husband, Gideon initially meets her by chance. However, his offer to intervene in a dispute with the local MP and council over the rerouting of the bicycle route seems more than altruistic. He appears attracted to Stella precisely because she lives outside – and is unimpressed by – the values of the world he inhabits. The return of a video camera, borrowed on Stella's insistence to capture Natasha's song, leads Gideon to suburban Southall where, in time, Stella leaves her guinea-pigs in the care of Hanif at the convenience store and introduces Gideon to the delights of the local Indian restaurant. Gideon risks missing an important meeting with potential client, Mr Badalamenti (Kerry Shale), to the dismay of his business partner Andrew (Tom Hardy) and his office team.

Ironically it transpires that Italian media tycoon Badalamenti (a thinly disguised Berlusconi of Mediaset) is himself two hours late for the meeting. Moreover, he admires what he takes to be Gideon's calculated rudeness as a measure of a man capable of standing up to him, unlike the sycophants who surround him. Again distracted by Stella to make a trip to an urban wasteland in Wolverhampton to hear her friend sing in a church choir, Gideon is inspired to improvise to government representatives on his ideas for the Millennium project to which his guru contribution has been solicited. It seems as if he cannot break free from other people's mystification of his capacities, even though Stella has persuaded him of an alternative perspective on reality more common to the majority of society's distinctive individuals quite unlike 'the sort of medium-sized, shrivelled-up blank sort of people – like I bet you have in your [focus] groups' (ibid.: 168). Ultimately, it is Gideon's deep feelings for his daughter which take him way beyond his comfort zone to a comedy venue in Edinburgh, where he loses all perspective and literally collapses.

Visually, Gideon's journey is marked by the patterning which – as in other of Poliakoff's mature television pieces – distinguishes this drama. From the grand first-floor office from which he initially looks down on the everyday world from a distance, Gideon is drawn first into the central London streets, then to the outer suburbs where he finds himself on all fours trying to recapture a wayward guinea-pig. Finally, outside the Edinburgh comedy club, Natasha finds her father sitting on the pavement unable to get up. Old-fashioned comedians figured in Gideon's early career and a new-wave comic derides him at the moment of its demise. Indeed, death resonates through *Gideon's Daughter*: from Princess Diana's death marked by initial television news and then elaborate coverage of her funeral, through to the death of Stella and Bill's son, and on to Natasha's mother's passing and to Gideon's fears about a possible fate for Natasha should she go to Colombia. Even when she decides to go to Edinburgh University, it is to Gideon, as Sneath notes, 'a little death' (ibid.: 195).[28]

A fear of Natasha's actual death is subsequently hinted at in Sneath's narrative prior to the news report of two young women having been found murdered in Edinburgh. The Poliakovian patterning motif of flowers, a two-faced symbol of the celebration of life and death, is accompanied by long-shots down office, apartment and hospital corridors and along VIP red carpets. In one fine visual sequence, Natasha is seen framed in a large doorway wearing a fifties-style dress for a party along a corridor in the spacious Warner apartment from the point of view of Gideon in a parallel room with one eye on his daughter and the other watching the video of Natasha singing 'Papa' and picking up the repetition of that haunting song.

Yet another atmospheric Adrian Johnston soundtrack subtly underscores *Gideon's Daughter*, a plaintive piano refrain bringing out the depth of the true grief in loss felt by Stella. But it is Thomas Tallis's

Spem in Alium sung by the Wolverhampton choir which undoes Stella in a powerful sequence in which Miranda Richardson portrays direct to camera in a close-up sustained for some considerable time, the inconsolable mix of anguish and guilt of a bereaved mother. Poliakoff returns momentarily to the sense of a visceral dramatic communication which marked his early dramaturgy. The weight of the performance grounds the thinking Stella articulates:

> Bill is right not to let go! . . . I was just thinking in there – however crazy it seems – he's absolutely right not to let go . . . Everything is over so quick now, on to the next thing, get rid of it – think positively! . . . But I come here . . . to this out of the way church – because I need to feel how much . . . (*she begins to cry*). (ibid.: 187)

In a seminal characterisation of postmodernism, Charles Jencks (1989: 16) cites Umberto Eco on the impossibility today of making a declaration of love without an ironic frame, since all the tropes of expression of feeling are outworn.[29] In this sequence, and indeed overall in *Gideon's Daughter*, Poliakoff reasserts his commitment to a humanism which defies the spin and irony of postmodern culture.

However, no simple solution is offered as a way out of a cultural predicament. Gideon invites virtually everybody he knows from his recent and more distant past to another version of the Poliakovian party, located this time at the Southall Indian restaurant, but dominated as usual by Poliakovian red furnishings, and with Stella wearing the red dress. The scene is a distorted mirror view of the movie première earlier in the piece, taking the grandees out of their comfort zone. Some are discomfited and others just puzzled by Gideon's idiosyncrasy, but they are at least brought together on a less hierarchical basis. Gideon, however, retreats initially to the kitchen and then away to Edinburgh in search of Natasha who fails to turn up. It is left to Sneath to summarise the situation: 'You know, it's like he has got all these people together, in this weird place, to say "Grow up . . . you don't need me, to hell with celebrity"' (2005: 205).

Having been reunited, and perhaps partly reconciled with Natasha,

Gideon takes up Stella's suggestion that they just 'go somewhere in the world and see where it leads' (ibid.: 211). The three are seen in long-shot walking away down a broad Edinburgh boulevard and '*they vanish off the street*' (ibid.: 212, s.d.) as bells ring out, pre-empting the Millennium celebrations Gideon has abandoned. It is left to Sneath as narrator, not so much to tie up all the loose ends of possible stories, but to suggest that he believes he has seen a happy Natasha in London (apparently confirmed by a visual sequence) and that he bets Stella and Gideon are still together. The broadly happy ending is under-scored by an image in a crane shot of the Wolverhampton church on Millennium night: '*The music of the oddly shaped choir is pouring triumphantly out of the church's doors into the night air*' (ibid.: 213, s.d.).

The strength of *Gideon's Daughter* over *Friends and Crocodiles* in respect of political commentary is that the critique of the Blair years and of a postmodernist privileging of surface style over substance is grounded in a specific narrative of grief over the loss of children which is drawn from Poliakoff's experience. A contrast between the public and private spheres is built into a dominant public event of the time, Princess Diana's death, particularly when juxtaposed with an intense private grief. The characters, unlike Paul and Lizzie before them, are not symbols caught up in a series of metaphors standing for political shifts over two or three decades, but representing instances, albeit located in a specific time and place, of one of the few experiences which might be regarded as a human universal. The time-frame of the narrative is much tighter, over months rather than the decades of *Friends and Crocodiles*. Moreover the paralleling of the Stella–Bill narrative with the Gideon–Natasha narrative lends structure to under-gird the plot coincidence which brings Gideon and Stella together, lessening a sense of implausibility which pervades the first part of the intended trilogy. The framing of the narrative with Sneath's commen-tary is a feature of Poliakoff's mature dramaturgy evident in *StP* and elsewhere in the 1990s. In this instance, it is used more to lead the viewer in and out of the story than as a distancing device but, as Sneath intermittently reappears with his own young son, it both strengthens the parallelism and draws attention to the principles of composition.

The detailed patterning, particularly evident in *Perfect Strangers* and *The Lost Prince*, is carried through to *Gideon's Daughter*, increasing the sense of authority of the work and lending more weight to the case for Poliakoff as a cinematic auteur, a number of Poliakovian tropes now emerging as identifiable. Critics might claim that the political critique lacks any proposals for meaningful change, but the first stage of making an intervention is to encourage broader recognition of the weaknesses of extant arrangements. In *Gideon's Daughter* the now recognised downside of New Labour, and Tony Blair in particular, is made visible. Bearing out Poliakoff's avowed aim, the piece invited people to see things differently at a time when, in respect of weapons of mass destruction, the Blair government acted upon the free-floating signifiers of postmodern culture rather than insisting on the evidence of substance.

Accounts of the final pairing in this 'second starburst', *Joe's Palace* and *Capturing Mary*, appear later in the book set against some of the earlier plays, film and television work. To conclude this chapter I emphasise the body of work's common concern with the way in which the past inhabits the present of lived experience. By intermixing still images with moving image reconstructions of the past as if in memory, Poliakoff deploys a range of media over and above his distinctive writing, accompanied by Johnston's soundscapes, whose timbres and rhythms parallel the structures of the words and visuals to create dense wefts. His strategies deeply engage both thought and feeling. The textures of the work and the sensuality and sensitivity of the perform-ances by a panoply of fine actors yield a distinctive style and an aesthetic viewing pleasure which is as hard to put into words as it is rare even in contemporary 'high-end' quality television. In an indict-ment of British television and a justification for turning to American quality TV, BBC Director General Mark Thompson complained that 'so much of it just feels dull, mechanical and samey. There's a perva-sive sense of predictability.'[30] He was demonstrably right to commission Poliakoff, in whom he has found a champion for the legacy of authored British drama transformed in a contemporary 'high-end' context.[31]

3 DEVELOPING A DRAMATURGY
FINDING A FRAMEWORK FOR CRITICAL REVIEW

This chapter takes up two interrelated but different aspects of this book. The first flips us sharply back to the outset of Stephen Poliakoff's career in order to foreground the marked difference between then and now and to start tracing the process of development of Poliakoff's dramaturgy which led ultimately to the television high point just discussed. The second aspect involves further articulation of my two key perspectives on Poliakoff's work to afford a framework for critical review: 'agency in structure' and 'complex seeing'. To introduce the first idea in outline, I proposed that circumstances make individuals as much as individuals make the structures they inhabit. This idea stands somewhat in tension with Poliakoff's strong sense of individualism but, in fact, the difference between us is one of emphasis.

As the account of a 'second starburst' has shown, Poliakoff asserted himself in standing against the trend of British television drama in the 1990s to establish a distinctive vision. But to do so he needed to engage with a system, not just in making a wager with the BBC, but in negotiating his approach to 'slow television' with the requirement to attract and hold audiences. As my account of the opening of *StP* indicates, for example, he was shrewd in finding his own ways to grab attention. Furthermore, I have demonstrated the relation between the emergence of his distinctive work and an industrial context in which the time for 'flagship' drama, as opposed to bland product, was right. These are examples in practice of what I mean by 'agency in structure': the need for individuals to function within – and at times against – extant systems, either society at large or microcosms of it such as the institutions of theatre, film and television. Poliakoff's emergence on the theatre scene affords another example of 'agency in structure', though the circumstances are very different since the world of the early 1960s and 1970s was very different from that of the early noughties. We'll revisit those times, and Poliakoff's place in them, before returning to the notion of 'complex seeing' which is increasingly a factor in Poliakoff's developing dramaturgy.

Negotiating the late 1960s/early 1970s

Structures of theatre and society

Poliakoff's beginnings coincided with a significant moment of liberation in society at large following the 'swinging sixties' and, in theatre specifically, following the Theatres Act of 1968 which finally saw an end to three hundred years of institutionalised theatre censorship. Given that theatre takes place in public spaces, involves collective audience experience and constructs partial viewpoints – if not ideological perspectives – typically in conflict, theatre has always been viewed with suspicion by the authorities.[1] Censorship under the Lord Chamberlain's office operated from 1660, becoming statutory under the Licensing Act of 1737 and continuing until 1968. The 1737 Act also restricted the performance of plays to patent theatres (also known as 'legitimate theatre'), non-patent (or 'illegitimate') theatres being allowed to perform only melodrama, pantomime, ballet, opera and music hall (burlesque). This early division between bourgeois and popular theatre influenced debate in the post-1968 liberated theatre, where battle lines were sometimes drawn between established or 'mainstream' drama, based in prominent buildings allegedly for middle-class audiences, and experimental, or 'alternative', theatre for the masses, to be performed wherever a popular audience might gather.

Thus Poliakoff emerged at a time of greater freedom of expression but also of greater questioning of the purposes of theatre than had been possible for many years. Moreover, 1968 is the last moment in recent history when a socialist revolution in Europe, if not the world, still seemed possible, typically signified by *les évènements*, the coming together of students and workers on the streets of Paris with the aim of overthrowing the government. Just as it may seem outmoded to consider the playwright as an auteur, the very notions of political theatre and political drama in Britain have gradually and quietly slipped from view over the decades since the 1970s. Scholarly attention has recently been paid to why this might be and we shall return to the viability of political theatre and drama in the twenty-first century.[2] But theatre culture in the late 1960s/early 1970s was unavoidably political and this was the circumstance Poliakoff had to negotiate to find a space and a voice. Committed views were strongly held by different factions not only about the overall purpose of theatre but also of the writer within it and the very places in which performance might be most effective.

Theatre, then, was a highly contested site and the full detail of its nuances and factions are beyond the scope of this chapter. Though it oversimplifies, a sketch of the Marxist and Situationist positions suggests something of the complexity of dynamic times when 'political ideals were well to the left of the Labour party and indeed quite outside the terms of parliamentary democracy' (Bull 1984: 2). The object of theatre was variously perceived as the promotion of revolutionary change through the education of the masses (Marxist theatre in non-traditional venues) or confrontational shock tactics (as in agit-prop theatre).[3] A significant number of practitioners – John McGrath and 7:84, for example – remained committed to a socialist revolution which Marxist politics understood as the inevitable outcome of the historical forces of class conflict. Marxists took the view that an expanded 'proletariat' (embracing the lower middle class) would inevitably overthrow the smaller 'ruling class' (the owners of the means of production and the attendant upper middle class). Thus, self-consciously Marxist theatre makers at the time sought ways to promote revolution through didactic theatre aimed at making members of the industrial working class aware of social injustice, its causes in capitalism's mechanisms, and their power to do something about it. On the other hand, they sought to persuade lower-middle-class people that their interests would best be served in the imminent power struggle by allying, not with the 'ruling class', but with the 'proletariat'. In short, in the discourse of the time, they sought to dispel 'false consciousness'.

To address the working class, it was thought useless to produce in mainstream buildings, such as national or regional theatres or even local repertory theatres. Would-be revolutionary theatre makers had to go to the factory gates or working men's clubs, mainly in the heartlands of heavy industry in the north of England, Wales and Scotland. At a time which favoured the collective action of working-class culture over the individualism of bourgeois culture, many theatre groups sought to eschew the hierarchy of the writer or director to function democratically by means of collaborative ownership and production. Joint Stock Theatre Company, founded by Max Stafford-Clarke in 1974, is a good example of such a company.[4]

With similarly radical aims, the Situationist tendency adopted a less educative approach seeking to make unsettling interventions to shock the bourgeois out of their complacency. Portable Theatre, founded by David Hare and Richard Bîcat in 1968, exemplifies this disposition. In Bull's summary account (ibid.: 16–17) Portable Theatre 'eschewed both the naturalistic tradition of social drama which had dominated left-wing theatre since the mid-fifties and the dialectical Brechtian model, in favour of a series of assault courses in which the audience was frequently as much the target as the ostensible subject-matter'. Stephen Poliakoff was very briefly part of Portable Theatre, in a position junior to the slightly but significantly older writers in the collective which co-operatively produced the play *Lay-by*.

Based on a report, cut from a newspaper by Trevor Griffiths, of an alleged motorway rape, *Lay-by* was instigated by David Hare, who enlisted Howard Brenton, Brian Clark, Hugh Stoddart and Snoo Wilson, along with Poliakoff and Griffiths, into the project. Ironically given Portable Theatre's aim to avoid established buildings, the final version of *Lay-by was* performed in a theatre in 1971.[5] The piece was, however, intentionally provocative and shocking. In Hayman's summary account of the final scene, 'naked male and female corpses were daubed with paint by two hospital attendants, who then stewed them in a large vat and started to eat them'.[6] Portable Theatre's notorious aggression and shock tactics, associated with the Paris Situationists (ibid.: 12ff.), arose from contempt for bourgeois constraint, particularly in theatre practice. Brenton has reflected that 'a really great outburst of nihilism like . . . the last act of *Lay-by* is one of the most beautiful and positive things you can see on a stage' (Hayman 1974: 94).

Different spaces required different dramaturgies, outdoor venues or working men's clubs requiring particular kinds of approach. Some, such as agit-prop, were theatrically crude with slogans and bold gestures,[7] while the more didactic Marxist political theatre companies discovered the need to work within recognisable popular forms. The touring work of Red Ladder, or the 7:84 companies mobilised by John McGrath and Liz McLennan in England and Scotland, serve as examples of such committed theatre, verging at times on populist forms.[8] In his influential series of lectures at Cambridge University (subsequently published in book form), John McGrath (1981: 95) acknowledged the compromises involved, but argued that theatres such as the RSC and the National were unable to make a left-wing political intervention since such attempts 'did not eradicate their "bourgeois" values'.

Despite the failure of *les évènements* in 1968 to mobilise a wider revolution, the possibility of fundamental political change was still eagerly anticipated in the early 1970s by most shades of left-of-centre politics. Indeed, disillusion at the failure of the Labour governments headed by Harold Wilson (Prime Minister, 1964–70 and 1974–76) to fulfil the post-war socialist agenda, drew many intellectuals to the conclusion that radical change could be effected only by revolution and not at all by parliamentary democracy. Contrary to McGrath, however, Brenton and Hare's disillusion about democratic means of reform was succeeded by a loss of belief in the class basis of revolution. In respect of theatre, in David Edgar's neat formulation (1979: 25–33), they moved away from the 'organisation of the working class at the point of production . . . [to the] disruption of bourgeois ideology at the point of consumption'. They now argued that the NT was exactly the place where serious writers might have impact.

Away from the Paris barricades, the chrysalis of the 1950s teenager had continued to yield the butterfly of 'beautiful young things' of the 1960s. It was a time, indeed, when young people might assert themselves in the theatre as elsewhere in society. Some were able cheaply to start 'alternative' or 'experimental' companies, while other young individuals became engaged by expensive, mainstream, building-based theatres. Peter Brook became Director of Productions at Covent Garden at the age of twenty-three, while Peter Hall headed up the Royal Shakespeare Company at the age of twenty-six with Trevor Nunn succeeding him at the age of twenty-nine. Even writers' theatre was undergoing change, however. As Simon Shepherd (2009: 14) has recently reflected, Peter Hall's displacement of Laurence Olivier as the manager of the National, and his invitation to Howard Brenton to stage *Weapons of Happiness* as the theatre's first new play in 1976, seemed, in Hall's words, to have opened the establishment theatre's doors 'to the fringe, to musicians, to poets, to the young with their experiments'. Indeed, when employed by the NT, Brenton brought his radicalism with him and a new dramatic technique which aimed to throw 'petrol bombs through the proscenium arch' (Bull 1984: 16).

Revolution by any of these means was not, of course, brought about. On the contrary, a marked rightward swing in politics, mobilised by way of the consumer individualism of the Reagan–Thatcher decades, the 1980s and 1990s, makes it hard, even for those who lived through the late 1960s, to remember that there was a time when a socialist revolution in Europe seemed possible.

Agents and agency

It was into the maelstrom sketched above that Stephen Poliakoff was drawn in the early 1970s. His driving ambition was to be an original playwright just as a sense of disillusionment with mainstream political drama had begun to lead to an explosion of 'alternative theatre'. He thus had to decide what kind of plays he wanted to write, with whom, and for which audiences. Though unquestionably on the liberal-left, Poliakoff's commitment was not as overtly radical as that of some of his peers. Indeed, knowing with hindsight the extent to which he has emerged as an auteur with a wish for maximum creative control over his output, it is not surprising that his early brush with Portable Theatre and collaborative approaches to writing was short-lived. Since most of the more experimental companies engaged in collaborative, devised production processes, it is no more surprising that Poliakoff gravitated quite quickly from writing plays for London's fringe theatres (Little Theatre, Hampstead Theatre, Bush Theatre) towards more mainstream institutions. Though it would be too simplistic to think of Poliakoff as simply electing for the establishment and not any of the 'alternatives', it will be evident why his sympathies and writing residency at the National might have placed him as an outsider on the mid-1970s theatre scene, frowned upon by the more militant and experimental practitioners. Some of his peers, indeed, unkindly considered him to be 'selling out' politically. David – now, ironically, Sir David – Hare wanted nothing to do, as noted, with the establishment and building-based theatres in his Portable years. David Edgar pursued an agit-prop touring theatre, the General Will, operating out of Bradford. McGrath, though established in film and television, also headed north with 7:84. Trevor Griffiths turned early in his career to television as an alternative space to the factory gates for speaking directly to working-class people.

At a time, then, when 'the emergent work was asking deep questions about the relevance of writing to performance' (Shepherd 2009: 114), Poliakoff's self-assurance as a writer of relatively conventional plays sets him at odds with the strong tides of the times. He became an 'outsider' in this respect, as well as by inherited disposition and by his age. It is important to recognise that Poliakoff, who went up to Cambridge in 1970, just missed the revolutionary fervour of student protest and 'sit-ins' which writers, a few years older than he was, experienced. Indeed, if nothing else, he feels he missed out on the fun of university in the late 1960s which his older brother had enjoyed.[9] Another factor which left Poliakoff as something of an outsider was the conviction in some quarters that performers should articulate in their work ideas and sentiments shared by their audiences. Some, indeed, advocated obligatory class solidarity among theatre practitioners.

As indicated in Chapter 1, Stephen Poliakoff has no natural allegiance with the working class since he is part of a family of upper-middle-class Russian Jews and was educated at Westminster

School and Cambridge. Having fled from the Stalinist pogroms, the historical consciousness of his family inevitably involves a sense of the dangers of the totalitarian state of Russia under Stalin which, though a caricature of the communist state envisaged by Marx as the outcome of political revolution, has often been confused with it in the Western imagination. Inheriting something of his father's Russian émigré sense of being an outsider, coupled with an embodied sense of the history of Jewish persecution, Poliakoff was personally disposed to be less of a collaborative participant and more of an outside observer. Furthermore, the family tradition of outstandingly able individuals perhaps helps to explain Poliakoff's disposition towards auteurism.

Poliakoff's outsider perspective leads him to resist trends. As society at large, and intellectual life in particular, has increasingly made accommodations with the apparently inexorable forces of commercial culture, Poliakoff has repeatedly, and in different ways, asserted a liberal-left resistance. There is a consistent critique of the 1960s brutalist environment in Poliakoff's early professional theatre plays along with attacks on mass commercial culture. Poliakoff's subsequent advocacy of 'slow television', as recounted, entails a conscious critique of the ever-increasing pace of contemporary television series driven by commercial imperatives. An espousal of individualism against mass society has been mistaken in some quarters, however, as indicative of a cultural, if not political, conservatism, and may have contributed to Poliakoff being under-represented in critical literature. In the 1980s academy, cultural studies emerged to valorise popular culture and undermine the hierarchies which privileged established, 'legitimate' culture. It shifted attention away from text to context, and it undermined criticism in the humanist tradition which had celebrated 'great work'. At this time, Poliakoff was writing primarily for the NT and the RSC and, even though his plays may have been counter-cultural in the ways indicated, he was perceived as being mainstream.

Moreover, his critique of commercially driven popular culture resonated with the increasingly unfashionable Frankfurt School. After the First World War, the Marx-inspired academics at Frankfurt am Main University's Institute for Social Research were sceptical about the capacity of the downtrodden working class to fulfil predictions of its role in a world revolution. They became critical of Marx's economism and turned their attention to other means of cultural critique. Their scepticism about commercial culture was fuelled by an urgent concern in the early 1930s at the capacity of Hitler's rallies to manipulate the masses. Indeed, leading figures, Marcuse, Adorno and Horkheimer, became Jewish refugees, relocating in New York in 1933 to continue the Frankfurt School's work. In Janet Woollacott's summary (1982: 105), their writing ascribed to the mass media and the culture industry 'a role of ideological dominance which destroys both bourgeois individualism and the revolutionary potential of the working class'. A number of Poliakoff's plays in the 1970s show a concern with individuals, and particularly young people, suffering oppression under the mechanism of what Adorno called 'the culture industries'. *City Sugar* and *American Days* in particular reveal the workings of mass culture to militate against individual expression. In D. Keith Peacock's summary (1984: 499), *American Days* exposes 'the American-inspired pop music industry which exploits young performers and even its own executives for as long as their commercial value lasts'. Both plays, however, show glimmers of potential resistance to the hegemonic power of the spectacle and commercial culture. While such a view of the 'culture industries' might have found sympathetic hearing among middle-class theatre-goers in the late 1970s, the rise of cultural studies in the academy saw an increasing critique of the Frankfurt School position. Poliakoff's unconscious allegiances and his lack of overt Marxist affiliations left him open to suspicion which this book aims to review.[10]

Poliakoff need not, of course, have turned to political drama at all and might have written well-turned plays for London's West End commercial theatre (to which some of his plays did indeed transfer). It remains, then, to consider in what sense, if at all, he might be considered a political playwright. Peacock (ibid.: 496) claims that he is 'not a political dramatist' and there is 'no analysis of [social problems'] economic or political causes' in his early work, while Oleg Kerensky (1977: 261) cites a young Poliakoff arguing that 'political drama is very remote from anything the audience can identify with'. In respect of theatre practice, Sandy Craig (1980: 30–1) makes a useful, if somewhat sharp, distinction between political theatre and political drama:

> [p]olitical plays seek to appeal to, and influence, the middle class, in particular that section of the middle class which is influential in moulding 'public opinion'. The implication of this is that society can be reformed and liberalized, where necessary, by the shock troops of the middle class – and, of course, such people are influential in campaigns for reform. But, further, political plays in bourgeois theatre implicitly realize that the middle class remains the progressive class within society. Political theatre, on the other hand, as embodied in the various political theatre companies, aims – with varying degrees of success – to appeal to, and be an expression of, the working class. Its underlying belief is that the working class is the progressive class within society.

Theatre makers in the early 1970s were confronted with overt, if not always conscious, choices about where and how they might make a social intervention. The stark choice, as Craig formulates it, was between revolution and 'gradualism', a term of insult from the point of view of the far left.

Among the very limited amount of scholarly writing about his work, Poliakoff is included in David Ian Rabey's review of *British and Irish Political Drama in the Twentieth Century* (1986). But Poliakoff's approach makes him hard to place politically. He is not included in Bull's seminal *New British Political Dramatists* (1984) which discusses Hare, Brenton, Barker and Bond. In a review of Michael Patterson's (2003) retrospective on British political theatre, Steve Barfield suggests that, from the point of view of most teachers, their students and play-goers, the term British political theatre indicates 'one of a dozen playwrights working in Britain between the late 50s to the late 80s. These would include: Arnold Wesker; John Arden; Trevor Griffiths; (early) Howard Barker; Edward Bond; Howard Brenton; John McGrath; David Hare; David Edgar; Caryl Chuchill; Peter Barnes.'[11] There is no mention of Stephen Poliakoff, either in the review or in Patterson's book. I propose, however, that he should be located, following Craig's distinction, on the side of political drama rather than political theatre.

Though not radical in form, Poliakoff's very early plays make a critique of established values, and *Clever Soldiers* (see Chapter 7) shows an awareness of a revolutionary spirit. Poliakoff has the young left-wing Oxford don, David, advise his tutee, Teddy:

> Very soon there's going to be such a holocaust you know. The world's biggest battle, bigger than anything ever before, and whatever the outcome, this revulsion is going to start working. This wave of revulsion – and revenge – that is building up all the time, is going to reach explosive proportions . . . It's going to completely slash through this stupor we're in – do you hear, boy, and everything will go down before it. This government, this place, and all its assorted barbarism – the whole hierarchy will collapse. (Poliakoff 1997: 59)

In the context of the play, David is referring to a sense prior to the First World War, that socio-political life was stagnant. But read in the 1970s, particularly by young intellectuals, it might resonate with a sense that even after the Second World War the repeated promise of fundamental social change had not been fulfilled but that, in accordance with the Marxist perspective, 'Socialism – it has to happen . . . It'll happen. There's no stopping it' (ibid.: 54).

In spite of his individualism, Kerensky (1977: 261) records that Poliakoff is '[l]eft-wing in his sympathies'. His work over forty years evidences a social critique and a liberal-left resistance to capitalist culture. That said, a number of questions remain about the mode of address of his developing dramaturgy and of his attitude to popular culture and the working class, since he has been criticised for writing about a culture he neither inhabited nor understood. Moreover, because his work, far from being direct agit-prop, is often metaphorical and ambivalent, his political position even as a mainstream theatre playwright was in question.

To write plays for middle-class audiences in established theatres with a view to enlisting that class's potential to influence gradualist, rather than revolutionary social change, involves a particular kind of dramaturgy. Rabey (1986: 2) takes 'political drama' (as distinct from 'social drama') to be 'that which views specific social abuses as symptomatic of a deeper illness, namely injustice and anomalies at the heart of society's basic power structure'. This definition well suits Poliakoff's early stance, which takes specific situations and, by exploring character in context, anatomises a moment or trend in history and reveals its ambiguities. To pick up again on one of my two keynote terms, Poliakoff himself sets 'agency in structure' for the ultimate contemplation of audiences, even though the experience in the theatre might also be more visceral. Unlike some of his peers' more didactic, overtly ideological writing, Poliakoff is less direct politically, espousing neither a critical naturalism nor foregrounding dialectical contradictions such as an avowed Marxist playwright (Edward Bond, for example) would see as inherent in the social fabric. Nevertheless, from the outset, Poliakoff is seeking a dramaturgy to elicit 'complex seeing' to fulfil his aim to encourage audiences to see things differently but not to take up any specific political perspective. This term now needs to be further unpacked.

Complex seeing

My adoption of the concept of 'complex seeing' as key to the framework for critical review of Poliakoff's work owes a debt to Raymond Williams (1981: 321ff.) who, in turn, acknowledges Brecht's reflection on his production of *The Threepenny Opera*. In question is the theatre strategy most likely to encourage audience members to engage with, and reflect critically on, what they are witnessing. Brecht (cited ibid.) concluded that '[t]hinking *above* the flow of the play is more important than thinking from *within* the flow of the play'. That is to say spectators should not just be drawn into involvement in the characters, plot and issues of the drama, however thought-provoking, but also be positioned outside (above) the play.

Williams comes at the question from another angle. Responding to 'the essential naturalist thesis of the "illusion of reality", in which an action is created that is so life-like that the verisimilitude absorbs the whole attention of both dramatist and audience', he notes that:

> [w]hat Brecht seized on was the exclusion, by particular conventions of verisimilitude, of all direct commentary, alternative consciousness, alternative points of view. At the simplest level, he is calling for their restoration: historically, these had been the convention of chorus, narrator, soliloquy; or, in more complicated movements, the achievement of a dramatic design which was more than a design of the action. (ibid.: 318)

Brecht was primarily interested in the impact upon the spectator, but Williams (ibid.) notes that this emphasis confused things: 'The issue is not in the spectator but in the play: whether in its dramatic design it is an essentially valued action.' Something in the dramaturgy is needed to mobilise complex seeing in the spectator – experience, that is, from more than one point of view simultaneously. Where Brecht emphasised the impact upon audiences, Williams insists that complex seeing 'had to be realised in a play' (ibid.: 321), within its principles of composition.

This insight validates both Poliakoff's sense of authorial power and the need for textual criticism such as undertaken in this book, because it is by exploring the principles of composition, as well as on occasion actual audience responses, that we come to understand how theatre, film and television function, and thus the quality of specific works. Developing Brecht, Williams wanted plays to show people's dreams and potential but also to offer a commentary on how the achievement of what was desired is constrained by social forces. In sum, he embraces the revelation of 'agency in structure' within the notion of 'complex seeing'. The plays and films which made Poliakoff's name in the 1970s (see Chapter 4) show young people trying to make their way through brutalist city environments in which a commercialised culture seeks to distract them from their limited life opportunities. Together, the plays offer a critique of a cultural moment and, Poliakoff's dramaturgy begins, within the context of political drama, to achieve his avowed aim, 'to make the audience look at the world slightly differently'.[12]

Though not a social realist, Poliakoff initially adopts a direct, visceral dramaturgy aimed at drawing audiences to share the lived experience of the characters under challenging circumstances. A term recently coined by Shepherd captures it. 'Expressive realism'

[c]reates the conditions in which an audience has the sense of recognising something as the characteristic expression of its own time. The form works with a stage image which is familiar generating emotions which are transparently communicated, and from here, in the best work, moves to the articulation of a larger feeling about 'society' and 'people' in general. It constructs the audience into a position where they agree to share this feeling and recognise its expressive truth. (Shepherd 2009: 141–2)

Through staging, powerful use of sound and scripting, Poliakoff conveys a strong sense of physical environments and the sensuous 'feel' of experiencing them. At best the grounding of the characters in context anchors the spiralling metaphors which afford a broader socio-cultural commentary. Another strategy frequently deployed involves shifts in character presentation which surprise audiences and invite a repositioning not only on the individual, revealed to be other than they seemed, but on the situation which brought the change about. Similarly, small but significant subversions of genre challenge expectations. These moves beyond strict realism led some critics to accuse Poliakoff of 'abandoning credibility both in his situations and in the behaviour of his characters' (Peacock 1984: 497), an aspect which is manifest in *Friends and Crocodiles*. But viewed through the lens of expressive realism, this attempt to make broader connections might be seen as strength rather than weakness.

Typically, a core antagonism demands that the audience shift their position in the process of witnessing. Rabey (1986: 3) argues that 'political drama is successful when the audience's morality is poised against contemporary society, so that the enforced fluctuation between two ostensibly congruent sets of norms reveals a contradiction'. In some early plays strong characters attract through their positive energy and capacity to achieve in the world, but aspects of their success invite an interrogation of the social fabric which facilitates it. For example, the charismatic DJ, Leonard Brazil in *City Sugar*, is contemptuous of both the anodyne popular culture he peddles and the young people who consume it. Ultimately he is offered a lucrative contract with a London company and a bigger platform on which to operate, which he accepts even though it is clear that he has neither interest in, nor respect for, the role. A middle-class audience might admire Brazil's enterprise and yet recognise the cynicism in his exploitation of young people. As Rabey suggests of what he calls 'satirical anatomies', such plays 'work by referring to a latent sense of morality all the more striking by its absence from a play's heightened image of our society engaged in its characteristic processes' (ibid.: 4).

The perspective of the outsider, developed beyond just the onlooker's fresh eye on a familiar subject, is, however, Poliakoff's distinctive contribution to strategies of 'complex seeing'. Towards his sophisticated treatment, Poliakoff explores a quasi-Brechtian use of narrators, framing devices and double perspectives of time and space in late-1990s plays such as *Blinded by the Sun* and *Remember This* which runs through to Oswald in *StP*. Though the perspective remains within (as distinct from above) the play, Poliakoff ultimately develops character – and camera – as participant observer. Though involved in the action, characters such as Johnnie and Daniel sustain a detachment from which point of view the action is observed, by them literally and by the camera more broadly, in the very process of its experience.[13] Particularly in the context of the recent television pieces, this double perspective leaves readers unsure where to place their emotional engagement. It gives rise to a productive tension in the viewing experience between intimate emotional involvement and detached thought, a sophisticated 'complex thinking-feeling'. Moreover, because the contexts of Poliakoff's plays typically embody a specific moment in history, the revelations about ordinary-seeming characters make them more resonant, inviting thought about the times which produced them. Thus, in a less programmatic way than a Marxist writer intent on illustrating the underlying forces of history, Poliakoff nevertheless makes connections between character and environment in time.

The strategy is not revolutionary in respect of fundamentally displacing the status quo, but it is political in so far as it aims to shock people out of complacent, habitual ways of seeing. In an entertainment medium, it displaces simplistic and narrow viewpoints which might be characterised in Prime Minister Thatcher's TINA dictum ('There Is No Alternative'). Under such regimes, to elicit complex seeing is to be radical.

The 'Poliakovian'

It is helpful at this point to summarise characteristics of the 'Poliakovian' which readers can identify and evaluate as they progress through their own viewings and my readings of the life and work. The notion will be revisited in Chapter 9.

The Poliakovian consciousness is embedded in European (notably Jewish) history and the *Poliakovian habitus* involves a disposition to be original in creative expression, picking up on socio-cultural trends but, on occasion, resisting them if they threaten to diminish human agency.

Themes include: family relations – particularly oppressive patriarchs; vulnerability in entrapment; the outsider perspective and suffocation of the individual spirit (oppressed youth, the Jew, the immigrant; the aged; the social eccentric, the resister of social erosion, the spy); and obsession. They also include: cultural trends; built environments – including the concealed corners and subterranean tunnels of London; urban despoliation of the environment; the impact of new technologies – downsides as well as progressive possibilities; and history – particularly Jewish experience;

Tropes (particularly in cinematic patterning) include: corridors and underground tunnels; parties and picnics; hot summer days; train and bus travel; colour in environment and costume – in particular red buses and red dresses; staircases – shot from above, below and through the banisters; cages – characters framed against doorways, windows; latterly, cats – offering comfort, even wisdom. Recursively looped, haunting soundtracks and intrusive noise.

These 'Poliakovian' traits are fully visible in the television work discussed in the previous chapter. Poliakoff's early work, though evidencing some of these features, is less concerned with the family and European history and more with the English urban contemporary. The next chapter deals with his meteoric rise from the London fringe into the 'institutionalised' theatre buildings of the NT and the RSC through 'expressive realist' treatments of urban youth in the 1970s.

4 'METEORIC RISE' (1970S)
URBAN YOUTH ON STAGE AND SCREEN

This chapter initially traces mid- to late-1970s plays concerned with youth culture in the urban settings of post-war modernity for which Poliakoff first became famous: *Hitting Town, City Sugar* and *Shout Across the River*. It brings out what Ronald Hayman noted as the 'remarkable intensity' (1979: 119) of Poliakoff's early dramaturgy and his feel for locations – particularly, but not exclusively, in London. Ultimately, the chapter follows the 'urban canyons'[1] through to the films *Bloody Kids* (1979) and *The Tribe* (1998), addressing an ambivalence in Poliakoff's attitudes to modernity and popular culture. Many of the protagonists are, in different ways, outsiders on the edge of society, but Poliakoff's positioning of audiences as observers, in spite of his strategies viscerally to draw them in, can be seen to be emergent.

Hitting Town (1975)

Hitting Town was first staged in April 1975 at the Bush Theatre.[2] It was a shocking play in its time partly because it addresses the potential for relationships between siblings, a topic to which Poliakoff returns in *Close My Eyes*. But the incestuous relationship between brother and sister in *Hitting Town* is less a specific focus than a manifestation in unorthodox behaviour of a need to break out of a context which dulls the senses. Though the theme of incest might have a timeless and ominous quality in theatrical precedents since Greek drama, the impact here arises from *Hitting Town* being very much a play of its time. Located temporally by specific references to the then recent 'Guildford and Birmingham bombings', *Hitting Town*, unlike Poliakoff's more overtly historical plays, is not concerned to investigate historical causation. The signifiers of time and place are more a means of creating a feel for the contemporary mid-1970s, a time when – as Poliakoff himself has, with slight exaggeration, remarked – 'as you walked down the streets you expected cars to blow up in front of you' (1997: 74). But anticipated bombings serve in *Hitting Town* as a signifier not just of the potential for actual explosions, but also of potential eruptions in a social fabric so bland that it perhaps demands rebellion. Likewise, the incest serves as a sign of the characters' perceived need to break out from the suffocation of life in a concrete jungle. In an instance of one kind of 'Poliakovian' ambivalence, *Hitting Town* affords a snapshot of a time at once sporadically dangerous and repressed. Poliakoff writes of 'the ugly mood of the mid-seventies, about people growing inward and private and lonely after the noise and frivolity of the sixties' (ibid.).

Hitting Town is a sparse, almost impressionist, play of just seven juxtaposed scenes, loosely shaped around a visit by Ralph to his sister Clare's flat in their home town, Leicester, in the UK Midlands. The setting for the initial and later action, Clare's room, is 'a featureless, nasty blank box' (ibid.) located in a post-war, inner-city precinct with a concrete tunnels and walkway. At the outset, Clare is depressed, having recently split up with her boyfriend. To cheer her up, Ralph, in his idiosyncratic way, offers to take her out to 'hit the town' in one ironic formulation of the play's title. This offer of a meal and a good time motivates a tour through the somewhat bleak, sub-modernist precinct which introduces the distinctive Poliakovian interest in the direct experience of character in the built environment. In respect of a restaurant, the town affords only a Wimpy Bar which fails to serve the couple any food but allows them to meet up with Nicola, an eighteen-year-old waitress, who, it transpires, also has a yearning to break out from her mundane job. She ultimately leads Ralph and Clare to a basement 'disco' playing 'bubblegum music' (ibid.: 103, s.d.) where, prefiguring karaoke, she has long waited to perform in the solo slot. She sings along to the soundtrack of 'This Wheel's on Fire', building up after a hesitant start to a 'clenched feeling' and culminating in a 'shattering scream' (ibid.: 108). The scream echoes a similar *cri de coeur* in the precinct where, she tells Ralph and Clare, she sometimes shouts in the vacant space (see ibid.: 97).

Poliakoff was determined in his early plays to create 'vivid, tactile, emotional theatre' (1997: ix). Prior to Nicola's scream, Ralph also actively expresses his frustrations. While at the Wimpy Bar waiting in desperation to be served, he begins to compose a 'meal' from the various condiments available. Enticing Clare to join him, he attacks with a fork the plastic tomato which in the early seventies was popular as a ketchup dispenser. The image is a memorable example of Poliakoff's ability to capture a mood in a graphic moment on-stage. The contents of the ketchup dispenser: 'Bit of chewing gum – half of a sardine . . . lots of cigarette butts' (ibid.: 90) and, finally a tooth coated in ketchup, viscerally convey the tawdriness of the times as experienced by the restless Ralph. His attack on the plastic tomato enacts a resistance to an anodyne culture. He remarks, 'You can always tell a town by what's in its tomatoes. All its undesirables are there. It spews them out' (ibid.), as if he has regularly encountered such gastronomic disappointments. Ralph's character is quirky with an unusual sensibility and, in Hayman's view, he is 'more plausible, more deeply thought-out than Teddy in *Clever Soldiers*' (1979: 122). In an early alert to Poliakoff's use of sharp sound, Ralph is very sensitive to intrusive noise, being troubled by music emanating from the room adjacent to Clare's, to the noise of the city as it filters up to Clare's high-rise room, and to the 'sound of musak' (ibid.: 86). In drawing the character, Poliakoff conveys through action as well as dialogue the overall impression of an unpredictable energy – in the precinct Ralph adds to the graffiti and, in the flat, he punches the wall in frustration. The ambiguity of his character, by turns menacing and playful, resonates with the unexplained disturbing mix of Pinter's celebrated characters in the 1970s.

Though the drawing of the character is vivid, it is not easy to pin Ralph down. Supposedly a student in London, Ralph is fanciful on a number of occasions. Initially he claims only to have been near explosions but, at the end of the play, he claims he was 'Right on top' (ibid.: 118). He makes a phone call to a radio DJ revealing to the world, but in the guise of an eleven-year-old child, his true relationship with his sister. At the end of the play, he attempts a hoax phone call, claiming to be 'the IRA speaking' and giving warning of 'a bomb somewhere in the Haymarket' (ibid.: 121). The phone calls mark the parallel between events which erupt from beneath an apparently calm surface, the bombs planted in a city-centre pub and the sexual attraction erupting in the relationship between Ralph and Clare, ten years his senior. The play's title, *Hitting Town*, thus comes to carry two additional accents: the bomb hitting Birmingham and the impact of the bombshell of an incestuous relationship in 1970s theatre and society.

Ralph places emphasis on the fact that Clare is his sister because Nicola has observed them kissing in public, first a possibly innocent kiss but then a '*sexual kiss*' (ibid.: 92). The kisses mark the beginning of their incestuous relationship which is consummated on their return, slightly drunk, to Clare's flat after the failed dinner and disco at the end of scene 6. Looking back, Poliakoff remarked that he wished *Hitting Town* had 'burrowed deeper into the incestuous relationship between the brother and the sister' (ibid.: ix). In marked contrast to *Close My Eyes*, in which the physical sexual engagement is graphically represented on screen, the consummation in *Hitting Town* takes place off-stage. Even the television adaptation does not go beyond bare shoulders and an overt sexual kiss.[3] In both, the pair appears half dressed the following morning when the breach of a profound social taboo is pointed up by a phone call from Clare and Ralph's mother, inviting audiences to think what her reaction would be if only she knew. Although the pair find the situation amusing, they are patently aware of its significance and the eerie quiet of the early morning in the flat is likened by Ralph to the aftermath of the Birmingham bombing. Poliakoff has himself drawn a parallel with the environment suggesting that the incestuous relationship should seem 'as fragile and impermanent as the architecture Clare and Ralph were passing through' (ibid.: xi).

A sense that post-war architecture deserved to be short-lived is betrayed in the hostility towards it manifest not only in Ralph and Clare's experience of *ennui* in the play but in the stage directions indicating the theatrical construction of the built environment. In the theatre, the environments beyond Clare's room 'can be suggested simply by concrete blocks etc.' (ibid.: 74, s.d.) front stage. In the TV adaptation, the 1970s interior is intensified by a cheaply furnished flat with an avocado bathroom suite. Poliakoff's attitude to tawdry environments is evident both in the stage directions (Clare's room is 'modern, hideous', ibid.: 74, s.d.) and in Ralph's remarking of the Wimpy Bar that 'They're multiplying all the time . . . They ought to be hounded' (ibid.: 87). Ralph tells Nicola that the '[w]hole centre has changed – me and my *sister* used to know a different place . . . You know most of the architects of this atrocity are probably in gaol or just about to be. But we're left with it. Something ought to be done' (ibid.: 96).

In sum, *Hitting Town* remains striking as an impressionist portrait of a historical moment. In the mid-1970s, its impact arose from its reflective construction of a graphically realised metaphor of an unhealthy society, captured in the mix of a brutalist built environment, sporadic bombings caused through political unrest and turmoil in an incestuous personal relationship. It mobilised Poliakoff's concern viscerally to convey the life experience of young people whose energies and potential were not matched by opportunities in their urban environment. The extent to which this amounts to a critique of modernity will be considered following discussion of *City Sugar*, the partner play to *Hitting Town*.

City Sugar (1975)

If *Hitting Town* introduced a scepticism about the post-war built environment, *City Sugar*, according to Michael Billington, is 'full of genuine animus against the brutalism of our provincial cities and of the society which treats its young as consumers ripe for exploitation' (*Guardian*, 10 October 1975). Billington's review relates to the first production at the Bush Theatre but the play transferred in 1976 to the Comedy Theatre, London, with Adam Faith replacing John Shrapnel in the lead role.[4] More directly, perhaps, than in *Hitting Town*, Poliakoff sets his sights on popular culture seen as 'bubblegum for the masses' in the form of commercial radio and, in particular, DJ Leonard Brazil. Brazil's broadcasts are first heard by Ralph, Clare and

Wimpy waitress, Nicola Davies, blasting out in the precincts of the earlier play. In *City Sugar*, however, the characters of Leonard Brazil and Nicola Davies are central.

Now employed in a supermarket, Nicola listens to Brazil's radio show at work as well as at home and she enters one of his phone-in competitions. Brazil is struck by the very flatness of Nicola's voice and bends the rules of his competition so that she wins a record by the Yellow Jacks, on condition that she enters another competition to meet the band. Listening at work, Nicola misses the question because of an intercom announcement. At the risk of being captured by the roving security camera in the supermarket, Nicola makes unauthorised use of the staff phone to chase the next question in pursuit of her dream of visiting the radio station. Assisted by her friend, Susan, she proceeds to make a life-size effigy of one of the Yellow Jacks to enter Brazil's 'Competition of the Century'. In another of Poliakoff's graphic metaphors, Nicola and Susan pile the entire contents of Nicola's bedroom – the posters on her wall, her collection of furry animals, and even the canned food she has stolen from the supermarket – into the model. Brazil, haunted by Nicola's featureless voice, changes his first choice of final contestants to ensure that Nicola is one of the two finalists. The device is used by Poliakoff to bring two key aspects of the play head to head: Nicola's seduction by celebrity in the form of a local radio disc jockey and a boy band; and Brazil's capacity to manipulate his audience while privately questioning the means of seduction and the credulity of his fans.

Though good at his job, Brazil is sceptical about its cultural impact, referring to his role as 'playing this mindless, milk chocolate pap, or manufactured synthetic violence endlessly to kids' (ibid.: 201). His interest in Nicola is in the very flatness of not only her voice but her demeanour. He contrives for her to progress in the competition so that he can elicit some reaction. As he puts it:

> I glanced at you before the first question and I saw that stare, that blank, infuriatingly vacant gaze, and then it just happened. I wanted to see just how far I *could push you*, how much you'd take – I was hoping you'd come back – that something would

come shooting back, that you'd put up a fight Nicola . . . What's the matter with all you kids now, what is it? (ibid.: 203)

He is finally moved to '*shake* [Nicola] *really violently for several seconds*' (ibid., s.d.) to no apparent effect, and, frustrated, he concludes, 'You almost feel Nicola Davies as if you're from another planet' (ibid.: 203).

The play is structured into two Acts of five and four scenes respectively. Each Act culminates in a soliloquy by Brazil. The first Act ends on Brazil's first telephone encounter with Nicola but, as he talks, he slides into a stream of consciousness reflecting critically, indeed cynically, on his role as a popular radio DJ. He reveals the boredom and frustrations of DJs between the records they play, suggesting that 'some long to scream obscenities over the air'. He proceeds to characterise the 'Mad DJ': 'And they use words sumptuously for your pleasure. Do you ever listen to your words, Brazil? Never, thank goodness, but never mind. Everybody needs us, after all – (*Lightly.*) – we're the new jokers of the pack, we're the new clowns . . .' (ibid.: 170). He characterises popular radio as a distraction from serious concerns:

We're going to make it aren't we, get through to the other side, of course we are – and if you've just seen something horrible on the television, bomb blasts, unemployment, politicians, and all that part of our good old England, and you've switched it off to listen to me, sensibly. Then remember, no need to fear we're going to lick it, so Shout it out! Things can only get better – so Shout it out! We have the greatest day of the century tomorrow, so there's something to look forward to. (ibid.)

The long piece to conclude Act I is a theatrical *tour de force* to leave the audience pondering its import over their interval drinks. Confused in his ranting, Brazil by turns critiques and advocates the contrived excitements of his Competition of the Century, ultimately seeing the attractions of popular radio as saccharine. This reading of contemporary culture is supported by a moment in Act II also bordering on frenzy, in which Brazil interrupts Big John's local news bulletin,

79

remarking on its mundanity: 'They call this news . . . Waste of Time isn't it?' In place of the news, he proposes to 'spin another circle of happiness and pour a little more sugar over the city' (ibid.: 195), that is to play another pop music track.

Throughout Act II, Brazil scarcely controls a seething anger. He taunts his producer, Rex, who craves a little airtime in his aspiration himself one day to be a DJ. Brazil's frustration is fuelled by the fact that Nicola and her co-contestant, Jane, seem willing to suffer any indignity in order to achieve the prize. Incredulous, Brazil openly confronts Nicola: 'You can't really like this shit, can you, do you really deep down inside, like this music?' When Nicola's response is at best non-committal, Brazil confides: 'You know, Nicola, if, ten years ago even – (*Mock voice*) – when things were very different, I'd been told that I'd be doing this job, playing this mindless milk chocolate pap. Or manufactured synthetic violence endlessly to kids like you, I wouldn't have thought it remotely possible' (ibid.: 201).

The irony at the centre of *City Sugar*, however, is that the DJ protagonist gains more and more success in a role to which he is wholly unsuited. Early in the play it is rumoured that Brazil has been offered a job at one of the more prestigious stations, Capital Radio. Given, however, his complete contempt not only for the product he peddles but, ultimately, for the young people who consume the sugar pap, the play appears to be heading for Brazil abandoning his audience and the career which he despises. In the final soliloquy (II.4), however, Brazil announces to his loyal audience that he has accepted the London-based post:

> I've got to tell you something now which is a big surprise because today I was offered a very big job in London, with the very splendid Capital Radio – and they offered me a lot of money and a large, large audience in London, the capital of this fine country of ours, and a fat programme, to do my very own thing. (ibid.: 207)

The contempt for the industry, and perhaps for himself ('What are you doing, Brazil?'), remains in Brazil's tone and in the rambling discourse of his final farewells to the Leicester audience. The play thus ends on a reversal of the expectations it has set up, as if Nicola's inability or refusal to resist the sugar-coating masking the brutalism of provincial city life (as Billington reads it) has convinced Brazil that no resistance is possible. Read thus, the play is indeed, to repeat Billington's words, 'full of genuine animus against the brutalism of our provincial cities and of the society which treats its young as consumers ripe for exploitation'. In the penultimate scene of *City Sugar*, however, the seeds of resistance might just be discernible.

Back in the supermarket (II.4) with her friend Susan, Nicola is in an aggressive mood. She '*pulls the leg of the dummy* [of the Yellow Jacket figure] *out of her bag*' (ibid.: 205, s.d.) and, smiling, drops it in a fridge, throwing packets of fish fingers out and tearing them apart. In dialogue with Susan, Nicola recognises that it is now too late even to queue for the Yellow Jacks' concert because she has lost time at the radio station. But she now feels anyway that 'It's not worth it. It really isn't!' (ibid.: 206). On edge, the two friends momentarily realise that they have some resistant power; if they wanted, as Susan remarks, they could pull the supermarket apart, 'do the whole place' (ibid.) in the dark after hours. Nicola feels such an act is also 'not really worth it' and a final interpretation of the play rests considerably on how her suggestion of 'Maybe next time' (ibid.) is read. She is not sure herself what her remark signifies but Susan has noted a change in Nicola and is '*bewildered by* NICOLA'S *aggression*' (ibid.: 205, s.d.). In the TV adaptation, the girls are figured in a crane shot lying amid the debris.[5] When, on hearing Brazil's broadcast, Nicola says, 'Forget it: it's only him', it may be that Poliakoff is signalling hope, strengthened in the TV version, in what Nicola has learned from her encounter. In itself this does not constitute a positive ending to the play, but it may offset the unmitigated bleakness of Billington's reading.

Shout Across the River (1978)

If Nicola Davies needs spurring into resistant action, Christine Forsythe in *Shout Across the River* (*Shout*) is non-conformism incarnate. As Poliakoff recalls, when the play first appeared 'some people found her a terrifying and ghastly creation' (ibid.: xiii). She is not so much a school 'refusenik' as a teenager whose behaviour breaches so many protocols of social orthodoxy that she goads the school, as well as her family and society more broadly, into rejecting her. Christine's attempt to dominate her mother is at the heart of the play's action and, as in other early work, Poliakoff is interested as a dramatist in the playing out in the theatrical here and now of a relationship located in a specific temporal and geographical context. Although the hinterground of the play, the urban sprawl of south London, is bleak enough, there is nothing in the broader environment to afford an easy social explanation of Christine's behaviour. Similarly within the family, though her father has left her mother, there is nothing so unusual as to account for Christine's vindictive drive. Her brother, Mike, though largely absent playing sport, does not appear maladjusted, though he does take a negative view of the future of the planet. Poliakoff does not write well-made plays gravitating towards plot resolution or thematic clarity. He is interested rather in 'trying to reach people obliquely working on their imaginations, instincts, memories' (ibid.: xiii). 'Like other playwrights of his generation,' as Irving Wardle remarked in the late 1970s, 'Mr Poliakoff writes in brief, angular scenes, leaving you to read much between the lines.'[6]

Shout, a play with ten such angular scenes, is centrally concerned with the troubled relationship between Mrs Forsythe and her wayward daughter. At the start of the play Christine has just been suspended from school with the threat that, if she does not report regularly to her social worker, she is in danger of being forcibly detained. The likely implementation of this threat increases as the play progresses and contributes to the dramatic tension. But there is little doubt where events are heading since Christine is uninhibited in her behaviour and fails completely to reform or report. Thus the real tension and interest in the play lies in the way that she strives to dominate her mother and her mother's weak, but occasional, resistance. There is a resemblance here to the goading of Nicola Davies by Leonard Brazil in the specific sense that the protagonist's taunting of others is not coldly malicious but undertaken at some personal pain. But here it is the socially disempowered Christine who manipulates. Christine is the first of Poliakoff's truly disempowered protagonists, Ralph and Clare in *Hitting Town* and Leonard Brazil in *City Sugar* having been drawn from the lower middle classes. Similar to Poliakoff's other urban youth plays, however, the specific situation is indicative of a broader social malaise, a lack of direction on the part of the young in a society which disappoints them in the loss of its bearings and values. The eponymous 'shout across the river' is a cry over the Thames from late-1970s south London to resonate with those from the Midlands in *Hitting Town* and *City Sugar* and with the *Bloody Kids* down the River Thames in Southend.

Shout begins with Mrs Forsythe summoned to Christine's school to receive notice of her daughter's suspension and a damning report from her teacher, Mr Lawson. The interview is halting since Lawson is defensive, hiding behind his unique 'completely scratch-proof, graffiti-proof' (ibid.: 213) desk and piles of stationery. The bogus sense of order in his room seems to afford an oasis in the desert of his life. In reciting the litany of Christine's alleged transgressions, he shows little concern other than to fulfil his pastoral tutor function. Though the assaults, sexual laxity, obscenity, wilful damage, truancy, smoking, pornography and general disobedience by Christine would seem to warrant serious address, Lawson explains that the school is 'turning our other cheek' (ibid.: 216). He seems resigned to the situation, while Mrs Forsythe, an agoraphobic, has found it a huge challenge simply to get to Mr Lawson's room and wants the interview to end as soon as possible.

Much of the play subsequently is composed of interaction and dialogue between Mrs Forsythe and Christine, the other characters besides Lawson – Christine's brother, Mike, and Martin, a sixteen-year-old youth who figures at the end of the play – being peripheral. The action is set in confined spaces, such as the 'small box sitting room' (ibid.: 219, s.d.) of the flat, or the launderette, which add to the sense of intensity in their relationship as they battle for the upper hand. In I.2, for example, Mrs Forsythe insists that Christine stays at home and threatens to lock her in while, in retaliation, Christine threatens her mother with scissors and superglue. Mrs Forsythe's repeated attempts to be properly assertive in her maternal role are largely ineffectual, often lacking the final words of command: 'you're staying in this room until we've . . .' (ibid.: 220). At the launderette, Christine kicks the machines violently and sticks pornographic images to somebody's folded clothes pile, remarking that 'Last term I cut several male parts and stuck them on my arm' (ibid.: 225).

However antagonistic their relationship seems to be on the surface, Mrs Forsythe and her daughter share confidences. Christine reveals that she has given up eating and her mother admits her agoraphobia. Indeed, Mrs Forsythe confides her fears of the outdoors and ordinary phenomena such as bus conductors in a stream of consciousness confession, breaking down into tears as her affliction overwhelms her. Christine observes her mother impassively until she ultimately resorts to threats to make her stop crying, but she seems to recognise that her mother is suffering, remarking that she is 'a real mess' (ibid.: 228). The moment heralds the development in the play of a *doppel-gänger* element: Mrs Forsythe cannot stop crying whereas Christine has not cried since the age of three. In the second half of the play, when Christine is largely in control of her mother, she makes her wear a black dress similar to the one she herself has adopted, and she introduces her mother as her sister, 'Marian'.

The action certainly plays out an intimately experienced relationship, albeit based on a will to power. In a telling moment, another of Poliakoff's graphic metaphors on-stage, Christine insists her mother takes off what she calls a 'hideous dress' (ibid.: 234). The scene (I.3) builds in tension towards this climax. In the cramped living room, Christine, wearing her great-grandmother's black dress which she has found in her mother's wardrobe, initiates a game of cat and mouse. She assaults the room, opening drawers spewing out Green Shield stamps and old copies of women's magazines. She moves ornaments and generally displaces the order which evidently serves as a reference point of security for her mother. In discovering a drawer of Mrs Forsythe's mementos of her husband, Christine appears to gain a psychological advantage which she forces home by insisting that her mother remove her dress. Crushed, Mrs Forsythe meekly complies. A further conflict over Christine's insistence that she must go out in the dress is interrupted by the phone ringing, an intrusion of noise which becomes a *leitmotiv*. Mrs Forsythe says she will not lie for her daughter if the authorities call but, inevitably in the drift of the power play, she does.

Mrs Forsythe opens a giant carrier bag Christine has brought home. She discovers a stash of goods which Christine has casually stolen. Christine does not want the goods and, indeed, there is an implicit criticism of a careless world in her explanation: 'You can go into any shop in the High Street, nobody is BUYING anything – there's no one anywhere near the cash desks! Everybody in the shop is squashed into corners having a quick grab. Even the store detectives' (ibid.: 235). The setting of the relationship between mother and daughter against a lightly sketched, but telling, backdrop of social indeterminacy makes it seem less abnormal. As Irving Wardle remarked in a review of the Croydon Warehouse production, 'the stage abounds in trading stamps, slimming magazines, television, thunderous traffic and the other junk of the 1970s all of it racing wildly out of control'.[7] When Mike arrives home covered in mud from a sports match and wanting his tea, he notices, not his mother standing in her underwear, but only the chaos of the room, wondering if there has been a break-in. In consequence, the antagonistic relationship between mother and daughter is tempered by a curious but mutual understanding between the *doppel-gänger* pair. It appears to be more a social product of the times than a matter of psychological breakdown. Indeed, Poliakoff has described *Shout* as 'a form of love story between mother and daughter' (ibid.: xii).

Act I, scene 5 finds Christine with her mother and Mike, all dressed in black, in an ice-cream parlour. Mrs Forsythe is already on edge when another phone mysteriously rings. Her state of mind is not helped by Mike's lengthy pronouncements of change for the worse.

Through Mike, Poliakoff is prescient, from a twenty-first-century perspective, in predicting global warming, having 'read somewhere the Arctic is going to melt quite soon and the whole of Europe is going to be drowned' (ibid.: 242). But Mike is evidently a prophet of doom, moving on to declare, 'There's a new disease too! From Africa' (ibid.: 243). Mrs Forsythe's horror is distracted, however, by Martin's arrival. In the rhythm of the play, the assault on Mrs Forsythe is rising to fever pitch. The young people talk of going into central London where heroin is passed around in a hamburger bar. Mike's view is that, '[b]y 1995 nobody will be living in the centre – it will just be full of rotting streets and businesses and garbage' (ibid.: 247). Mrs Forsythe is shaking, either laughing or crying. Martin propositions Christine on the basis of her well-known sexual laxity and, deliberately in front of Mrs Forsythe, she offers a deal at a higher price with her 'sister here thrown in for free' (ibid.: 249). The scene ends with a totally speechless Mrs Forsythe, finally reduced to a potential sex-slave by her daughter's insistent determination to dominate, as again the phone rings insistently. Through shrill sound, Poliakoff plays also on the audience's nerves.

At the end of the week of the play's duration, Mr Lawson and Mrs Forsythe encounter each other again at the school leavers' ritual party held in a '*huge Pleasure Palace*' (ibid.: 262, s.d.). Having shared with Mrs Forsythe his sense of the pointlessness of teaching people who do not wish to learn, Lawson takes up a theme from *City Sugar* in evoking what he sees as the more authentic entertainments of the past: '[t]hey used to have really good shows in the pubs round here, before this pleasure palace opened . . . Now it's all plastic girls done up in cellophane' (ibid.: 269). It is Christine's final night of freedom since she – and everybody else – is well aware that enforced detention looms. There is a sense of danger in the air since she has nothing to lose and has promised Martin that sexual encounter with both her and 'Marian' for which she has demanded payment. Ironically, since Christine has no intention herself of having sex with Martin, Mrs Forsythe, when left alone with him, kisses Martin several times sexually, in full view of Mr Lawson. It is a moment of calculated ambiguity in Poliakoff's presentation since she is acting on her own volition though she acknowledges she might also be 'doing exactly what Christine wanted' (ibid.: 276).

The thought proves prophetic since, back in the flat in the final scene of the play, Christine tries to effect another shock. The dialogue has emphasised that she has not eaten, drunk or slept for two days and that she is ghastly white and painfully thin, as if she were planning to become a casualty of bulimia. Out of nowhere, however, she suddenly reveals to her mother that she's 'going to tell them you refused to feed me properly, refused to feed me at all! And so I'm not answerable for my actions' (ibid.: 290). All the extraordinary things she has made her mother do in the course of the week will be presented by Christine as evidence of her mother's ineptitude, if not insanity. It is an extraordinary moment of theatrical reversal since everything the audience has witnessed as an apparently out-of-control and self-destructive trajectory towards either Borstal or death on Christine's part, must now be refigured as a cold and conscious plan to save herself from incarceration at the expense of her mother. Where it might have seemed that Christine's forcing her mother out of the flat into the world of cafes and pubs might have involved at least an element of cruelty-to-be-kind in helping her to address her agoraphobia, it now appears simply cruel in the extreme. Christine says: 'I'm going to brick you up again in here, for ever . . . I'm not having you staying here as you are now, while they take me away, I'm *not* letting that happen' (ibid.: 291). But the situation and the characters are complex. At this moment, in fact, Mrs Forsythe is regaining control. She stands up to Christine and even asserts that she is 'going to get a job again' (ibid.). In contrast, Christine is hurtling out of emotional control:

CHRISTINE	Don't you *understand*? Haven't you learnt anything at all?
	She moves round room.
	I've shown you everything. I've taken you out and shown you it all. (*Loud*) And you've seen how horrible it is!
MRS FORSYTHE	No I haven't.
CHRISTINE	CAN'T YOU UNDERSTAND! I *hate* all this muck they give us!
	She kicks the magazines violently all over the floor.
	They throw it at us. They try to drown us with it. (*Screams.*) And I hate all men!
MRS FORSYTHE	No you don't. Only some of them!

This dialogue illustrates well something of the complexity of Poliakoff's presentation of characters experiencing situations. Here Christine is articulating a similar cultural critique to that of Leonard Brazil in *City Sugar* but it is evident that her viewpoint is not entirely reliable. Though Mrs Forsythe's perspective might itself be called in question, the surprisingly quiet but firm contradiction of Christine for the first time in *Shout Across the River* carries some weight. It does not, of course, completely negate Christine's cry that 'This is the worst time to be alive, *everybody* knows that!' (ibid.: 292), but it does trouble any easy reading of the socio-cultural critique the play embodies. The clash of views in the live dramatic situation requires a reading of shifting dynamics, changing character as well as the utterances themselves. The play ends with this ambiguity or complexity, with the two women sat waiting for the intervention which will separate them possibly for ever. In Mrs Forsythe's view, whether or not she sees Christine again 'depends if [she]'ll want to' (ibid.: 296). In sum, in spite of all that has happened under the constraints of the environment, the characters have a measure of choice about their ultimate destinies.

American Days (1979) is more a follow-up play to *Hitting Town* and *City Sugar* than to *Shout* in that it traces a group of young people's aspirations to celebrity through interviews at a recording studios. It is memorable for jet-setting media executive, Sherman, who insists on finding identical environments – with replica contents in the fridge – whichever country he is in. Though he plays power games, keeping the young hopefuls wondering if they will actually be auditioned, he is ultimately as much a victim of media commercialism as they are. Lorraine's ultimate resistance – building upon Nicola's karaoke outburst in *Hitting Town* and attack on the supermarket in *City Sugar* – further suggests that the trap of 'cultural dupe' is avoidable. A decade on *Sienna Red* (1992) affords a comedy treatment, not so much of urban youth, but of commerce. A manager in a DIY store, Harry starts the play almost unintentionally subversive, not only in being unambitious, but by being more able to exploit marketing than the corporate chain's managers. His individual imagination, in this respect, trumps their research as he constructs elaborate domestic interiors as in-store advertisements of the company's wares. Urban sprawl passes by on the flyover outside as the pressure on middle management extends the sense in *American Days* that all of us, not just the young, are trapped in the capitalist system. Limited space prevents further discussion of these plays since a reflection on developments in Poliakoff's early dramaturgy is required before we trace his continuing concern with urban youth into later films.

Developing dramaturgy

Along with some historical plays (*Clever Soldiers*) and the unpublished pieces – *Sad Beat Up*, *The Carnation Gang* (1974) and *Heroes* (1975) – the two urban canyon plays discussed mark a prolific twelve months, 1974–75, in which Poliakoff had five plays in production in London. Victor Davis recorded that 'there is hardly a dramatic critic in Britain who does not have Stephen Poliakoff earmarked for greatness'.[8] There were, however, reservations. From the point of view of 'political theatre' devotees, Poliakoff's voice and dramaturgy lacked the authenticity of somebody speaking about youth from within the culture. Reviewers struggled to identify a style in Poliakoff's dramaturgy. Eric Shorter, writing about Poliakoff's professional debut play *Pretty Boy* (1972) complained that the young author did not know how to end the play, but acknowledges that he has created 'an engaging monster' – perhaps a prefiguration of Christine in *Shout* – in Benny (Michael Pennington), 'a fascinatingly malevolent but sentimental lout . . . in the tradition of Jimmy Porter'.[9] John Barber, reviewing *Clever Soldiers* (1974), suggests, however: 'more is expected than an angry dissatisfaction with the way things are, and an adolescent eagerness to bust them wide open. Mr Poliakoff conveys something of his hero's sensual delight but otherwise demonstrates few dramatic skills. I am not sure theatre is his medium.'[10]

In similar vein, but writing of *Heroes* at the Royal Court in 1975, he opines that 'the piece has little dramatic merit, is full of loose ends and veers uncomfortably between symbolism (the mysterious, rioting city) and reality (an elderly drunken blackmailer comes and goes without explanation)'.[11]

Frank Marcus, reviewing *Shout* in 1978, is still unsure about Poliakoff's dramaturgy, suggesting 'the style might best be described as uneasy naturalism'.[12] Such remarks may well reflect critics' difficulties with coming to terms, not just with Poliakoff, but with early-1970s experiments in dramaturgy more broadly.[13] Indeed, there was considerable debate in respect of theatre – and subsequently in respect of television – about the relative merits of realism and naturalism. The former was sometimes understood as a narrative form (classic realism) leading both to storyline and ideological closure, while the latter was sometimes understood to denote just the accurate capturing of surface appearances.

Entering the debate, Raymond Williams made some useful distinctions between the naturalist emphasis with 'its demonstration of the *production* of character by a powerful natural or social environment' (1980: 127) and 'high naturalism' in which: 'the lives of the characters have soaked into their environment . . . Moreover, the environment has soaked into their lives. The relationship between men and things are at a deep level interactive, because what is there physically, as a space or a means for living, is a whole shaped or shaping social history' (ibid.: 140–1).

Poliakoff aspired to the simplest sense of naturalism, 'lifelike reproduction', in his wish to avoid Brechtian distanciation in favour of a more tactile, emotional theatre. But his interest in the built environment inclined him, as noted, to set agency in structure suggesting, under Williams's naturalist emphasis, the production of character by environment. It is this aspect which sets up a contemplative, 'outsider' viewpoint in addition to feeling for character. Identification is not strongly invited in that Clare, Ralph, Nicola and Christine are engaging but not particularly attractive protagonists. Emotional involvement is further tempered in that they are to be understood as products of their environments, though Poliakoff avoids any sense of absolute determinism by offering glimpses of agency in fight-back, or even escape. As Poliakoff remarked at the time:

My plays are aware of dangers, but they're not saying they're definitely going to happen. They are not despairing screams of

'Oh God, we're all being killed in this concrete jungle', because I don't believe that . . . My plays are about people coping with that, and I'm coping with that myself . . . I'm not a Marxist . . . I suppose I am a Socialist . . . but through that I have grown an anarchic belief in people; that they can stop themselves being exploited, falling into the prevailing greyness . . . I believe there's a certain resilience in people. In my sentimental moments, I think there's a terrific resilience.[14]

Furthermore the disposition to observe and capture significant cultural moments leads Poliakoff towards 'high naturalism', as defined by Williams, in that his graphically depicted spaces and means for living serve also to stand for 'a whole shaped or shaping social history'. Thus the concept of 'expressive realism' captures well, and values positively, what some have seen in Poliakoff's dramaturgy as an awkward slippage between strikingly graphic stage realisations (Ralph and Clare attacking the ketchup dispenser; the construction of 'Marian' in the black dress) and a looser use of poetic metaphor. To repeat Shepherd: 'the form works with a stage image which is familiar generating emotions which are transparently communicated, and from here, in the best work, moves to the articulation of a larger feeling about "society" and "people" in general' (2009: 141–2).

Poliakoff's 'meteoric rise' was based on his seeming ability to capture the contemporary moment of the early to mid-1970s, to articulate to relatively middle-class audiences at the Bush, the Court and the RSC the frustration of urban youth negotiating the concrete jungle and bubblegum culture. His dramaturgy may have been in formation, and his output uneven, but, in his remarkable achievement, the seeds of his more mature work are evident. In the next piece for discussion – a film of urban youth – Poliakoff's script again mixes realism with metaphor and he was drawn towards expressionism, perhaps by his director.

Bloody Kids (1979)

Significant credit for the film *Bloody Kids* is properly attributed to director Stephen Frears since, at this stage in his career, Poliakoff was primarily perceived in respect of film and television as a writer, credited here for the screenplay and the original idea. There are distinct resonances, however, between Poliakoff's dramaturgy, as evidently emerging in the 1970s plays discussed above, and Frears's treatment.

The narrative base of the film involves a fight staged as a joke by two 'bloody kids' in which one of them actually gets stabbed. It remains ambiguous as to whether Leo (Richard Thomas) ultimately stabs his friend, Mike (Derrick O'Connor) deliberately, or whether it was an accident. In any case, the stage blood they have stolen from school to lend authenticity to the supposedly mock fight is augmented by actual blood, and Leo ends up in hospital with the police only half-heartedly investigating what they consider to be an attempted murder. It is clearly deliberate on Leo's part to frame Mike subsequently since he constructs for the investigating police an image of Mike as 'weird' and 'aggressive', and says he has talked of 'attacking', and even 'killing' people. As in the plays discussed above, however, Poliakoff is less interested in psychological explanations of character than in establishing a dramatic springboard for observing young people as they function in a specific environment. Because Mike must go on the run, an opportunity is created for the camera dynamically to explore the social and urban environment (in this case of Southend) from inside and outside perspectives, creating, in Chris Allison's summary, 'a fictional world both familiar and yet mysteriously foreign'.[15] While in no way wishing to deny the strong contributions of director, cinematographer (Chris Menges), or composer (George Fenton) to the film, it will be evident from what has been established thus far in this book, that the concerns of *Bloody Kids*, its style and structuring devices, are distinctively Poliakovian.[16]

Though Poliakoff's interests in observing youth in action in urban environments might sound documentary-sociological, his constructs are typically more metaphorical-poetic. It is one of the features of his writing which makes him, as noted, at once distinctive and difficult to place. He cannot be located simply in the British Realist tradition of cinema or in the lineage of the Loach–Garnett school of television documentary drama. Frears's expressionistic treatment of the screen-play in shooting the film, however, is a perfect complement to Poliakoff's writing. In Allison's summary: 'Frears draws on iconography from American *film noir*, mostly shooting in a brooding darkness occasionally illuminated by the neon signs of amusement arcades, the strobes of a disco or the flashing lights of police cars and ambulances.'[17]

In his treatment, Frears in effect realises with the extended apparatus of the cinema the feel of the built urban environment at which Poliakoff has gestured in the stage directions for his plays. In a low-action, but expressionistically stylish, opening sequence of some nine minutes' duration, the eleven-year-old Leo comes across an 'incident' while wandering the streets after dark. Though the visual imagery never offers a fully explanatory account, a major traffic accident appears to have occurred in which a lorry has careered off a fly-over, potentially damaging the structure of the bridge in the process. People are hurt, possibly killed, and the emergency services are on the scene. Organisation is poor, however, with the chief inspector of police trying, but failing, to gain control. That Leo is able to wander through the scene is a testament to his failure just as it is opportune in affording the important dimension of an outsider perspective on it. The treatment, as if from Leo's point of view, is literally very dark with the imagery almost indiscernible and voices muffled as if in a fog. Leo steals the chief inspector's cap from an unattended car and drifts away past a nearby police station where the perspective of the outsider looking in on an apparently incomprehensible minor activity, or inaction, is sustained. That the position might shift, however, is realised when Leo is caught on a surveillance camera.

The impression of aimless drifting through an environment spinning out of control is reinforced in subsequent sequences in Leo's school. The stolen police cap becomes a *leitmotiv* bringing Mike into complicity with Leo in transgressing boundaries to retrieve it from the roof of the senior school where an older boy has tossed it. The impression sketched of school life for the boys resonates with that of the organisation of broader society in the opening sequence. As he progresses down the corridor of the senior school, Leo casually runs an indelible felt tip marker along the wall. Though the teacher who catches him does not duck the issue and instructs him to remove the ink, there is no conviction in his approach. Leo and Mike are more keen to avoid the senior boys who lurk in the corridors threatening to bully.

The atmosphere conveyed is not, however, so much one of fear and danger as of obstacles to be negotiated in an unpredictable, careless and alienating environment. There is a semblance of social control – television monitors and surveillance cameras being much in evidence throughout the film – but, like the society overall, it is verging on the dysfunctional. For example, the uniformed caretaker at the end of the school sequence, like his police counterparts, has a television monitor but appears to be watching a TV police drama rather than keeping an eye on security. When Leo goes missing in the hospital, nobody can be found to operate the sophisticated telephone exchange. Leo's parents when phoned by the hospital nurse are not at home (indeed they are never seen in the film), while calls to the school find only the answer-phone. The police fail to communicate with each other or to connect with the public in their investigations. They are frequently distracted, on occasion walking past the very person they are seeking. A sense of almost comic lawlessness is underscored by the 'spaghetti western' soundtrack covering the sequence of a police car taking Leo to hospital after the football match stabbing. The police drive their cars fast as if in *The Sweeney*,[18] with screeching tyres frequently heard on the soundtrack even of scenes in which cars do not feature.

The plot, like the imagery, progresses in a picaresque manner. In a sea-front cafe where Mike eats a banana split, a group of teenagers returning from the match joke about seeing a fight, leading Mike cautiously to approach one of them for information. Mike is dragged along with a gang led by Ken (Gary Olson) to a disco, affording further *flânerie* observation of social phenomena – bingo and the seventies disco. In the disco, Mike observes everybody but finds himself being watched dancing by two of the teenagers. Ken leads the gang and the film through into the early hours, stealing cars and defying the surveillance cameras and the police to catch him. From Mike's point of view, which the camera frequently takes, there are scary moments – for example, when another gang surrounds and kicks Ken's stolen Cortina – but ultimately the mood is typically one of teenage boredom fuelled by surges of testosterone rather than real danger. Ken throws a waste bin through the window of a shop sporting television monitors as his gang saunters through a precinct which might have figured in *Hitting Town*, *City Sugar* or *Shout*. Indeed, lengthy sequences in the last third of the ninety-minute film serve expressionistically to realise the feel of a brutalist urban environment inhabited by kids who are unruly because bored which typifies Poliakoff's urban youth plays. Working with Frears on *Bloody Kids* must at once have revealed to Poliakoff the possibilities for the moving picture medium to realise his dramatic ideas and the relative limitations of theatre. It is not surprising that the next decade saw him working increasingly in film and television, though he continued to write plays for the theatre.

That urban youth culture remains a preoccupation of Poliakoff's is evident in that it features in a minor way in other works. In a film for television, *Caught on a Train* (see Chapter 6) the protagonist is haunted on his train journey across Europe not only by the formidable Frau Messner but also by a group of young men who appear at the station in Ostend, join the train and intermittently intercept Peter (Michael Kitchen) throughout the film, either in the train's corridors and compartments or at station stops. In the feature film, *Hidden City* (see Chapter 8), a young woman stalks statistician James Richards (Charles Dance) and leads him, in the course of their search of London for confiscated film footage, into a different kind of 1980s youth culture. In another film for television, *She's Been Away* (see Chapter 6) a tribe of what today might be called eco-warriors emerges from the woods when Harriet (Geraldine James) and Lillian (Peggy Ashcroft) are stranded after their car grinds to a halt. The painted 'warriors' leer through the car windows but do not otherwise attack the women who nevertheless feel forced to make a speedy exit. The final example for discussion in this chapter, however, was produced almost two decades later than the early flurry of urban youth plays. It is a film, *The Tribe*, ultimately distributed on television in the 'Screen Two' strand, in the absence of a cinema distribution outlet.

The Tribe (1998)

Poliakoff has remarked – at least through the figure of young Mary in *Capturing Mary* – that early success is hard to sustain. Though he was to achieve even greater renown with his post-1998 television work, *The Tribe*, a film transmitted on television having not achieved cinema distribution, did not match the success of his meteoric rise in the 1970s. A quarter of a century on from his first engagements with the urban environment of *Shout*, Poliakoff again ventures south of the River Thames to 'the pits of the universe . . . the most violent part of town'. These are the views of young executives in a chic property developer's office when their assertive boss, Kanahan (Trevor Eve) announces that Goldlease Holdings has acquired some real estate there. He has an ambitious scheme – inadvertently spurred by Jamie in an improvised presentation – to reclaim the inner urban and suburban wastelands of Europe and turn them into lifestyle real estate for those for whom electronic home-working has done away with the commute.

The problem is that there are sitting tenants in the acquired property, a 'tribe' of late-1990s urban youth quite different from those of the 1970s. Indeed, these young people, headed up by Emily (Joely Richardson) – a charismatic figure who has attracted the others to join her in an unconventional commune – are disciplined but without set rules. They all dress in versions of 1990s trendy Gothic black and are more twentysomethings than teenagers (with George Costigan's Micky being significantly older). A trip to 'the badlands', to attract the tribe to sell out, is assigned by Kanahan to Jamie (Jeremy Northam) who is seen travelling by train through bleak suburbs and industrial wastelands to a rather impressive Victorian brick edifice on a hill inhabited by the tribe. Initially Jamie thinks them to be a religious sect – a parallel to 'the Moonies', perhaps – and, indeed there is another 'cult' group whose leader suggests that disciplined gated communities such as theirs are the future in an otherwise anarchic world. Emily is scornful of this sect, however, and deliberately exposes its bogus leader, Delario (Michael Feast), in front of his deluded followers.

Following his initial professional curiosity about the tribe, Jamie gets increasingly caught up in their allure, finally leaving his wife to join them just as Emily's reign is over at the end of the film. These young people are intriguing to him in that they appear free and physically attractive but, above all, are not easy to pin down. Though most are escapees from troubled pasts, they are clean and healthy-looking and their lifestyle, unlike that of the teenagers of the earlier urban cultures, is well organised and purposeful. They are not squatters but hold the lease legally and have permission for changes made to the building's layout in order to construct variously designed, but attractive, living spaces. Though they eat some unusual – and to Jeremy's taste, delicious – Eastern foods, they also go to the local cafe and order sausage chips and beans. It transpires that they finance their closed community by selling from an impromptu stall discounted consumer goods in the form of high-tech gadgets, acquired through contacts in the Far East. Some of them also hold conventional jobs – one is a traffic warden. Their sexual relationships are fluid, though not quite the 'free love' of the 1960s. Poliakoff shows interest in the impact of AIDS on sex lives in the 1980s and 1990s in comparison with the worry-free 1960s. Before Jamie is seduced into a threesome sexual encounter with Lizzie (Anna Friel) and a young man, he is required to take an HIV/AIDS test. The tribe is partly bonded in the knowledge that they are all 'clean' and thus able freely to indulge in unorthodox sexual relationships contained within a safe frame, as the brother and sister do in *Hitting Town* and, more explicitly, in *Close My Eyes*.

Ultimately the tribe is destroyed only incidentally by the property developers since it is first undone in a not very convincing brawl with the less disciplined local youth culture which has intermittently threatened Jamie on his visits, and has been spoiling for a fight with the group. Hitherto, Emily has kept them at bay by the sheer strength of her personality and, once the myth of her invincibility is punctured, the whole world of the tribe begins rapidly to fall apart. The rival cult joins the local youth to enter the tribe's sacrosanct compound, threatening death and destruction. Lizzie breaks ranks and reveals an insider view to a local newspaper journalist who, predictably, runs a sensationalist story giving Kanahan the excuse he has been seeking to reclaim the property. Though Jeremy rescues Emily as the building is being knocked apart around her – and finally gets to sleep with her, ironically in his marital bed – a romantic ending is disavowed as Emily cannot return to a conventional life. She proffers to Jeremy a self-consciously bogus romantic notion that somewhere, sometime, they will meet again.

Though *The Tribe* evidences a number of Poliakovian tropes and to some extent picks up on the picaresque style of *Bloody Kids* and *Hidden City* in that the tribe is shot endlessly wandering around town, it does not successfully combine its features. At the level of the 'lifelike representation' of expressive realism, it fails to convince. The tribe members may be intriguing but, picking up on an accusation less justifiably levelled at Poliakoff's earlier work, they do not seem to be written from experience. It is clear that Poliakoff is aiming by way of expressive realism also to capture more abstractly the urban spirit of the late 1990s, constrained by economic as well as sexual fears, by drawing comparisons with the relative freedom of creative expression in the 1960s. As Chris Allison summarises, '*The Tribe* taps into two major trends characteristic of the 1990s: the exploration of alternative modes of living, itself a reinterpretation of 1960s communal experiments, and the proliferation of religious cults.'[19]

The need to contain sexual freedom within a closed community, noted above, is mirrored when, at the end of the film, a gallery of artworks created by tribe members is discovered hidden from the world. The creative energy of the 1990s has shifted to property developers such as Kanahan whose prime interest is in making money and, far for being community-spirited, he tramples on anybody who gets in his way. But the comparison is clunkily made in fragments of dialogue such as when Jamie interrogates his boss about his 1960s indulgence with the conclusion that they were the 'lucky generation'. Poliakoff, who just missed the full flowering of the 1960s, seems haunted by an issue which did not perhaps resonate with late-1990s audiences. Another improbable sequence occurs when the tribe announces from nowhere its penchant for occasional bingeing on television, sometimes by way of arbitrary access to recorded material. By this means, random television clips feature 1960s footage of Woodstock and Timothy Leary in a way which feels too evidently imposed to make a point. Thus, curiously, the abstract point in *The Tribe* is made too literally where the setting of agency in structure lacks conviction.

Stylistically, the film instances Poliakoff's interest in colour symbolism, with a strong red, starkly contrasting with the tribe's habitual black dress code and linking characters, places and objects – Jamie's car, Emily's 'secret' dress with the red-brick house and its interior light. The property developer's office, in contrast, is depicted in streamlined glass and steel, with cool greys predominant. But, despite some visual flair, expressive realism is not fully achieved. Another trope which Poliakoff had more successfully explored in previous work is the subterranean world beneath London. When the tribe invites Jeremy to an open day, they show him 'what's behind the façade of a bland suburban street', the twenty-five-mile underground network of the Chislehurst caves, before extending Poliakoff's own fascination with the built environment in moving on to Darwin's house and the site of Crystal Palace. And that is the point; it appears again that Poliakoff's interests are being presented rather than those of the tribe members. Where, in his successful pieces, Poliakoff works his passions and interests into credible, if quirky, characters, strong narrative and/or telling symbolist or expressionist atmosphere (both on stage and in film), *The Tribe* disappoints on nearly all fronts.

Cultural pessimism or cultural critique

To sum up Poliakoff's achievement and developing dramaturgy in his 'strikingly unique urban canyon plays' (Martin 1993: 1), and to revisit Poliakoff's avowed turn away from Brecht, the final section of this chapter draws upon analysis by Matthew Martin. Martin concurs with my sense that Poliakoff sets agency in the structure of the built and cultural environments. He proposes that the works

> share one common basic principle that helps to determine their thematic and dramaturgical style. Characters tend to define themselves not so much in terms of their own independent beliefs and attitudes, nor in terms of other characters, but in terms of environment. The environment has become canyon-like – monolithic, encircling immutable, inescapable – yet manmade, filled with TVs, radios, bizarre lighting, muzak and more muzak . . . Their reactions to these environmental forces reveal not so much how we should judge the individuals, but how we should understand the dynamics of their lives in connection with contemporary urban life. (ibid.: 1)

Through an expressive realist dramaturgy, Poliakoff at his best grounds a socio-historical moment by locating strong characters in credible situations while at the same time articulating that 'larger feeling about "society" and "people" in general'. While to achieve 'complex seeing' Poliakoff draws in the later work upon a double perspective which resonates with Brechtian dramaturgy, in the early work, he achieves a broader abstraction through atmospheres and tensions created by heightened realist treatments which, at times, border on expressionism.

In respect of Brecht, Martin opens up a different perspective, distinguishing Poliakoff from Brecht not so much in respect of dramaturgy but by arguing that, where the modernist Brecht saw the potential of increasing human agency by way of new technologies affording greater control over the environment, Poliakoff's plays of the 1970s

> inform us that the spirit of the scientific age has passed, and that we live among that age's decayed ruins . . . The physical environment of Poliakoff's world has been so altered by a decadent science run rampant, changing things for no apparent purpose or improvement, that it has become bewilderingly

oppressive, as monolithic and immutable as nature once seemed to be. (ibid.)

This view of the decline of the individual in post-1960s culture affords a recognisable account of some of Poliakoff's preoccupations and his engagement with the downside of the modernist project. His distinctive vision in the 1970s is in part a documentation of the socio-cultural impact of technological progress – sanitised living among concrete blocks of flats and shopping malls with pervasive surveillance and muzak. The perspective chimes indeed with Billington's contemporary critique. But his account seems unduly negative and at odds with both the glimmers of hope in the plays as well as Poliakoff's overt assertion that he does not 'share this revulsion with modern life, with the urban world, expressed by some of [his] characters' (1997: xv). Martin's stance does, however, focus the question of Poliakoff's Frankfurt School cultural pessimism. It is an aspect of interpretation which perhaps led to the recognition among mainstream theatre audiences of that distinctive voice which informed his 'meteoric rise' on the London theatre scene, but denigrated by those positioned to champion the resistant powers of youth culture.

In my reading of the plays, though the signs of hope of escape from oppressive environments are little more than glimmers, they do offset an utter pessimism. They are evident in Ralph's volatile energy, in Nicola's attack on the freezer contents and in Christine's manipulation of her situation. It may be difficult to identify targets amid what Martin (1993: 1) calls 'the anonymous powers of all sorts [which] seem to be controlling all of Britain's urban environments', but the plays suggest that agency might still assert itself against a sense of entrapment.

Certainly there is no rational political analysis such as might be found in Brecht to assist in translating critical thinking into political action. In *American Days*, however, as Poliakoff reflects, he set out 'to show the reverse side of *City Sugar*: young people not as victims, but as avengers, coming out of the mass culture and spitting it back, manipulating it with equal contempt' (ibid.: xiv). In addition, though it is short-lived, the tribe's accommodations with consumer culture, with urban degeneration and sexually transmitted disease, at least suggest the possibility of negotiating cultural change and even of creating modes of living contentedly in a fragmented society.

In subsequent discussion, these aspects will receive further consideration but, rather than trace the ups and downs of Poliakoff's career in a simple linear history, the next three chapters cluster selected works according to other distinctive features of Poliakoff's *oeuvre*. The first cluster for consideration is 'issue plays'.

5 ISSUE PIECES

'I don't write about issues, but about characters,' Stephen Poliakoff told Lyn Gardner.[1] This chapter begs to differ by way of inviting readers to see Poliakoff afresh. It is acknowledged that the selection here – as in the following 'cluster' chapters – is arguable, though not arbitrary. The accounts of the plays and films to follow – *Strawberry Fields* (1977), *Stronger than the Sun* (1977), *Close My Eyes* (1991), *Century* (1994) and *Blinded by the Sun* (1996) – illustrate a distinction between the broader 'spirit of the times' concerns of the pieces covered in the last chapter and a tighter focus here on, respectively, the rise of reactionary right-wing politics, the threat of nuclear fallout, incest and professional ethics. There are, of course, fascinating characters and socio-historic contexts in these works and the metaphors may spiral, but they centre upon these specific issues.

Strawberry Fields (1977)

Strawberry Fields was the opening production on 31 March 1977 of the Cottesloe, the NT's 'black box' studio theatre. At a moment when Brenton and Edgar were writing plays which demanded the large-scale resources of the National and the RSC,[2] Poliakoff continued to convey with a small cast a 'pervading sense of isolation in supposedly crowded locations', as John Bull (1994: 585) puts it. *Strawberry Fields* has been associated with the 'urban youth' plays but, though some of its locations are at 'non-places', motorway services rather than shopping malls, this is a 'journey play' along a motorway from London to the north of England. *Strawberry Fields* nevertheless has a claustrophobic cauldron atmosphere, adding tension to what at the outset appear to be innocuous events.[3] It is a kind of inverse *Easy Rider* rather than a play in which the built environment entraps the characters.[4]

The play follows two twentysomethings, Kevin and Charlotte, who scarcely know each other but who have met up to take a van northwards. They are members of a minority political party and their mission is to distribute publicity and to collect donations from supporters on the way. The short scenes are stations of the journey. The events of the play, apart from two moments of high drama, are unremarkable, but interest is held by an increasing mystery about their identities, purposes and politics. Kevin, who has ostensibly come to drive the van, turns out to have very poor eyesight, indeed to be on the verge of blindness. Keen to do a good job, he has the loaded 'the literature', prepared the van and bought 'hundreds of maps' (1977: 6). He is 'a sixties' left-over' (ibid.: 25) whose inner confusion about the greyness and inertia of the 1970s, in contrast with the colour and optimism of the 1960s, finds expression in his obsession with old films, particularly those with macabre elements. Charlotte, in contrast, appears to be in control of herself and of the situation. She is unconcerned at the prospect of embarking on a journey with a strange man, her request for a replacement drinking straw because the one she is using is 'a little dirty' (ibid.: 6) merely betraying a slight preciousness. She decides to drive and she has prepared a timed itinerary.

It is not until the pair encounters Nick as they picnic on the motorway verge that the true nature of their project is revealed. Aiming to cadge a lift to Scotland, the would-be teacher 'in his early twenties' (ibid.: 9, s.d.) becomes increasingly curious about Kevin and Charlotte, the more so when he discovers one of their leaflets, which he reads with incredulity:

Have you thought about England lately, England now . . . the ordinary long-suffering English people. *Pollution* . . . the length and breadth of England polluted, every river, every *field*! Pollution on a gigantic scale. *Urban wastelands* . . .

Impersonal Government – ordinary people offered no chance or choice, crushed by impersonal government. *The Mauling of the countryside* – the countryside has been mauled . . . disastrous series of mistakes . . . the worship of the motor car . . . internal combustion engine eaten away the fabric of the country, the very fabric of ordinary people's lives destroyed. Preserve. (*He turns the page.*) Preserve. (ibid.: 12)

This citation yields the fullest articulation in the play of the English People's Party policies and ideology. Reread from a twenty-first-century perspective the emphasis placed upon the ruination of the countryside resonates, as Poliakoff has himself remarked, with green concerns. Indeed, writing in 1989, he ascribed the fact that the play is 'regularly performed all over the world' to its resonance with green issues and 'a European terrorism both from the left and the right' (ibid.: xiv), postdating the play. In its 1977 context, the play reso-nated more with 'the time of the National Front, of racist demonstrations, of a minority Labour government lurching from crisis to crisis' (ibid.: xiv). That the British National Front was posing an insidious threat is reinforced in *Destiny*, David Edgar's analytical play on the subject, which was simultaneously in production just across the river from the NT at the Aldwych, the RSC's London base.

In contrast with *Destiny*, *Strawberry Fields* comes at the issues from an oblique angle rather than politically head-on. Poliakoff's drama-turgy again resonates with early Pinter in bringing together a group of distinctive and, in Nick's view, cranky characters who have little in common other than the cause they support. Mrs Roberts, an 'ordi-nary' woman who meets them at a motorway services and seems preoccupied with her family and bus home, makes racist allegations against 'black boys' (1977: 18) and is drawn by Nick to admit she is a member of the National Front. But Charlotte emphatically denies Nick's suggestion that the English People's Party is 'the conservation wing of the National Front' (ibid.: 19). It is as if she is in denial about the implications of her beliefs and actions, since she does not elabo-rate on where she personally stands, either at this point or subsequently.

While Charlotte awaits her contact at a stop in Doncaster by a hot-dog van and disused picture house, Nick provokes Kevin – who seems to have spent much of his life at the cinema – into reliving some of the more violent film sequences he can recall. Kevin's 'little Englandism' emerges when he remarks that, '[w]e can't even keep our cinemas open any more, in this country, can we? Used to be the centre of the community didn't it. No British movies any more, nothing really' (ibid.: 22). After an edgy confrontation between Nick and Charlotte in the adjacent Gents' lavatory, Kevin breaks into the hot-dog van and its drinks vending machines. When a young policeman arrives on the scene and asks to see in Kevin's bag, Charlotte suddenly shoots him with a gun concealed in her handbag. In what might be seen as a Poliakovian reversal, the most controlled character takes the most violent action without warning. Poliakoff uses strong sound to mark the dramatic moment: Charlotte '*empties the gun into him. Silence. Fast fade down. On the soundtrack a loud electric buzz lasting 50 seconds in the blackout*' (ibid.: 28). It is the end of Act I.

Act II opens with the same noise but *at full volume* before the lights come up on a '*motorway cafe, stark dirty, very late at night. The neons are overpowering*' (ibid.: 29, s.d.). All of *Strawberry Fields* is set in public spaces which get increasingly ugly or threatening as the play progresses. Even the moorlands, on which the trio ultimately hides out, are being closed in by a ring of searching police vehicles. At the motorway cafe, Charlotte requires the two men to wait while she changes out of her blood-stained dress. Nick shouts out that he is 'nothing to do with these two' (ibid.: 33) but Charlotte will not allow him to leave and, '*really savage*' (ibid.: 33, s.d.), instructs him to 'SHUT UP' (ibid.: 33).

While Charlotte changes, Kevin drinks heavily and reminisces again about the 1960s and the Glastonbury festival. He recalls a 'wonderful feeling in the air' (ibid.: 34), a mood of 1960s optimism envisaged in the image on stage of 'this *small white boy* [David Bowie] . . . standing with sun on his hair, smiling, really smiling you know, it was like the future' (ibid.). Against the contrast of '*Muzak playing*' (ibid.: 35, s.d.), Kevin plays down the shooting of the policeman, suggesting it is little different from road deaths in a context where 'there are too many cars out there' (ibid.: 35). Nick is cautiously cynical, prompting Kevin more fully to articulate his position: 'I've felt these things for a long time. Oh yes. Like a lot of people now. Know this place, this country, belongs to them. Know it has to be protected . . . It's not just a question of race – it's a question of England' (ibid.). In the face of Nick's increasing incredulity, Kevin argues that he speaks for a lot of people and explains that is why they are conducting their campaign.

Envisaging a police hunt for them and their arrest, Kevin, perhaps recalling another 1960s road movie, *Bonnie and Clyde*, imagines that he and Charlotte will become 'famous . . . a sort of myth' (ibid.: 36). Charlotte returns cleaned up and in fresh clothes and ready to drive on. She appears to have won the battle of wills with Nick who, though he remains sceptical and cynical in what he says, goes with them to the van. The tension between them, already high, increases when the trio learn from their portable radio that they were seen leaving the crime scene and that a wide-ranging police search has been set in motion. A minor confrontation with a seventeen-year-old drug abuser causes Charlotte finally to snap. It is not just his arrival at a very awkward and tense moment that riles her but his being 'filthy' (ibid.: 40), representing the kind of culture she cannot abide. She screams, 'DON'T YOU UNDERSTAND, I CAN'T STAND HIM BEING NEAR ME – DON'T YOU UNDERSTAND' (ibid.).

When Kevin goes to refuel the van, Nick insists that Charlotte talks to him. Unlike her predecessors in the plays discussed in the last chapter, she offers an image of hopelessness. She recalls challenging herself to swim in a dirty pool: 'thick with mud and oil and things . . . I couldn't see anything except a sort of horrid muzzy darkness. It went all over me and in me. It feels like that now doesn't it, all the time . . . That's what it felt like – feels like – all the time, for a lot of people' (ibid.: 42).

Nick reads her as a spoilt middle-class child, blaming anything and anybody for things she personally finds offensive. But when he asks Charlotte why she came armed, she tells him she is protecting herself from 'all the leftist groups that know what we're doing' (ibid.: 43).

In a climactic moment in respect of the play's core issue, Charlotte continues to rail against 'those wasted years of grey government, letting the country be overrun by people who just don't belong' and 'the mess everywhere, just totally grey' (ibid.). She turns to comment on the environment, 'This sprawling mess, those lights up there, that savage light have you ever seen anything so horrible, anything so inhuman, more disgusting, it's just degrading' (ibid.: 44). In sum, taking up a Poliakovian theme, she points to industrial despoliation, a downside of the transition to modernity.

In the final scene, set on a hillside as they try to lie low, Nick again taunts Charlotte and Kevin about their vision of being martyrs. Charlotte finally scribbles down on paper what they stand for, as if for posterity, while Kevin again recalls a lost creative past in the hippy communes of the 1960s. He waxes lyrical about an imminent change in this summer of heat, a revolution from the right which will protect the unspoiled countryside around them from ruin. He builds up to: 'They've got to be sent back now! Back to where they came from. Yes! Even the kids in school are beginning to feel it, feel their Englishness, know this place belongs to them . . .' (ibid.: 49). Nick can listen no longer. He grabs Kevin and shakes him hard. Fading sirens suggest the police have gone past so Charlotte decides it is a good moment for them to move on. Having told Kevin to go on ahead to the van, she is left with Nick listening to the stillness on the hillside. Instructing him not to turn around, she draws her gun and shoots him at very close range, before picking up the thermos and leaving. The lights fade to an increasingly loud soundtrack of scrambled traffic news '*blasting out fiercely*' (ibid.: 52).

In *Strawberry Fields*, Poliakoff has not written a 'State of the Nation' play such as Edgar's *Destiny*, analysing politically the rise of the extreme right in the UK. In contrast, as Bull (1994: 584) has remarked, 'Poliakoff's is a theatre of individual gesture'. Where *Destiny* features a British National Party rally and, using the device of formal speeches, is overt about the party's racist policies, Poliakoff's treatment of issues in *Strawberry Fields* is set against the question of how seemingly harmless individual characters might, in given socio-historical circumstances, get drawn into extreme beliefs and, indeed, violent action. Matthew Martin has drawn attention to *Strawberry Fields'* echo of John Lennon's 1966 song, the fragmentary lyric of which evokes not only the 1960s hippy dream but its nightmarish dark side.[5] The words encapsulate Kevin's confusion of 1960s pop aspirations, distorted film images and disillusion. Rather than foregrounding political structures and organised movements, Poliakoff's *Strawberry Fields* picks up on the dangers which can arise from individuals' confusion when a progressive trajectory falters. Though the link to European history is not made explicitly here, Poliakoff is alert to the latency of fascist tendencies.

The reasonable and sceptical Nick is offered perhaps as a participant-observer point of identification for the more liberal members of the NT studio audience, but others might have been called upon to face up to their own rightward leanings in sympathising with what Charlotte and Kevin have to say, even if they cannot fully empathise with the characters. That Charlotte's background and general cultural outlook might not be so far from their own, demands reflection on the fine line between a wish to defend establishment values and reactionary militancy, highlighted in the two shootings. It is through increasing shocks of discovery as the journey progresses, and ultimately through the violent deaths, that the play invokes the disturbance of complex seeing. Audience members are required to face up to distinct political possibilities of which they might previously have been only half-aware but, which, in the late 1970s, they were to be called upon to confront, possibly in themselves.

In an interview, David Edgar remarked that neither he, nor his fellow-playwrights, had seen Thatcher coming.[6] *Strawberry Fields* was prescient, perhaps, not only in its treatment of ecological issues, but in glimpsing a lurch to the right in British politics. Charlotte's cool shooting of Nick might serve as a warning about a social group which appears respectable on the surface but has the capacity to be more ruthless than the socially disempowered. In the decade to follow, the Conservative Prime Minister, Margaret Thatcher (1979–90) was to act upon at least some of the reactionary tendencies espoused by Charlotte and Kevin in *Strawberry Fields*.

Stronger than the Sun (1977)

Stronger than the Sun marks Poliakoff's breakthrough specifically as a television playwright with a commission in 1976 to write a single play on the pressing issue of nuclear proliferation. *Stronger than the Sun* (*Stronger*) was produced by Margaret Matheson and directed by Michael Apted for BBC1's prestigious 'Play for Today' strand. The core issue was topical in that it concerned workers at a fictional Caversbridge (echoing Calder Hall) at a time when weapons-grade plutonium was being produced in the UK.[7] An atmosphere of menace is constructed both visually and sonically. Beyond the mere barrenness of Caversbridge's isolated and faceless industrial buildings, security at the plant is militarily tight as guards with aggressive Alsatian guard-dogs patrol the perimeters, and everybody is required to show their ID at the gate. Inside, a bleeping geiger-counter accompanies the personnel, dehumanised in contamination suits, being checked as they finish their shifts. The visual sense of repressive control and menace is underscored from the outset by a dramatic soundscape with strident strings and a percussive piano.

Alan Whitely (Tom Bell), Head of Section 502, becomes concerned about unusual movements on the site that suggest there might have been an incident. He deliberately befriends attractive 'new girl', Kate Cowley (Francesca Annis), who has begun work in the Health Physics records office, inviting her for Sunday lunch. While she awaits him on the sea-front at Whitby, a group of young bikers circle around the bandstand where Whitely, by arriving with two boxes of chicken and chips, disappoints any romantic expectations. He quite bluntly explains to Kate that he wants access to the confidential records on the plant and seeks her help. He is taking a risk in this approach but, as he says, since they do not know each other, there's no reason to be distrustful.

Querulous strings and a high-pitched percussive piano continue to mark the tension as they secretly enter Kate's workplace together out of hours. In a telling conversation in which Kate, mysteriously back-lit such that her face is in shadow, asks the questions, Alan shares his view that 'what we're doing here is wrong'. As a scientist he had joined the programme to develop fast-breeder nuclear reactors in the sincere belief that 'plutonium is the cleanest, cheapest form of energy ever' and that they were 'saving the world'. Now he has fundamentally changed his position and wants to stop the work from within. Framed in a big close-up, he asks Kate if she is 'shocked by this heresy'. But Kate, a local girl who watched the site being built, turns out ultimately to have even stronger reservations than Whitely. The initial dialogues between them are punctuated by detail shots of the plant in which protracted hand-washing becomes a motif, echoing Lady Macbeth's seminal attempts to wash away her guilt after the murder of Duncan. The implications for the health of the tacitly complicit local workers are evident in the measures needed to protect them. The plutonium is handled through built-in gloves in sealed laboratory compartments accompanied by the ever-present bleep of the monitor. After work, a screening follows their personal cleansing to check that they have erased all traces of radioactivity.

Having resumed employment following a failed marriage of seven years, Kate's professional life advances when she is somewhat surprisingly promoted to metallurgy. Though her secretarial role has given the impression of a relatively uneducated woman, Kate, it transpires, has Advanced Level qualifications and has read and digested the technical manuals which line the shelves of her unheated bed-sit. This revelation may be justification of a plot device but it also exemplifies the Poliakovian strategy of revealing characters to be more complex than they might at first appear. When Kate invites Alan back to her place, Poliakoff eschews the easy option to catch viewers' attention and swell ratings, preferring to draw upon the attractions of the thriller genre than on-screen sex. The mystery of Kate's character is deepened when she proves even keener than Alan to expose and stop the Caversbridge experiment. Indeed, as Alan becomes more cautious, Kate argues portentously that 'there are very few moments in history where you actually have the chance to stop something as big as this'. Such an attitude bears out a strain running through Poliakoff's *oeuvre*, of individuals apparently on the edge of political life having the opportunity to do something to make a difference. This view is in stark contrast with that of the biker who takes Kate on a joy-ride, in a reprise of the sea-front scene earlier, who says, 'there's nothing you can do about it; nothing you can do about anything'.

The risks of Kate's mission are emphasised when she is summoned for an interview with Higsby, the head of the Caversbridge plant and his PR manager. Prior to her arrival, their profile review reveals that she is 'extremely intelligent' with an 'obstinate tendency' and their concerns are aroused since Kate has posted a notice inviting anybody with worries about the plant to sign. Since nothing has come of this notice, she manages to persuade them that it was done for a bet. But Higsby warns her about her conduct, pointing out that 'it's a sensitive time now . . . with the national debate everybody's aware of'. From this point on, Kate becomes more determined to do something to stop the plant but also more paranoid about being watched and followed. Together, the two features crank up the temperature of the drama.

Kate proposes to smuggle some plutonium out of the plant. Alan is dismissive about the feasibility and the purpose of this action, angrily pointing out that Kate is 'not some nuclear Joan of Arc'. But, despite his practical and principled objections, Kate is determined, retorting that 'the effect would be devastating . . . it would be front-page news'. Having quarrelled with her former ally, Kate becomes increasingly isolated but unshakeably determined. Her gaze when she asks Alan to leave is steady and she is seen to be putting a plan carefully into action. Having chatted up her section manager, to ascertain the weight of incoming plutonium samples, she carefully files down metal to replace in the phial a weight identical to the plutonium she plans to steal. In a tea-break, she dons the scientist's gloves to access the sealed laboratory unit and introduces her bogus phial, swapping it for the plutonium. The tension of this sequence is marked in the action when one scientist does not quit the lab and then bangs the door on his subsequent exit, sounding as if somebody is returning. It is underscored by the percussive piano and strings which are nerve-janglingly ascendant in these moments. The risks are very high as she must conceal the phial in a bodily orifice in the toilets before she can exit the plant at the end of the shift, hoping not to trigger the various alarms. Intercut with a delay in the departure of the workers' bus, close-ups of the patrol dogs' snarling jaws at the gates offer a visceral reminder of the possible consequences of discovery, but Kate ultimately makes her getaway and, back home, recovers her smuggled goods.

What follows appears to be an object lesson in political naïveté though, structurally in the drama, it also serves as the lull before the final storm. Travelling to London, Kate first approaches an environmental pressure group and subsequently a national newspaper journalist, confident in the sense that, once they knew what was in her possession, they would raise a national alarm. They do not. The first group is concerned about its political credibility, having made recent advances by democratic means and fearful of risking its political influence from within the established political frameworks. The latter is too busy to take her seriously. Increasingly strained, if not paranoid, by the sense that she is being followed, Kate returns deflated to Whitby. The ambiguity sustained in the filming of her journeyings as to whether she is actually being followed or not serves only to heighten the overall dramatic tension. Having drawn in *Stronger* upon the political thriller genre, Poliakoff skilfully scripts the requisite dénouement.

In a three-and-a-half-minute sequence, cinematic in that it comprises only images underscored by a strong soundtrack, Kate is seen deliberately exposing herself to radiation. Entering her apartment, she empties the contacts of her handbag on to the floor, seeking the phial of plutonium, as yet still safe in its vacuum-sealed pack. She places the phial on the glass coffee table in front of her and thinks what to do. The sequence is set to stirring strings accompanied by a querulous, tinkling piano. Kate gets up and goes to the bathroom to run a bath. On her return she again sits to contemplate the phial. An over-the-shoulder, point-of-view shot of her invites the viewer imaginatively to share her thoughts, before a close-up of the phial is set to a rising phrase from the interrogative, percussive piano, emphasising the phial's significance and leaving no doubt about Kate's preoccupation. A cross-cut shows the intensity of Kate's expression, full on in close-up. A tear dribbles down her right cheek: cut back to a close-up of the phial. Kate gets up and fetches scissors from a desk to breach the vacuum pack and open the phial. She has made a conscious decision.

In opening the phial she spills a little of its powdery contents, which she proceeds to sniff, first one granule on her figure and then strongly, as if snorting a narcotic drug. A cut to a tight shot of the full bath embraces Kate's arms as she arrives in the bathroom to turn off the taps before sprinkling the radioactive plutonium into her bath water. The music reduces to a single cello refrain and then the percussive piano over a full-screen shot of the bath water infused with the grey particles of plutonium. A strong percussive pulse signals Kate's moment of decision before the strings of the soundtrack become increasingly agitated. The cello bassline is augmented by violins in a higher register, suggesting heroic effort amid profound perturbance. Kate, having sprinkled some plutonium directly into one cupped palm, puts her hands in the water and splashes her face, the medium close-up from the side picking up her almost sensuous indulgence in the act as she licks her palm clean. She returns to her bedroom and gulps down another handful of plutonium before lying on the bed to await the consequences. The soundtrack settles and comes to musical closure as she turns on her side to sleep.

This sequence has been recounted in some detail partly because it is the moment of dramatic crisis in *Stronger*, but more because it fully illustrates Poliakoff's ready move from theatre to a moving image medium. Though he begins his career as a playwright – and the use of well-chosen words plays an important part in his later work – the film-maker's capacity to work with images in a carefully constructed relation with sounds is evident in this, his first piece for television. Working closely with composer Howard Blake and editor David Martin, Poliakoff uses heightened ambient sound as well as musical underscore to create atmosphere and narrative tension. Noise is important in Poliakoff's theatre work, as seen, for example, in the sustained loud electric buzz which marks the change of Acts in *Strawberry Fields*. As Beth Meszaros (2005: 124) has remarked, 'for Poliakoff, noise is not just an invasive force; noise is a given non-negotiable presence'. Where, in his theatre plays, often intrusive sound (muzak, for example) is an inescapable part of the environment, in his 'film' work Poliakoff sets visuals against sound for a range of purposes.

The sound of geiger-counters intensifies as a team of specialist police in white plastic suits and breathing apparatus approach Kate at the end of *Stronger*, echoing the sound of Caversbridge workers being screened for radiation at the opening. The men remove Kate from her bed-sit on a stretcher canopied in sealed plastic and reminiscent of a funeral bier. The soundtrack is now magisterial as the bier, featured in high-angle long-shot, is carried slowly down the front steps of the house to an awaiting white hearse rescue vehicle, the formality ironically suggesting a state funeral. The only words spoken in the final sequence are those of the Caversbridge boss, who claims, 'the girl is completely mad' and instructs his colleague 'when this gets out . . . tell them the girl is mad'. A final zoom in to a close-up of Kate breathing in an enclosed system like her rescuers, shows her still to be alive but effectively asks for how long.

Though the structuring of *Stronger*, and in particular the sequence detailed above, invites some sympathy with Kate and the anti-nuclear lobby of the late 1960s and early 1970s through the use of sound and the positioning of the camera, Poliakoff ultimately leaves it open for the viewer to judge where the madness lies: with Kate or with the nuclear reactor industry. A harder-left, more socially critical filmmaker might have loaded the piece more heavily against the dangers of nuclear research. Troy Kennedy Martin's later critique of the nuclear industry and its secrecy, *Edge of Darkness* (1985) may sound a bleaker warning of nuclear dangers.[8] But Poliakoff creates a powerful drama, successfully negotiating the political thriller genre in a medium new to him without abandoning his distinctive vision of a strong individual character resisting an oppressive environment, albeit at a cost to herself. In my judgement, *Stronger*, largely overlooked in television histories, bears comparison with the more celebrated *Edge of Darkness*.

Close My Eyes (1991)

Produced by Beambright with FilmFour International, *Close My Eyes* is Poliakoff's second self-directed feature, made in a period when he parted company with the BBC to take up opportunities afforded by FilmFour (Channel 4). He moved because:

you made films that might get into the cinema, which was good, but, more important, they had a long life because Channel Four showed them several times . . . *Close My Eyes* was successful in the cinema and won prizes and things but, much more importantly to me, it still shows . . . After 14 years, it was still playing on terrestrial television.[9]

The shift marks another stage in Poliakoff's transition from playwright to moving-image auteur that this book traces, introducing, as Matthew Bell has remarked, 'a rich look, a world away from his gritty dramas of the late 1970s'.[10] Indeed, *Close My Eyes* is very different in look from the television version of *Hitting Town* and the environment of the stage play on which both are based. As Poliakoff has acknowledged, 'ever since I finished the play I'd had a desire to explore the central relationship more deeply . . . but I wanted to create a new story involving a brother and sister that would reflect some of the anxieties that pursued us in the nineties' (1998: xi–xii).

Though the aim here is not to offer a detailed study of the adaptation from play to film, the transposition does afford an interesting example in which to observe how a cinematic approach refashions a pre-existing construct. Attention will be paid particularly to visual story-telling and visual style (with Witold Stok as director of photography and Luciana Arrighi as production designer), and to the soundtrack (composed by Michael Gibbs) working with and against the images. For *Close My Eyes* is a sensually atmospheric mood piece setting the issue of incest from *Hitting Town* in a new socio-historic context of AIDS and in a built environment removed from the run-down urban mall to the postmodern make-over of London's docklands.

At the core of *Close My Eyes* is the overtly sexual relationship between brother and sister, Richard and Natalie Gillespie, performed with an edgy conviction by Clive Owen and Saskia Reeves. Although the siblings are aware that their relationship is against the law and that, if discovered and arrested, they might end up in jail, Poliakoff does not foreground a psychological or ethical perspective. Instead, the Poliakovian approach juxtaposes a visceral specific, the incest, against 1980s London, using the commercial regeneration of the city, with buildings such as Richard Rogers's Lloyds Building (completed in 1986), as an expansive metaphor. Though possible comparisons between the one and the other are drawn, the overall effect is interestingly dissonant. In David Wilson's view the relationship 'may be seen as double-edged: as a perverse celebration in toppling of a last taboo, but also as a swan-song for the unchecked licence of the age'.[11]

The film starts somewhat unsatisfactorily with a number of short scenes and jumps through time. In his later work, as we have seen, Poliakoff becomes a master of revealing backstory to deepen understanding of how past experience locates and informs character in a present predicament. In *Close My Eyes*, the handling of time is relatively clunky. It takes thirty minutes of film time over five years of fictional time to reach the core experience under scrutiny. In marking and jumping through time, Poliakoff appears to have seen a need to establish a distance between brother and sister such that their re-encounter might be seen as fresh, and to show that Natalie had tried to contain her impulse over time. When their parents divorced, it is explained, the siblings also went their different ways, Natalie with her father and Richard with his mother. Thus they lived apart and were not brought up in close proximity, as typically in a nuclear family. As young adults, they see each other only intermittently with Richard proving unreliable in respect of keeping appointments.

The first images, like those in the televised *Hitting Town*, suggest incursions of the unpleasant into an otherwise comfortable world. As Richard walks the London streets one Sunday in 1985 to visit Natalie, a group of punks in leathers – also echoing *Bloody Kids* and prefiguring *The Tribe* – interrupts a game of bowls where litter strews one corner of an otherwise immaculate green. As in *Hitting Town*, Richard insists on taking his sister out and, following a coffee in an empty cafe, they make their way home. Richard is awoken by a rowdy party upstairs and finds Natalie curled up on the lounge floor by a candle-lit shrine to her lost love. Apparently seeking consolation, Natalie asks Richard to kiss her but, when he embraces her, she kisses him on the lips with some passion, immediately apologising, saying she just needed a hug. In the first overt sex scene, they lie naked together on the floor of Richard's flat with Natalie weakly proposing that they go no further, but moments later, her lust overcoming her better judgement, she falls upon Richard and their sexual union is consummated. The following sequences marked 'two years later', 'one year later' and again 'two years later' create the distance noted.

Away from his sister, architect Richard is seeking a career change in an eco-conscious direction. His disillusion with grand project building is reflected in a sequence of wide-angle views of London's dockland, figured as a maze of cranes as it enters a postmodern phase of fundamental redevelopment. In response, as it were, Richard takes a less prestigious and less well-paid job with a firm which aims to be a kind of 'urban Greenpeace' monitoring the alien landscape. Immersed in his new role, Richard seems irritated to receive at the office a call from his sister alleging he has not been in touch for six weeks. In the passing of time, it transpires that Natalie has married, and she invites Richard to meet Sinclair (Alan Rickman), her entrepreneur husband, over lunch at their impressive riverside residence in the Home Counties. Though Richard agrees, he appears more interested in chatting up the office junior over a take-out pizza. When they meet, both are sceptical about each other's change of circumstances but only by way of minor reservation. Richard expresses surprise at Natalie's move into the *haute bourgeoisie*, although he gets on with Sinclair, who constructs himself as something of a bohemian. Back at work, when asked by a colleague if he and his sister are close, Richard replies 'not at all'.

The overall situation at this point is typical of much of Poliakoff's later work, in which well-heeled characters located in architecturally stunning settings are not entirely comfortable with the excess of fine food and material plenitude at their disposal. An underlying restlessness informs Paul in *Friends and Crocodiles*, Mr Elliot in *Joe's Palace* as well as Natalie in her marriage in *Close My Eyes*. It might also be remarked that Poliakoff would appear himself to have something of a conflicted attitude to material wealth in that, though critical of commerce, he is patently attracted, in his 'films', to fine buildings, particularly in and around London. The camera in Poliakoff's work sensually explores the built environment with a sexiness of visual style, which, in *Close My Eyes*, resonates with the sexual tension between the protagonists. In addition to lingering in the memory, the design and cinematography of *Close My Eyes* serve to make the familiar strange, the docklands environment in particular serving as a metaphor for both the specific predicament and the times in general. The ambivalence is captured in Wilson's summary: 'Docklands is a wasteland of half-empty buildings, obscenely parading their icons of see-through lifts and monumental ash-trays. The interiors are darkly lit as if hiding from the glare outside just as Richard and Natalie are forced to hide their secretive life behind closed doors.'[12] Poliakoff can be seen, however, to be further developing from a playwright understood primarily as a wordsmith, into a film-maker, conveying ideas and telling his stories and making his commentaries obliquely through visuals and sound rather than more directly through dialogue.

Up in London for a wedding, Natalie and Sinclair drop in unannounced on Richard's office and again Natalie suggests that Richard is wrongly situated as though she knows him better than he knows himself. She says she wants to speak with him about something important and makes an 'appointment'. Arriving four hours late at his flat, perhaps to get her own back, she finds an impassioned Richard, furious at being restrained from pursuing his own interests that day. In passing him in the hallway, Natalie kisses him on the lips in a manner beyond the sisterly. Clearly impassioned herself, she makes for the kitchen to take a glass of water. Richard, shocked and disturbed, follows her and they embrace passionately with Natalie ultimately pulling away. They move to the lounge and, on Natalie's insistence, sit apart making small-talk. But, as the tightening close-up on Natalie's face reveals, the attraction between them is overwhelming and it is only moments before they are naked on the floor. Her words contradicting her actions, Natalie implores Richard to stop her but when he does move away, she follows him and jumps on him. A tight close-up on a relieved smile confirms the incestuous consummation while the strings of the soundtrack mix romantic strains with modernist dissonances to invite a perturbed but not unsympathetic view of the siblings' plight.

Poliakoff is clearly at pains to establish that Natalie in particular has tried to resist the temptation of the illicit and is not merely acting on the rebound of her first broken love affair – as perhaps in the first stolen kiss – but is subject to a passion which, despite a conventionally good marriage, she simply cannot control. The focus on the experience of a supposedly misplaced lust is presented without prurience. Ironically, the cover of the DVD issue cites the *Guardian* review judgement that *Close My Eyes* is 'the sexiest film of the era'. And, indeed, the film does capture the sensuousness of the passion of two explicitly sexual encounters in which, like fresh lovers, the pair simply cannot keep their hands off each other, tearing off clothes to achieve fleshly encounters. Cinematography and sound score are used in both instances to present the liaisons, in Poliakoff's words, 'as almost natural' (1998: xi–xii). Natalie's casual remark to Richard at the end of the encounter that Sinclair wishes to have lunch with him affirms, however, that, for her at least, the liaison she has instigated is no more than a passing affair. Other aspects of her life are to continue as before, it would appear. Richard's confusion suggests things may turn out otherwise.

Two more charged meetings develop Natalie and Richard's fractious relationship. Sombre strings underscore another beautifully shot sequence, not of urban London, but the surrounding Home Counties and, in specific, a Poliakovian picnic on a hot summer's day by the river. Having established the location and ambience, the camera dwells in close-up on the face of Natalie being photographed by her brother. Her facial expression suggests her thoughts and feelings are not at her husband's picnic as Sinclair, taking centre stage, prattles on about parasols making a come-back with global warming. Overcome by more than ennui, Natalie is still attracted to Richard, but is partly in denial, wishing she could 'close my eyes and wake up and it would be gone, this feeling'. Nevertheless, she agrees to contrive a future meeting.

The next encounter, underscored by softly stirring strings which evoke a depth of emotion, sees Richard arrive on time to meet Natalie at the in-laws' empty London apartment as arranged. The pretence that they will just talk is soon overtaken by a passionate embrace. Though the camera is again not prurient, it leaves the viewer in no doubt about the nature of the relations as the couple are ultimately viewed from a high angle lying naked and exhausted on the bed. A frisson of anxiety is injected by the unexpected arrival of an Italian housekeeper, but Natalie deftly turns her away. Following a phone call to Sinclair and further coition, Natalie is relaxed, walking by the Thames with Richard, who speculates on a possible future abroad together in the face of Natalie's suggestion that he simply enjoy their last moments. Nearby, adolescents are hanging out in the first flush of sexual awareness. Richard, in observing them, notes that being single no longer seems so simple for him.

The driver of plot suspense, such as it is, is that Sinclair comes to suspect his wife is having an affair and is determined to discover with whom. But the detection element serves merely to augment the suspense concerning the illicit lovers' capacity to sustain, or break free from, their intensely powerful sexual attraction. Natalie's cover that she is staying at a hotel in Nuneaton on a business trip is blown when Sinclair needs to call her. Surprisingly, given his apparent self-assurance, Sinclair quickly becomes haunted by the idea of her infidelity. And, indeed, the relation between Natalie and Richard is like an affair, cinematically presented as such. The lovers are figured the next morning waking up in the 'time-warp' of the old apartment block which the camera explores as Richard opens the bedroom window. Dressed casually and barefoot, they amble in the grounds of a nearby church, but the relaxed mood is disturbed when Natalie becomes concerned about Richard's repeated suggestion that they might spend their lives together. Against a soundtrack of church bells, she refuses to see him again until has got a girlfriend, as if this will somehow balance and legitimate their incestuous relationship. Natalie talks down their predicament but Richard tries to emphasise the strangeness and illegitimacy of what they are doing by daring Natalie to enter the church with him without feeling any guilt. Observed by choirboys, Natalie is at least embarrassed, imploring Richard to refrain from touching her as she does not 'want it to be wrong'.

In the following days, Sinclair's sense of betrayal by Natalie grows while Richard crassly tries to chat up Jessica (Lesley Sharp) in the office. Being rebuffed here, he seeks out a former casual partner who works in an arcade cafe. He is merely trying to meet Natalie's stipulation that he have a girlfriend before she will see him again and even his 'girlfriend' senses she is being used as an alibi. On the way back to her bed-sit through run-down London backstreets, Richard stops off to get condoms from a vending machine. Refraining from copulation back in her room, however, they talk about it, Richard saying that sex used to be so simple prior to AIDS. Interestingly, Richard declares that the revelation that his boss, Colin (Karl Johnson), has AIDS strikes him as a sign that what he's 'doing is right'. The dialogue invites consideration of a moral balance between incest and AIDS, resonating with the contemporary context in which some commentators ascribed the epidemic to a punishment for sexual promiscuity. Perhaps this scene comes closest to articulating the issue central to *Close My Eyes*, namely an examination of the ethical implications of sexual, and related, licence from the 1960s into the 1980s. A heady and reckless pursuit of desire, it would seem, cannot escape consequences. In this allusive sense, *Close My Eyes*' visual preoccupation with the building of a shrine to corporatism in London's docklands overlays the specific relationship between Natalie and Richard. As Chris Allison puts it, *Close My Eyes* offers 'a metaphor for the moral and political irresponsibility of the Thatcherite 1980s . . . [and] highlights the ambiguous nature of economic progress and its effects on individuals and relationships'.[13]

Richard and Natalie's relationship is certainly having a corrosive impact on Natalie's marriage, she being unable to break free from her obsession with Richard, and Sinclair becoming increasingly obsessed with discovering her lover. When the siblings meet again in the foyer of the in-laws' apartment block, Natalie will not let Richard touch her and, in an echo of the moment prior to their first sexual encounter, insists he sit apart from her. But the physical separation as before does not last, moving from a skirmish between them to a passionate embrace before Natalie breaks away to set Richard another task. An interim sequence between sexual encounters finds Richard, having temporarily liberated Colin from hospital, travelling again on the docklands railway. They speak of an unfulfilled architectural vision: 'It was going to be this great new city: the New Venice, modern but

magical, one of the wonders of Europe . . . But look what's happened.'
The camera scans a panorama of sites building office block on office
block, dwarfing human scale in the mirror-glass reflecting the train as
it traverses the docklands landscape, a monument to late capitalism in
the making.

Following the revelation that Natalie and Sinclair are leaving to
live in Connecticut, an encounter in the lobby of a grand London
hotel sets the emotional charge between Natalie and Richard against
the constraints of the faded gentility of afternoon tea-dance. Natalie is
self-collected on this occasion, amused to imagine the reaction of the
elderly tea-sippers if they only knew what was between her and
Richard. He, in contrast, becomes increasingly desperate in tearfully
imploring Natalie not to leave him and the country. In turn, Natalie
asks Richard to 'let it go'. Sinclair arrives and Richard narrowly avoids
betraying the situation by causing a scene. Only the intervention of a
doorman allows Natalie to escape with Sinclair. A querulous soundtrack introduces the sequence in which Richard, back home in his
flat, attempts suicide by swallowing all the pills he can put his hands
on before wandering among the mechanical diggers working on a
nearby building site. Natalie, presumably alerted, arrives at his flat to
comfort him as he throws up. She tells him he is precious to her but
she will not let him 'destroy us both'. In the interim, Colin has actually died, in contrast with Richard's melodramatic 'cry for help'.

Richard attends the film's final garden party, an inevitably extrava-
gant affair, with colleague Jessica, but he mopes around on his own,
tracking down Natalie – who is visually distinguished by the
Poliakovian scarlet dress. In his desperation, he physically attacks her
and, unlike the unconvincing brawl in *The Tribe*, the fight between
Natalie and Richard is protracted and visceral. When they limp back
to the party, apparently unconcerned now to keep up appearances,
they are blood-smeared and bedraggled. Observing them, Sinclair
remarks, 'something tells me this is the end of the party'. And, indeed,
it is the end of the actual party and of Richard and Natalie's relationship but, as a forgiving Sinclair emphasises in the closing dialogue,
'there's something extraordinary between you two'.

Demonstrating Poliakoff's versatility in yet another powerful treatment of contemporary issues, *Close My Eyes* was a considerable critical and box-office success. As Poliakoff reflected: 'No one could have predicted that a drama about incest – what you would have pigeon-holed as pure art-house – could have made £500,000. And that was only five prints.'[14] This success gave him clout within the industry to move further into feature film and the films for television which distinguish his later career.

Century (1993)

Following *Close My Eyes*, Poliakoff takes on issues equally as contentious as incest in his next feature film, *Century*. As Geoff Brown records, '[o]n the back of that success, enough finance was finally attracted for this multi-layered drama about science, morality and the sins of the future century'.[15] The broad question of the film concerns the justifiability of the pursuit of scientific progress at all costs. In the process individual scientists face highly sensitive ethical dilemmas.[16] The specific focus in *Century* is on eugenics, the study and practice of selective breeding, in which advances had been made as part of a rush of medical and scientific developments at the turn of the twentieth century. Indeed, eugenics taken as a social philosophy – a means of improving human hereditary traits and hence, supposedly, the human condition – was taken up worldwide in the first two decades of the twentieth century.[17] This theme is interwoven with a *leitmotiv* across Poliakoff's work since his protagonist's family in *Century* is Jewish. It was Hitler's espousal of eugenics – involving racial hygiene by way of compulsory sterilisation and mass extermination of the *Untermensch* (subhumans) – which ultimately brought eugenics practice into disrepute. Thus the question of ethics in science maps on to the Poliakovian concern with the position of Jews in European history.

In *Century*, Poliakoff deploys a double time perspective to mobilise complex seeing. Viewers of the film are positioned as looking forward to a new century, the twentieth century, from a position at the end of that century with prior knowledge of the Holocaust, and other atrocities. In addition, by exploiting an ambiguity as to whether a new century starts at the end of its last first year (that is 1 January 1900, rather than 1 January 1901) in respect of the turn of the twentieth century), Poliakoff is able to frame his piece with two 'New Year' parties thrown by a Romanian Jewish immigrant to the London suburbs by way of Scotland. Mr Reisner (Robert Stephens) has established a successful building business and encouraged his son, Paul (Clive Owen) in his educational aspiration to be a doctor. Reisner's self-assured eccentricities – his insistence, for example, on a large illuminated sign announcing his party against local authority advice and regulations – have begun, however, to embarrass his son. Paul is thus relieved to be leaving the family home to take up a research post at the prestigious, though idiosyncratic, Whiteweather Institute, headed by an eminent figure, Professor Mandry (Charles Dance).

Paul Reisner joins a team of ambitious young doctors believing in their abilities to find remedies for a range of medical and social ills. Behind and below the fine façade of the institute – which Mandry sustains to give science research a positive image – the doctors inhabit basic communal accommodation and the ancillaries work in near squalor. Though the laboratory facilities are quite good, the doctors must, in true Darwinian fashion, compete for Mandry's favour and the best-equipped laboratories by pursuing their specialisms to treat such outpatients as present themselves. Paul achieves highly, though his self-assurance and strong views bring him into conflict with some colleagues. In short time, he is invited to work alongside Mandry. When, however, another exceptional scientist, Felix Russell (Neil Stuke), convinces Paul of the value of an ambitious project to treat diabetes, Paul comes into direct conflict with Mandry who, for some unexplained reason, will not sanction the research. Paul's opinionated, if not arrogant approach achieves banishment from the institute, for a month in the first instance and subsequently for good.

He is saved from penury by a woman ancillary worker, Clara (Miranda Richardson) to whom he is clearly attracted. Having lost an illegitimate child, Clara lives alone, achieving less than the potential evident in her sharp intelligence and scientific knowledge. Independent of spirit and sexually demanding, she represents the 'new woman' of the early twentieth century not yet empowered in society.

Paul and Clara have an affair while considering how Paul might find work. In returning together to assist the poor who inhabit makeshift accommodation on a hill near the institute, Paul discovers that Mandry has been sterilising women without their consent. He seeks to confront his mentor at a Christmas lecture but cannot quite find the courage. He appeals to Mrs Whiteweather (Joan Hickson) whose late husband's money funds the eponymous institute. When she is initially unsympathetic, Paul achieves his ends by resorting to an underhand tactic and claiming that Mandry is experimenting on dogs and monkeys. The institute is summarily shut down.

At the second of the New Year parties thrown by Mr Reisner, Paul and Clara meet Mandry, who is an invited guest. They resist the professor's request to recant and, in a reverse echo of earlier scenes, they require him to leave the premises. Viewers are left questioning the ethical basis of Paul's actions since his headstrong ambition leaves an element of revenge on Mandry at least as partial motive. The murkiness of the personal ethics colours the broader theme of hope in scientific progress to cure social and medical ills to produce a better society. From the vantage point of the late twentieth century – and with resonances for the twenty-first century – the ambivalent position of science is foregrounded. Modern viewers are invited to consider whether the undoubted advances in medical science – the discovery of insulin to treat diabetes; the ability to at least hold some cancers in remission; the improvements in housing and social welfare which leave the poor relatively less vulnerable – outweigh the downside of modernist obsession, namely the devastation of industrialisation and atomic warfare, and the evil inherent in attempts at enforced genetic selection?

Some slightly clunky editing apart, the achievement of the film is that its weighty themes are well brought out by visual and narrative patterning and appropriately contrasting imagery. As part of the self-presentation of the institute, Mandry insists the doctors wear the finest morning dress, while underlings such as Clara are more modestly dressed. When Paul formally invites Clara out, he impertinently hires a grand gown for her to wear to an event at which new inventions and futuristic schemes are presented, equivalent to the Great Exhibition a half-century earlier.[18] When he falls from favour, Paul is lent ill-fitting everyday clothes by Clara, an outfit which offends Mr Reisner when he makes a surprise visit to London. Thus costume affords markers of class distinction throughout the film. A similar visual distinction is afforded by the built environments, initially between the fine front of the institute and its non-public spaces. Similarly, the grand exhibition hall and the tea-rooms, in which Paul twice encounters Mrs Whiteweather, contrast with the tenement housing where Clara lives and the improvised slum dwellings on the hill near the institute. Witold Stock's camera roams the environments, appropriately creating a range of atmospheres and a sense of the powerful attractions of the new by picking out detail in the environments. Couples kiss openly and voraciously in public parks and industrial machines steam on London's streets.[19] Paul returns with Clara from London through mist in a single horse and trap paralleling the horse-drawn waggon of the telephone company in which he cadged a lift to London at the outset, refusing the six horses planned by his father. Though on occasion (the interior of Clara's tenement, for example), an element of romanticism renders the environment more appealing than a grittier realism might have done, there are darker undertones in the lighting and coloration of much of the film to underscore its themes. Poliakoff aimed to avoid nostalgia in making a period picture 'that told an arresting story with a modern resonance'.[20]

The garishness of the huge, illuminated sign at Mr Reisner's first party, and the grotesque fancy-dress costume in which he and other family members are attired at the second, pinpoint a *nouveau riche* taste formation, grand-scale but garish, which mark Mr Reisner's – and, to a lesser extent, Paul's – outsider status. At the very beginning of the film, the local burghers who object to Mr Reisner's illuminated sign challenge the timing of his party on the grounds that 'Your New Year's different – because of your religion', and a neighbour, invited to pick garden fruit, remarks under his breath, 'nasty little Jew'. By the time of his second New Year's Eve party, which on this occasion the worthies do not boycott, it transpires that they have driven him to move out of town – in parallel with his son's fortunes – by depriving him of business.

The theme of antagonism to Jews is woven subtly but unmistakably through the piece mainly in brief but telling remarks. Paul is made conscious of his Jewish origins when in London first through a direct question of Felix Russell's and, secondly, when Mandry observes that he is 'from relatively humble origins – Scottish Jewish'. In banishing Paul and threatening that he will never work again in medical research, Mandry exhorts him to 'remember who you are'. Subsequently Paul is arrested amid talk of an 'Aliens Act'. In the second meeting of Paul with Mrs Whiteweather, she observes that she is 'not anti-Semitic [her]self but that some of [her] friends have their own opinions'. Thus the variation in reprise on a celebratory theme at the respective parties manifests a superficial gloss thinly masking a deepening unease. As midnight strikes, Mr Reisner is tearful about what he has not achieved; Clara is not absolutely convinced that the common-law relationship proposed by Paul will work; and Felix is unable to make any sure predictions about the future. Paul's final voice-over confirms mixed fortunes but more successes than failures. It informs the audience that he never heard of Mandry again and that he and Clara set up a rural medical practice. Hopes for the future of the new century thus remain not entirely dashed but uncertain and ambiguous.

Blinded by the Sun (1996)

Blinded by the Sun, like both *Stronger than the Sun* and *Century*, is concerned with ethical issues in the scientific workplace, in this instance a modern, albeit established, university science department. Its location is more specific than Poliakoff's urban canyons, though a shopping mall does figure.[21] As in *Century*, the ethical issues concern the breach of sacrosanct protocols for career advantage, in this case research scientist, Christopher's, apparent rigging of an experiment. But the concern expands into a broader, more abstract consideration of ethics under 1990s socio-cultural pressures such that the sustained viability of established standards of evidencing truth-claims is called into question. This account of *Blinded by the Sun* (*Blinded*) will foreground developments in Poliakoff's dramaturgy to enhance complex seeing of an issue from unresolved multiple perspectives. Though the first Act concerns an unacceptable breach of ethical standards in academia, the complication of perspectives in Act Two takes up Poliakoff's interest in socio-political contexts. The specific issue of scientific ethics is set against an emergent culture of popularisation and celebrity alongside managerialism introduced in the Thatcher years (as in *Friends and Crocodiles* and *Gideon's Daughter*). The play's treatment ultimately opens up the even broader issue of cultural relativism, its dramaturgy leaving a range of possible viewpoints with no simple means for audience members to determine between them.

Blinded by the Sun juxtaposes three approaches to science. The talented young Christopher appears to have faked an experiment to perfect the Sun Battery; department senior, Elinor, having gained a reputation from her early career research on vitamins, stands up for pure, 'blue skies' research but produces no new results; and Al, a forty-year-old of modest achievement, on being unexpectedly promoted to the department chair, first turns managerialist and, secondly, jet-setting international populariser of science. The first new feature of Poliakoff's dramatic treatment is the use of a character as participant observer.

Blinded is narrated by Al, who introduces his story in direct address to the audience by opening – and revealing the contents of – bags containing objects from his scientific collection. He begins to unravel a 'science detective story, a tale of greed, deception, jealousy, and a touch of hate, in the unlikely setting of the chemistry department of a northern university' (1996: 4). The role of narrator, which Williams noted as one of the lost means to complex seeing (see Chapter 3), affords a double perspective on the action, which is presented as happening before the audience in apparent real-time, but which has in fact already happened. Seeming to serve a similar function to that of Alfieri, who comments on the action in Miller's *A View from the Bridge* (1955), Al rhetorically invites a response to the difficult ethical predicament he finds himself in. Audience members are thus encouraged from the outset to think about the issues from more than one point of view.

An initial tension arises when newly promoted Al, having taken us into his confidence, behaves questionably. Adopting a managerial stance, he conducts a workload analysis and proposes 'Energy Studies' as a snappier department title with a view to attracting sponsorship. He suggests that his mentor, Elinor, might vacate some of her lab space since her research, protected by 'funding for life from the university' (ibid.: 45), appears not to be yielding quality outcomes. Though Al does not press his suggestions, which are met with universal contempt by his colleagues, a conflict between two sets of values begins to emerge.

The first Act is largely taken up with the success of Christopher's Sun Battery experiment, which raises Al's suspicions since it is not achieved in a known area of Christopher's research. When his attempts to find out whether other colleagues have doubts about the experiment draw a blank, Al consults Elinor, who supports Christopher and advises Al to 'do nothing' (ibid.: 61). Her position – which Al can't believe he is hearing from a respected scientist – appears to be that, even if Christopher has faked the demonstration, he is very near to proving his theory. Obtaining Christopher's research note-books, however, Al finds what he takes to be evidence of Christopher's fraud. Feeling that he cannot ignore the evidence before him, Al is left at the end of Act I on the horns of a professional ethical dilemma.

Act II, set four years later, takes another direction. To mark a comparison with Act I, Al appears with an even larger plastic bag, containing a variety of documentary artefacts, at his feet. But Al's star has now risen on the waning of Christopher's. Following the publica-tion of a number of books popularising science and questioning the experts, he has become a media celebrity, making international lecture tours and giving media talks. But, returning to the department for a possible reconciliation with Christopher at Elinor's retirement celebra-tion, Al is consumed by a genuine scientific idea he has come up with, namely a feasible method of turning waste matter into usable fuel. His growing confidence that his idea is original and that his model has potential is tempered, however, by the recognition that its develop-ment needs the assistance of more talented colleagues.

At an edgy reunion with his disgraced colleague, Al invites Christopher to join a unit he proposes to form, 'a real Powerhouse of

Ideas' (ibid.: 84). Christopher responds only with a '*distant smile*' (ibid.). He and his lawyer wife, Ghislaine, believe that any damage to Christopher's career has by now been repaired and that they certainly do not need Al's assistance. Despite Elinor's offer of coffee on her arrival, relations remain strained, with Christopher revealing his awareness that Al has come in part to offer Elinor a place in his unit since he plans to close down her laboratory. Before Christopher leaves, Al wants to know why he faked the experiment. The response is tellingly ambiguous:

> I know you want an admission, a confession, even. But there is nothing to admit, Al. I just couldn't repeat the experiment, that's all. (*He moves.*) It's really very simple. (*He smiles.*) Don't think about it any further. I know it's galling – *but there is nothing more to discover.*
> *He exits with Ghislane.* (ibid.: 88, original emphases)

This may be a statement made on legal advice but, in the absence of other evidence and in the light of his apparently restored career, he may just be telling the truth.

Al, in contrast, is being not entirely straight with Elinor about his purposes. He is keen to get a response to his new idea and Elinor gives him positive feedback, though she expresses surprise that it is 'all [his] own work' (ibid.: 90). She proceeds, however, to dress down Al, not for accusing Christopher but for 'the way you have used what has happened' (ibid.: 91). In another shift of perspective, she invites a view of Al as a self-seeker on the back of other people's misfortune. She accuses him of 'using the wave of anti-science feeling for your own purposes, feeding people's cynicism . . . You've always described yourself as a hack, Albie – but now you've become slightly more dangerous. Somebody who reduces everything to their own level' (ibid.: 92). Even though Al has been absent from the department on his lecture tours, Elinor feels he has been omnipresent: 'One can't move anywhere without being urged to tailor things to the marketplace, justify everything in commercial terms. (*She moves.*) I see you everywhere, Al, and I dread seeing you' (ibid.: 93).

Such an accusation will undoubtedly resonate with any audience member who worked through the Thatcher years in the British university system (and it should not be forgotten that Stephen Poliakoff's brother is a chemistry professor). In a major cultural shift, cost accountancy rather than the pursuit of knowledge for its own sake became the guiding principle. Poliakoff again has his finger on the cultural pulse and, with Elinor's speech, locates the debate building in *Blinded* between truth, knowledge and commercial interests in a shifting political climate. The monetarist ethos, expounded by Mrs Thatcher and her advisers (and largely sustained under the subsequent Blair administration), infused all aspects of culture in the 1990s, and universities, which had hitherto stood at arm's length from market influence, became subject to its dictates. 'Blue skies' research of the kind undertaken by Elinor, allegedly irrelevant to industry and market economics, became a rarity.

Though some ambiguity remains about whether Elinor really is pursuing something of scientific value, her words frame a debate of great significance in the academy, and in culture more generally. The variability between claims to factuality and interpretation coloured by personal interest continues. Al questions whether there is anything at all in Elinor's work: 'THE WORK IS SO PURE – IT IS INVISIBLE' (ibid.: 94). He accuses her of being hurt by the fact that he has come up with a good and workable idea. As the argument moves to a climax, Elinor exhorts Al to do what he's come for. Al confirms the closure of the department in September – a year too soon for Elinor to complete her research. Elinor summarises the situation as: 'Everything I've done in my life – whatever my achievements are, my reputation, years of work – and it comes down to me pleading with an administrator. To be allowed to exist' (ibid.: 98). Her revenge lies in knowing that Al's new idea will haunt him, since 'He can't finish it on his own' (ibid.: 99).

The final scene serves as a reflective coda on the play's issues. It brings the protagonists back to the university department for the presentation of an honorary award to Elinor, marking her lifetime achievement. Interestingly, Al does not open this scene with his plastic bags of evidence and a direct address to the audience. He is, however, managing the event with great efficiency and ensuring it is documented with a multi-camera set-up. Building work – presumably for the new university development to replace the chemistry department – sounds noisily off-stage and does not stop as planned when the bells herald the ceremony. Elinor is self-ironic, commenting that 'they only give you these lifetime achievement awards when they think you're no longer a threat' (ibid.: 115). Reflecting on the events they have experienced, Elinor amusedly undermines Al's attempt to delineate primary causes for effects. When he tries to assert his view of the truth, Elinor retorts, 'I'm sure it's one of the aspects' (ibid.: 116).

More than in earlier plays on contemporary issues, the open-endedness here more pressingly demands audience reflection since the overall means of achieving complex seeing are new. This is not a play conveying a visceral sense of character in situation. It is rather a play of ideas and issues, a debate play, in the lineage of Shaw, Ibsen and Miller. However, where a privileged viewing position is typically afforded by the plays of these forerunners, the strands of argument in *Blinded* are either left unresolved, or are resolved in such a way as to be inconclusive, left open for the audience to ponder. The use of a narrator as it were to frame the events and afford another perspective is a device Poliakoff will develop (in *Remember This*, for example). It is particularly interesting that, unlike Alfieri in *A View from the Bridge*, Al proves not to be impartially distant from the events. *Blinded* affords no such privileged point of view.

From *Blinded*, different readers might conclude: that, motivated by lust for fame and advancement, Christopher broke the cardinal rule of modern science by faking an experiment; that Elinor was a spent force after her early success with vitamins; that Al is merely a time-server who struck lucky, his popularising and cost-accountancy approaches to knowledge just happening to resonate with a period of monetarism and relativism. They might equally conclude: that Christopher was telling the truth when he claimed he simply could not repeat the first successful experiment; that Elinor would have again achieved some remarkable discovery given a little more time; that Al was distracted by circumstances from his true scientific vocation. Partly because Al is an unreliable narrator, it is not at all clear with which character, or which position, we are invited to identify.

The undecidability is crucial. Poliakoff, though his own passions and interests are sometimes too apparent in his work, develops here a provocative, multi-perspectival dramaturgy which invites thinking about the broader issues. Like Al, he remains 'a detective patrolling the Zeitgeist' (ibid.: 102), but his commentary on the times here is freshly open-ended. The title of the play might be read on several levels. Christopher is evidently blinded by the Sun Battery, if he did indeed fake the experiment; Elinor perhaps stares too intently into blue skies; and, if *The Sun* (the popular British newspaper) affords another accent, Al is perhaps blind in his tabloid approach to popularisation and self-publicity.

Other works of Poliakoff's might be included in a chapter on 'issue pieces'. *Coming in to Land* addresses the issue of immigration while *Playing with Trains* addresses the lack of development funding for British enterprise. The purpose of this chapter has been to demonstrate, through the juxtaposition of works which have a tighter focus on a specific issue, the versatility of Poliakoff's treatments of matters of concern across theatre, film and television. The next chapter similarly takes a cluster of pieces in different media, but this time bringing out his capacity to write 'quirky strong women'.

6 QUIRKY STRONG WOMEN

Conversations with feminist colleagues have drawn attention to what appears to be a Poliakovian penchant for very attractive young women, quite frequently featured in scenes involving nudity. While this observation is demonstrable, Poliakoff has also created a range of interesting and demanding roles for more mature women, otherwise notably lacking in the British repertoire. Moreover, for the wide range of roles of all ages that he has created, he has attracted an extraordinary number of the most prestigious British actors, male and female, to work with him on his projects. Female performers who have worked with Poliakoff early in their careers have often returned some years later to take on even more challenging women characters. Besides finding young talent almost fresh from drama school (Ruth Wilson, for example), and repeatedly attracting up-and-coming stars (Jane Asher, Saskia Reeves, Jodhi May, Romola Garai), Poliakoff has drawn mature female actors to some substantial women character roles. Starting with (Dame) Peggy Ashcroft in *Caught on a Train* (1980) and *She's Been Away* (1989), the estimable performers include (Dame) Maggie Smith, initially in *Coming in to Land* (1987) but subsequently in *Capturing Mary* (2007), (Dame) Helen Mirren in *Soft Targets* (1982) and Billie Whitelaw (CBE) in a cameo role in *Shooting the Past* (1999) which also stars Lindsay Duncan who returned in a central role in *Perfect Strangers* (2001). Miranda Richardson first worked with Poliakoff on *Century* (1994), but subsequently played the repressed Queen Mary in *The Lost Prince* (2003),[1] and stars two years later, alongside Bill Nighy, in *Gideon's Daughter* (2006).[2]

In Poliakoff's early life, he was was surrounded by two sisters, an actress mother and a Russian grandmother of few words, and their influence on his writing is overtly evident in his very first play, *Granny*. Whatever the genesis, Poliakoff developed an ability to see the world from the point of view particularly of women who suffered oppression by patriarchal forces. To examine some of the quirky but strong women Poliakoff subsequently created for stage and screen this chapter begins with a theatre play, *Coming in to Land* (1987), and then turns to the second of his screen pieces to feature Peggy Ashcroft, *She's Been Away* (1989).

Coming in to Land (1987)

Though *Coming in to Land* (NT directed by Peter Hall) might have been included in the last chapter since it addresses the issue of immigration, the development of the central character is at the crux of the play.[3] In two Acts, each of six scenes, the play recounts the attempt by Halina (Maggie Smith), a Polish would-be immigrant, to 'land' in the UK, by persuading the Home Office of her suitability for residency. Halina's opportunity is by way of a marriage of convenience to Neville, a solicitor, whom it suits 'to be unavailable, for a certain time' (1986: 9) and who owes a favour to lawyer friend, Andrew, who assists immigrants. Andrew and Neville appear to be in a controlling position, insisting that a marriage of convenience is the only available option even though it is risky and stands little chance of success. The question of whether Halina will be granted residency in this context thus appears to be the driving force of the plot of the play. But twists and reversals reveal the character of Halina to be less malleable than might at first appear.

The focus of this discussion, then, is on the character of Halina as illustrative of Poliakoff's quirky and surprising mature women, but her development is effected by another Poliakovian interest, new media technologies and the mediation of experience in the contemporary world. Indeed, *Coming in to Land* illustrates Poliakoff's increasing use of new media in 'live' theatre events (see also *Remember This*, Chapter 7). The scenes are punctuated by fragments of media noise relevant to the play's context. The sound device is established at the outset over an empty stage and reinforced to cover subsequent scene changes. For example, between scenes 2 and 3: '*News items, as if radio channels are being changed: late-night music, and then domestic news settling on an item about whether the Russians are going to retaliate over the expulsion of three members of their embassy staff in London'* (ibid.: 13, s.d.). But key aspects of the plot also rest upon the deployment of media technologies, involving actions first by Halina and subsequently by Neville, and the play's emphasis upon mediation opens up a broader theme of whether truth and integrity are more effective than a plausible story with the right media spin.

Early in the play, Halina is self-effacing, apologising for 'causing too much bother' (ibid.: 9) and not wanting 'to be such a nuisance' (ibid.: 10). Her awkward appearance in a *'very large, bulky old grey coat and carrying two huge plastic carrier bags which are stuffed to the brim'* (ibid.: 2, s.d.) is a visual intrusion into Neville's minimalist apartment. That Halina might not be so submissive and compliant as supposed begins to emerge in scene 3 when, *'wearing a new dress, in vivid garishly coloured squares'* (ibid.: 15) she repeats to Neville the story of how she has spent her life supporting her father after he was ousted from his post as a party official in Warsaw. She also vaguely reports a phone conversation with a journalist interested in 'the group of us at the college – in the present climate' (ibid.: 18). Further, she implores Neville to use his connections to find her part-time employment even though such a step is both illegal and very risky. However, scene 4 finds Halina at work in a hi-fi and video emporium assisting Waveney, 'a black woman of 31 . . . beautifully dressed in very carefully chosen, stylish clothes' (ibid.: 20, s.d.).[4]

The true shock reversal of the first Act comes, however, when Waveney replays – at first muted and in black and white – a sequence of Halina talking to camera in a news report across the multiple screens in the emporium. Halina is dwarfed side-stage by *'the enormous silent image of herself, her head in close up'* (ibid.: 25). When Waveney brings up the sound, Halina is recounting a story about how she and a group of friends were arrested and mistreated by the police in Warsaw. Attention is drawn to Halina's performance of her story by Waveney's critique of her self-presentation. This serves as a kind of momentary distancing device on the content and its veracity – as Neville's scepticism will do in II.6. Waveney makes a joke that '[t]he hat was a mistake' (ibid.: 25) and suggests that 'the hands are far too busy' though 'the stare is good' (ibid.: 26) as if coaching Halina for a media career. Halina is aghast at what she sees as 'a creation from another planet . . . It seems they have photographed somebody else' (ibid.: 25). She has only just focused on the consequences of her action and its irreversibility when Neville arrives having read newspaper coverage of Halina's decision to follow her own course. Halina tells Neville that she does not wish to marry him or make an arranged marriage with anybody else, and that she will only accept advice on an unofficial, voluntary basis. She has made up her mind to make her own case for residency.

The tone of this pivotal scene is relatively light, given the weight of the issues involved. Waveney makes amusement out of the failing business at the outset of the scene, slapping fanciful reduction notices on to hi-fi kit nobody wants to buy, even though her job is at stake. She and Halina make fun of the unseen supervisor for getting his pleasure from media catalogues ('[t]he trade magazines are erotic for him', ibid.: 22). Neville is, perhaps surprisingly, not angry at Halina's independent track but makes a joke of the women misusing the merchandise. The scene ends with Neville offering to buy something: 'make sure this place lasts until Christmas at least' (ibid.: 32).

A more sombre note is sounded, however, by the interspersed scenes (2 and 5) featuring the ponderous machinations of Peirce and Booth, officials of the UK Immigration Office. Peirce, the senior man, proceeds at his own pace, even changing from casual clothes to his work attire by order. The large piles of files and his dismissal of many of them as 'too late' or 'filled up the wrong form' (ibid.: 11) convey a sense of a bureaucracy grinding along unmoved by the fates of the individuals which hang in the balance of its decisions. There is, from Halina's position, a disturbing sense that such minimal enjoyment as Peirce gets from his job is catching out applicants in their various duplicities. There is mordant humour in Peirce's descriptions to Booth of the efforts and endurance of the applicants in their attempts just to get a hearing, let alone to 'land'. In I.5, Neville visits Peirce's office to sound out the current climate of immigration policy and is surprised to learn that a great deal of information comes in to the office by, sometimes anonymous, recorded telephone messages. Curious about the motives of such informants, Neville learns from Peirce that '[t]hey do it to get rid of "friends" and relatives they don't like – or detest' (ibid.: 37).

Media technologies open the final scene of Act I with Halina's experience being discussed on a late-night radio phone-in which mixes with the ambient sound of carols being sung outside Neville's apartment. It is Christmas time and, untypically for London, snow is falling heavily and settling. Despite there being no date set for Halina's interview with immigration officials, Neville proffers champagne to Andrew and Halina. The voice of an old woman, first heard in scene 3 on Neville's answer-phone, interrupts the conversation demanding Neville's attention. When Halina is out of the room, Neville relates to Andrew his impression of her, having shared his flat with her for a few weeks. He sees Halina as 'slightly batty . . . but curiously interesting' (ibid.: 40).

Just as Poliakoff's father had glimpsed significant historical events from the apartment window in Red Square, Halina has been witness to – or claims to have seen – significant events in war-torn Warsaw. Neville recognises that Halina is 'a long way from being wholly admirable' (ibid.), but he is disposed to support her against that 'real shifty little creep' (ibid.), Peirce. Indeed, Neville rightly suspects that Halina has made up her story to the press claiming that she was arrested by the police and tortured. In fact she was merely held with friends overnight for a driving irregularity, drinking and smoking with her guards.

Halina, however, is growing in confidence. Neville sums up the chameleon which is Halina now dressed in a fashionable sweater and skirt: 'one moment you're this comic character emerging with a heap of scabby plastic bags that you won't let out of your sight. And now you look like this' (ibid.: 46).

Neville even connects the un-English weather and the 'weird psychopathic carol singers' (ibid.: 47), who are singing highly irregular lyrics to traditional tunes outside the window, to Halina's personal transformation. Neville's neat, minimalist, rational world has been disturbed to the point where he feels he is 'inhabiting one of those infuriating East European cartoons' (ibid.). Halina is now determined that her plan can succeed and the Act ends with her declaiming her hopes and fears while symbolically crushing the coloured balls on the Christmas tree in her bare hands. Her deepest fear – and perhaps she speaks here the feelings of all would-be immigrants – is that she will end up 'Not just without a home, but with nowhere to *be*. Ending up in the last possible airport, surrounded by plastic bags' (ibid.: 50).

Act II of *Coming in to Land* is set largely on the premises of the Immigration Service, in and around Peirce's office in which Halina finally gets her interview. She nearly succeeds in duping him but inadvertently reveals her detailed knowledge of sound equipment gained in her time spent working illegally in the hi-fi shop. The game is up and Peirce has won out with a devious ploy, as Andrew predicted he would.

Between interrogations, II.3 serves as a reflective interlude pointing up the emotional impact from an immigrant's perspective as Halina and Waveney recount their experience of officialdom and racism on entering Britain. Their stories are framed, however, by Neville's unease at hearing Halina tell her story to Peirce when he knows she's lying. Thus, a 'participant observer' distancing device demands complex seeing from audience members: sympathy for the immigrants' experience perhaps accompanied by a certain scepticism about their motives and behaviour. This complex response is emphasised when Peirce and Booth interrogate Neville about his interests in Halina's case, and question his origins and ethnicity. It transpires that Neville was actually born in India with a Belgian parent. As Booth remarks, 'a little chipping away and we find you're not quite as wholly British as you make yourself out to be' (ibid.: 78). Poliakoff has skilfully turned the tables with this dramatic layering, shifting attention away from Halina as immigrant at the heart of the plot to Neville as representative of the indigenous Britons in the audience, making them feel uncomfortable.

Back at Neville's, up-rooted floorboards are tossed on to the stage as the apartment is literally torn apart by investigating officers, Andrew summarises his sense of failure: 'The people I *manage* to get in usually have a pretty miserable time. It's such a waste. Some of them disappear without trace. They think they are coming to a land of opportunity, a multi-racial society! A home! (*very sharp*). God knows if I've actually helped anybody!' (ibid.: 91).

In explaining to Neville why Halina would not agree to the bogus marriage plan Andrew asks, 'Who would want to land right *here* – if they could possibly help it? *Blackout*' (ibid.: 92). In doing so he calls in question the assumption that Neville's middle-class apartment and lifestyle is desirable beyond question and, by implication, any audience members' easy assumptions about immigrants envying and wanting to adopt, if not steal, their lifestyle.

Coming in to Land may not be a wildly radical play but, by deploying Poliakoff's distinctive dramaturgy in an NT context, it draws audiences to see character in situation from one perspective, only to shift their viewpoint in ways which at least invite complex seeing and even, perhaps, some critical self-reflection. The use of recorded media, sound fragments and video projections underscore scepticism. Neville believes he is the cause of Halina's deportation, having left a message on the Home Office answer-phone, but Halina assures him she was betrayed by other Poles. Media devices are thus at once theatrically functional – to cover some scene changes – and thematically insightful. Act II, scene 5, for example, opens with rapid changes of channel, fragments of '*a news story about HALINA . . . Red Halina . . . Home Office spokesman, her story under investigation has proved a pack of lies . . . Future uncertain*' (ibid.: 89, s.d.). The Home Office has patently done a good job not only in discrediting Halina but refabricating her in an elaborate double-bluff. As Andrew realises: 'They are making out she was sent by the Russians to be deliberately rumbled, so as to discredit any future unfavourable reports coming out of the Eastern Block' (ibid.: 90). Besides showing officialdom in a questionable light, such narrative spin locates truth-telling in fundamentally modern contexts.

In addition to the dramatic methods noted, *Coming in to Land* is marked as a Poliakovian play in its adoption of the perspectives of the outsider, not just of the immigrant to the UK of Poliakoff's family history, but of the apparent insider (Neville) who, because he does not quite fit in to established society, becomes a 'participant observer'. But Halina's development, visually tracked in costume changes, is at the heart of the play, the shifting perspectives gravitating around her. There is further ambiguity at its end when Halina's deportation is delayed because no country will accept her. Despite the seriousness of Halina's plight, it may be that Neville needs her more than she needs him, leaving the narrative outcome and the play's thematic concerns open for further thought after the final blackout.

Another take on this play is noted in Chapter 9.

She's Been Away (1989)

She's Been Away also deals with an outsider's perspective on British society but, in this instance, the outsider is a native who has been exiled as a young adult into an institution for the mentally unstable because she was unable – or unwilling – to suppress her emotional and sexual desires to comply with the protocols of upper-middle-class Edwardian respectability. Lillian Huckle (Peggy Ashcroft) is rescued after sixty years of internment by her well-meaning, but uncomprehending nephew, Hugh Ambrose (James Fox), who has created living space for her in the elegant London family home he has inherited. Lillian will not speak, however, and disturbs the household by creating unpleasant odours in her inept attempts at cooking, and by rhythmically banging a metal plate in the night. When taken to a supermarket by Harriet Ambrose (Geraldine James), she causes havoc, destroying a stack of tinned biscuits and checking out a trolleyful of frozen ducks. At a family party (a prefiguration of *Perfect Strangers*) to celebrate Hugh and Harriet's wedding anniversary, Harriet's pregnancy, and Lillian's return, the family members patronise Lillian, treating her as a brainless curiosity. A stirred memory leads, however, to a series of flashbacks which afford viewers insights into what might be going on in Lillian's mind. The flashbacks reveal that it was the intense and uncontrollable passion Lillian felt as a young adult for one of two twin brothers, and her subsequently fierce defiance of her father and a series of psychologists, which led to a life-long incarceration.

It is Harriet who recognises that there is something more going on in Lillian's mind than she is revealing and, initially, she accuses Lillian of being a fraud. When Lillian runs away back to the institution, however, Harriet is genuinely concerned to the point of running through the streets in her nightdress in search of her. Having retrieved Lillian with her friend George (Hugh Lloyd) from the near-derelict institution, Harriet begins to establish a kind of *doppel-gänger* relationship with her which is at the heart of *She's Been Away*. The drawing into parallel of two women who, at the outset, seemed poles apart is another instance of the Poliakovian character surprise strategy. It reveals that Harriet is also trapped, in her case within an oppressive marriage with a domineering husband and an irritatingly proto-bourgeois son. Indeed, James Fox's measured performance as an overtly charming and civilised, but deeply self-centred and manipulative patriarch is matched to great effect by the irritating public schoolboy, Dominic (Jackson Kyle), who, at eight years old, gives unwanted legal and financial advice to his parents. Though the latter figure has an element of comic caricature, the function of these male roles is to convey that it is the institutional, rather than personal, oppressiveness of middle-class patriarchy at work now, just as it was in post-First World War Britain sixty years ago.

In consequence, Harriet is very uncertain about her feelings towards the second child she is carrying while her husband is overbearing in his self-satisfaction, smothering the house with flowers even before he knows for sure of the pregnancy. To stave off panic attacks, Harriet opts to make her escape by going for a drive and, in one of her first voluntary utterances, Lillian indicates she wants to join her. Harriet gouges the side of the Jaguar as she exits the driveway, marking a symbolic attack on her husband's proprietary wealth and attitudes which climaxes in the car getting further smashed and ultimately burned out. The two women run out of fuel, having driven aimlessly into the countryside and, despite her protests, Lillian survives a night sleeping in the car. At dawn, the car is surrounded by a group of eco-warrior teenagers sleeping rough, and the two women make their escape by hitching a ride by truck to a smart hotel in the nearest town, where they arrive dishevelled but undaunted. For Harriet it is an outbound journey of increasing liberation as she vents her own feelings of frustration, irrespective of what the censorious guests and hotel staff might think. For Lillian it is an inbound journey, returning her to the everyday world in a situation which nevertheless licenses her eccentricities.

Excessive eating, drinking and dancing, however, bring Harriet into a serious bodily collapse on the hotel stairs and it is now Lillian's turn to seek support for her *doppel-gänger*. At hospital, the baby has to be induced prematurely and has a questionable chance of survival. While Harriet rests to regain her strength, Lillian protects her, barricading the door against the ringing footsteps of approaching authority in the form of Hugh Ambrose, doctors and police. The final shot is of Lillian's face pressed against the glass in close-up, nominally expressionless as ever but, in Peggy Ashcroft's telling performance, saying all.

Structural features of the film bring out the predicaments between the two women protagonists. Both are shown through frames as if caged. Particularly when Harriet returns to the institution to retrieve Lillian, a number of objects fly across the shot, narrowly missing the characters, as demolition is in full swing. Similar imagery is constructed by the flying objects and suitcases Harriet flings from cupboards and across corridors in her home as she searches for her own suitcase to pack for her leaving. The film opens with a pan in close shot across a range of objects on a large oblong table which turn out to be the lost property of past inhabitants of the institution. An excess of food on a buffet table at the Ambroses' party ironically echoes the redundancy of material superfluity. The grand Ambrose house is in stark contrast to the bareness of what is left of the decrepit institution. A minimal music soundtrack comprises variations on an old love song which Lillian recalls from her youth, and indeed sings briefly at the party, but noises, as in other work of Poliakoff, are also literally and metaphorically resonant. They range from Lillian's rhythmic metallic banging in the night to the repetitive buzz of Dominic's aggressive computer game, and from the scraping of the Jaguar's bodywork along walls to the 1960s pop music in the hotel where Harriet dances wildly. In sum, visual and sonic patterns are repeated and varied to underscore the patterning of the characters and narrative across time in a world where the surfaces have changed since Lillian's incarceration but patriarchy remains firmly in place. And given Dominic's precocious self-assurance, it looks set to continue beyond the closing shot.

Caught on a Train (1980)

In *Caught on a Train*, in contrast, it is a woman who assumes dominance in the grand personage of Frau Messner (Peggy Ashcroft), a Viennese bourgeois remnant of a world prior to the Second World War. The situation is a journey on the post-1977 Orient Express,[5] running across what was then East Germany, en route from Ostend to Vienna. Peter (Michael Kitchen), a young businessman, is confronted on the train by the formidable Frau Messner, who initially demands his window seat and then, in the wake of his refusal to give it up as he holds the ticket for it, haunts the rest of what turns out for him to be a nightmare journey.[6] Since the piece, written for 'BBC Playhouse', is well-known – indeed 'one of [Poliakoff's] most popular works' (1997: ix) – and readily available for viewing, it is not necessary to recount all the details of narrative incident, but a focus on the dining car scene serves to bring out the characters of Frau Messner and Peter and something of the clash of values at stake in the developing relationship between the two protagonists.

As is her custom, Frau Messner has bought breaded chicken legs to eat on the journey but they mysteriously disappear. She effectively accuses Peter of stealing them, forcing him by her imperious manner to stand up to show he is not concealing them. Having nothing to eat, and having subsequently acquired the necessary ticket for dinner from an American fellow-passenger, Lorraine (Wendy Raebeck), she follows Peter to the dining car. Taking the only available table, Messner obliges Peter to join her and proceeds to complain about the loss of quality of the furnishings: 'They have tried to make the carriages look old, but none of it is real. It's all false. See this table. It's plastic' (ibid.: 37). Peter's preoccupations are brought out, in contrast, when Messner asks him where he is going and whether he is to do something important. His reply about his destination, a book fair in Linz, reveals much about his own slightly superior air: 'Very [important], as it happens. I've got to meet two famous authors that we handle. Big European celebrities . . . medium-sized celebrities, 10.30 tomorrow morning. It's the first time I've represented my firm abroad (*slight smile to himself*). Naturally if I handle things well . . .' But Frau Messner is not listening. Increasingly impatient, she is preoccupied with catching the attention of the waiter and worrying whether other diners were there before her, or indeed, hold dinner tickets. Peter finally explodes: 'You really can't wait for anything can you? It's like a disease. I have never seen somebody quite so unable to wait their turn. It's almost as if the effort would kill you.' Frau Messner retorts: 'If you are going to be rude to me you can leave my table. (*Her tone changes, still quiet.*) I *cannot* wait. Ever. They have to give you service, that is what they are paid to do' (ibid.: 41). Throughout she has berated the waiter for his failure to attend immediately to her needs and, when her threat to report him does not yield the desired result and he does not take away the plates she is proffering, she smashes them on the floor. She proceeds to make a grand exit leaving Peter deeply embarrassed under the gaze of all the diners, including a secret policeman who has been watching them throughout.

Though there are aspects of *Caught on a Train* which are distinctly 'cinematic', this is a very theatrical scene, building its tension to a literally noisy climax. But it is pivotal in the piece in bringing into focus what Poliakoff has generalised as 'the deep feelings of unease, we, the British, have about Europe' (ibid.: ix). If, however, there is a representative of Little England-ism on board the train, it is Preston, a mildly irritating nerd who joins Peter's carriage, only to complain about the price of everything on the boat, the tardiness of trains and the unavailability of porters. That his point of view is ultimately unattractive is underlined in that he turns out to be the culprit in the theft of Messner's chicken legs. In relation to the film overall, Poliakoff's remark about attitudes to Europe would seem to overlook the particularity of the figure of Frau Messner, a domineering woman by dint of class (and a strong hint of Aryan ethnicity evident in her dismissive remark on a possibly Jewish servant girl who 'disappeared one day') who could scarcely be said to be a typical European, even in the Cold War period of European history. Moreover, the remark would seem to assume that Peter's point of view, on the receiving end of Messner's imperious manner and a more broadly grim experience, is adopted by spectators. Though Messner may, indeed, embody an aspect of a fear of continental European 'otherness' at a time when travel abroad by Brits was not a common phenomenon, *Caught on a Train*'s concern with values is, in my reading, a more complex matter than an articulation of Little England xenophobia.

The film sets up a strong point of identification with Peter at the outset. It is Peter who is first to arrive at the station, who is jostled by the unruly youths waiting to join the train, and whose perspective the camera invites us to adopt when he finds himself sharing a carriage with a woman who speaks his language and whom he finds attractive, the American, Lorraine. The subsequent arrival of any 'foreigners' is set up as an intrusion upon their happily shared space by their agreed attempts to 'look hostile' (1998: 7). Thus, spectators are initially invited to share Peter's perspective on Frau Messner's overtly obtrusive imperiousness, a point of view which is sustained for a considerable duration but is not entirely singular. Though we do not see it happen, we learn that Lorraine has given up her window seat opposite Peter and she subsequently also gives Frau Messner her dinner ticket. She tells Peter he should have yielded his place and distances herself from him when he suggests that together they might look for seats in another compartment (see ibid.: 22). This small, but significant, shift begins to unsettle the initially privileged perspective and, much later, Lorraine overtly affirms her own different point of view when she tells Peter that both England and Europe give her 'the creeps' (ibid.: 61), and does not exempt him from a dislike of the majority of people she has met. Lorraine's viewpoint, though not fully developed in the film, importantly affords another perspective anticipating a further shift whereby Peter becomes the object of Frau Messner's gaze.

Following incidents involving a snack, improbably taken at the Opera House in Frankfurt am Main, whereby Peter believes Frau Messner has deliberately caused him to miss the train, and after his subsequent arrest by East German border guards because he has lost his ticket, Peter has a final conversation with his apparently serene tormentor. She suddenly observes, 'we're rather alike in many ways, you know' (1997: 78) and invites him to stay with her in Vienna. She proceeds to summarise her perception of his character:

> You're good-looking. You're quite clever. You notice things. And you're not at all cruel. (*She suddenly looks directly at him, then louder.*) *But you don't care.*
>
> *The train has stopped.*
>
> You pretend to of course, you pretend. (*She is staring straight at him.*) But you don't really care about anything do you? (*She stares at his pale, young face, as he stands holding his case.*) Except maybe success in your work. Becoming very successful. It's all you have. You don't *feel* anything else. *Nothing. You just cannot feel anything else.* (*She looks at him.*) Can you? (1998: 80, original emphasis)

This summation has greater impact for being unexpected. For most of the film Frau Messner's preoccupation with her own needs, and with manipulating others to fulfil them, has betrayed little sense of awareness of other points of view. The words in the moment thus invite a considerable revaluation of character in context. As a representative of a former, trenchantly hierarchical Europe with a deeply troubled recent history, Frau Messner's claim to have a greater sense of the worth of things than Peter can scarcely pass unqualified. Nevertheless, her remarks about Peter hit home, making spectators aware that, though his personal manner may be more restrained (more 'English' even), he is ultimately as single-minded as she.

That for much of the film spectators have been encouraged to identify with Peter's point of view makes the shock of recognition all the greater. The audience is now invited to consider that there may indeed be a loss of value in the shift from the finer fabrications available to at least the few in a world of highly policed social boundaries. A hint of vulnerability in age and a possible illness, strengthened in the portrayal of Frau Messner by Peggy Ashcroft – whose capacity to convey a less secure inner life beneath a feisty exterior is legendary – comes to the fore. The dark, rain-sodden images of an industrialised

Europe which dominate the film serve additionally to emphasise the question as to whether a more democratic, but blander, world of self-seeking – which would emerge in the 1980s as a culture of consumer individualism – is so obviously preferable to the one it has displaced. Such a loss of certainties reverberates through the range of images and minor incidents which enrich the texture of *Caught on a Train*. Indeed Chris Allison detects Hitchcock's influence in 'the gradual accumulation of mysterious and often insignificant details'.[7]

The unruly teenagers who jostle Peter and make fun of him at Ostend station reappear intermittently throughout the journey. They do not overtly threaten him but they close down his personal space in a slightly intimidating manner, at one point snatching his passport. They are disrespectful of the authorities when they come to check travellers' documentation, and they taunt the Belgian border guards, once the train is pulling out. After the stop at Frankfurt, they have occupied the carriage where Peter was sitting, hiding his luggage, and a fight breaks out between the youths as the older passengers move to their sleeper cabins, the Ostend ring-leader having his face slashed with a broken bottle. When Peter tries to assist Lorraine in finding a bathroom where she might clean her teeth, the youth has left the hand-basin filled with bloody water into which he tosses the photographs he had earlier tried to pass off on Peter. Particularly when contrasted with the strictly hierarchical structure Frau Messner represents, all these incidents and images contribute to a sense of an erosion of social order.

In one important sense, *Caught on a Train* is about a struggle for space. Though the many young people shown have claimed a space in the world and are no longer objects of the oppression of social place, packed into third-class compartments and corridors as they are predominantly shown in the film, their liberations are not unequivocally positive. Even the peaceful youths singing Bob Dylan songs to an acoustic guitar on Frankfurt station are strewn across the concourse amid the detritus of a new Europe. It might even be observed that the old class distinctions remain more or less in place, the only change being that Messner perceives herself to lack the resources for a first-class ticket.

Contributing to an even starker vision of an alienating world are the East German border guards who arrest Peter on a pretext, as if instructed to do so by the secret policeman who watched him in the dining car. For some moments, he appears to have been drawn wearing only his underpants into a Kafkaesque world where a removed light-bulb, the inability to produce a ticket and the lack of a familiar face to corroborate his story will lead inexorably to the gulag. Alsatian dogs snarl, police car sirens blare, and blue lights flash as he is removed from the train at night, handcuffed and bundled into a police car. The strident jazz soundtrack (composed by Mike Westbrook) of *Caught on a Train* is at its best here, though, throughout, as Chris Allison has remarked, 'it perfectly complements the atmospheric images of urban European landscapes'.[8] It serves particularly well to cover the exterior shots of the train travelling through the night which punctuate episodes of on-train action and lends the dynamic to *Caught on a Train*'s journey, both literal and metaphorical, into the unknown.

Capturing Mary (2007)

Though a quarter of a century divides *Caught on a Train* (1980) and the much more recent *Capturing Mary*, both are concerned with the weight of history as it impacts upon women. Even young people – young Mary in this instance – while inhabiting more liberated times, can remain haunted by the forces of class. The entrapment of women in high society is, indeed, a theme to which Poliakoff returns in *Glorious 39*.

In *Capturing Mary*, an up-and-coming young woman journalist (Ruth Wilson), 'the Voice of Youth' (2007: 129), is confronted, haunted and destroyed by an old-guard socialite Greville White (David Walliams) who is too deeply entrenched in a racist and colonial past, in spite of his relative youth, to adjust to new times. The experience is reviewed from the point of view of old Mary revisiting her past both literally and metaphorically. Both relationships, as often in Poliakoff's work, ground metaphors of the return of the repressed in British and European history.

Capturing Mary, in the view of Mark Kermode, is 'a horror story'.[9] In the same impressive west London house as its partner piece *Joe's Palace* (Chapter 7), uninhabited but meticulously kept, Joe (Danny Lee Wynter) functions as a janitor on behalf of the wealthy owner, Mr Graham (Max Dowler) who lives across the road. When elderly Mary Gilbert (Maggie Smith), an elderly woman, rings the bell in passing one day, Joe breaks the house rules to admit her. It is evident that she knows the house and Joe gradually presses a reluctant Mary to revisit parts of the house in which she underwent profound experiences. In a Poliakovian device to draw viewers into the narrative through fascination with characters who are not what they first appear, Joe, from an observer's position of initial lack of interest, poses the questions viewers would want to ask, and probes a secret history waiting to be unfurled.

As in several of Poliakoff's mature works, a double time-scale is used, intercutting young Mary in the late 1950s with old Mary's memories in dialogue with Joe from a standpoint in the present, a half-century later. The construction, as it were in flashbacks, of the late 1950s and early 1960s affords three key action sequences as young Mary attends a series of soirées at Mr Graham's house. Old Mary's voice-over recalls and comments upon the 1950s 'present action' as it unfolds to viewers. The double time-scale affords viewers a lens for critical reflection on history.

The group of guests at Mr Gilbert's soirées is very select, including E. M. Forster, Alfred Hitchcock, Evelyn Waugh, Ava Gardner and other celebrities, politicians and intellectuals of the period. Among them, Greville appears to wield a mysterious power based on insinuations of knowledge about the celebrities' private lives which he never divulges but rather uses as a means to social control by way of tacit blackmail. Greville has apparently worked on the memoirs of both Lloyd George and Winston Churchill and has strong associations with newspaper barons, such as Beaverbrook and Rothermere, facilitating the publication of memoirs of other old-guard dignitaries. An air of menacing energy is manifest in White's hitting a table-tennis ball against a wall, when young Mary first catches a glimpse of him, '*moving from her seat in the reception room to watch* GREVILLE *from the shadows hitting the ping-pong ball in the passage*' (ibid.: 125, s.d.).

The visual perspective of *Capturing Mary* might also be said to be characteristically Poliakovian. Young Mary also adopts the observer's position; being originally from Manchester she is something of an outsider in respect of class background, as well as representing 'the voice of youth'. She is observed by old Mary who, in turn, is observed by Joe, creating a multi-layered text, whose density is reinforced by a camera which glimpses the socialites in shadowy long-shots along corridors and through half-open doorways. At the outset, the camera draws viewers slowly into the story: a Poliakovian crane shot from the top of the stairwell leads to the elaborately tiled ground-floor entrance hall and from there very slowly back up a stone staircase to find Joe sitting Buddha-like on a landing. The impression of being drawn increasingly into a web of intrigue is created. The domestic interiors and decor are sumptuous as might be expected of 'number eight [in] the list of the richest people in the world' (ibid.: 111), and the costumes of the guests at the soirées are likewise rich in materials and impressive in style. Where Poliakoff's earlier work – particularly that set in run-down urban spaces – may have been visually stark, his later work is visually replete to the point of splendour. Resonating with the period drama genre, its visual pleasures are afforded by the trappings of bourgeois materialism. But, in Poliakoff, there is always a dark undercurrent, as there undoubtedly is in *Capturing Mary*, to unsettle viewers in their armchairs. In this piece, it lies literally in the cellars.

After a number of events in which Mary is conscious that Greville is aware of her presence, she finally meets him in the kitchen. Against his ethic of discretion, Greville feels compelled to reveal to Mary some titbits of gossip about his celebrity friends. Having drawn her into the cellar on the pretext of choosing a bottle of wine, he shares even darker insights – an archbishop who thrashed little boys, an anti-Semitic senior politician, and 'one or two things so disgusting, I have never been able to get them out of my head' (ibid.: 141) – obscene behaviour and prejudiced opinions which Mary finds truly shocking. In sum Greville reveals to Mary 'a line of cruelty . . . running from before the war right through to where we are now' (ibid.). Less consciously, he also reveals his own elitist political disposition towards an establishment he knows from direct personal experience to be

deeply corrupt. He continues to believe that: 'the alternative is worse
. . . Reducing everybody and everything to the same level (*He smiles*).
Letting the great unwashed run everything . . .' (ibid.: 142).

The horror story aspect, noted by Kermode, is at its height here.
As young Mary makes a dignified but speedy retreat through the labyrinth of the cellars, Poliakoff deploys a receding shot, tracking away
from Greville until he is reduced to a small, but still sinister, figure.
Then, '*Suddenly the image bursts into bright white electric* light' (ibid.:
143, s.d.). It is a powerful cinematic moment, evoking tropes of
horror movies in which vampires in evening dress suck the blood from
vulnerable young women, as Greville has metaphorically done to
Mary. Indeed, Greville, as young Mary is well aware, is always accompanied by particularly beautiful and very young women. The contrast
between the world of beautiful people, fine things and apparent civilisation and its dark underbelly is graphically made as Mary emerges
from her shock in the cellar to the drawing-room in which operatic
arias are still being sung. From this moment on, Mary is haunted by
Greville.

Much of the emotional impact of this experience, as well as reflection upon it, is carried by Maggie Smith's performance of the enduring
hurt caused not just by these revelations but by Greville's oppressive
destruction of her career when he finds she will not enter his inner
circle. Nothing is said, but Greville apparently uses his influence over
newspaper proprietors to annul the 'voice of youth' and shut Mary
out of journalism. Mary meets Greville again on revisiting the house
in the 1960s when she is in a relationship with a painter and the
balance of the times has shifted away from the old guard towards
sixties liberation. Although a young man interrupts Greville's
unctuous conversation telling him he is talking 'utter bollocks' (ibid.:
169), young Mary is unable even then fully to confront him and what
he stands for. Indeed, it is not until the twenty-four hours of the
dramatic present of *Capturing Mary* that old Mary, in revisiting the
house and prompted by Joe, finally addresses her demon.

The three richly textured sequences at Graham's soirées in the
1950s and early 1960s which punctuate *Capturing Mary* are literally
juxtaposed in the construction by intercutting stark versions of the

same spaces as Joe leads a reluctant old Mary through the house to revisit the scenes of her youth. In a conscious strategy, old Mary and Joe frequently assume the same positions and spatial relations of earlier scenes, notably those in the cellar, allowing visual resemblances to enrich the weblike texture of the cinematography. Now empty, 'like [they've] been preserved' (ibid.: 134), the rooms are nevertheless recognisable although their atmospheres are completely different. In a camel coat with court shoes and neatly set hair, old Mary's self-presentation initially belies the tormented alcoholic she has become.

The slow revelation of the woman she is, rather than the woman she might have been, is carried almost entirely by Maggie Smith's performance. Her clipped, 'well-spoken' delivery may be a result of the forced suppression of a Manchester accent as she indicates, but it might equally be a mask for the slurred speech of a drunk. For the first eighteen minutes, Smith sustains a voice-over in which even Greville's words are repeated rather than spoken 'live' in the 1950s scene carried in the visuals. Her face, frequently in close-up, is taut and lined but with small glimpses of a smile as if to reassure that she is in control of the evidently rising emotion discernible in her eyes. An unsteady hand reaching towards a marble pillar for support is another small performed signifier of instability. After Greville's revelations to young Mary, the camera finds old Mary in a short intercut sequence with Joe in the cellar in the present, and zooms from mid-shot in tight to her now haunted, and deeply wrinkled, face. It is forty-five minutes into the piece, when, like her younger self, old Mary beats a hasty retreat from the cellar to the surface, before she is seen taking a drink from her hip flask: 'Just keeping out the winter cold . . .' (ibid.: 147). Later she acknowledges that she 'started – having a little tipple' (ibid.: 172–3) in the early sixties when her painter boyfriend was a rising star and when she was unable to write because haunted by the cellar and the sound of the ping-pong ball. In a role whose challenge is to play an alcoholic but only slowly to reveal the condition, Smith's perform-ance is finely judged. By sixty minutes in, she is swigging openly from her flask in front of Joe, but she retains an air of dignity throughout.

In the end-game, Mary reveals to Joe that she has seen Greville that very morning as she took her regular walk in Kensington

Gardens. A cut to the action under Mary's voice-over relates how Greville first appeared through the mist at a distance and then much closer to the bench where Mary regularly sits. Though she protests to Joe that, 'if it was an hallucination, it was a very sustained one' (ibid.: 147), Greville's appearance – his age, his immaculate suiting – has evidently not changed. When the moment is sharply interrupted, by a strident sound which turns out to be a passing boy on rollerblades, there is no trace of Greville. It is this 'encounter' which has led Mary back to the house and to an ultimately therapeutic revisioning of her youth and what might have been. She stresses to Joe, however, that her life has not been filled with self-pity and that she had even rebuilt a moderately successful career. Her alcohol dependency betrays, however, her deep unhappiness to Joe (and viewers), but it is not until she ironically takes up a recommendation of Greville's and sees herself as others might see her, that she acknowledges how – stretched out on the park bench, *like her younger self lying on the bed in the blue room*', and sobbing uncontrollably – she appears to be a *madwoman in the park* (ibid.: 191, s.d.). The emotional breakdown avoids outright self-destruction in Mary's resistance to the oppressions of a panic attack. In the park, the following day, Mary does keep an appointment to meet Joe but, at her request, he leaves her on the park bench 'looking quite elegant reading a book' (ibid.: 194), having apparently got rid of Greville and her demons. A zoom outwards dissolves to a long-shot.

Though *Capturing Mary* is introduced in BBC publicity and the continuity announcement as 'a film by the award-winning Stephen Poliakoff', its success lies in its Poliakovian mix of rich cinematography and the intimate narratology often described as the strength of the television medium in respect of screen fictions. Though it goes beyond 'talking heads', much of old Mary's dialogue is in close-up and voice-over, both intimate television devices. The dialogue with Joe is largely shot in conventional shot/reverse close shot, drawing viewers in by use of a conventional television grammar. As noted, the soirées at Mr Graham's house afford in contrast a richness of *mise-en-scène* redolent of the period drama genre, while the ghost story – or horror movie – dimension of *Capturing Mary* invites the shadowy cinematography effected by Danny Cohen. Nevertheless, the settings are mainly domestic interiors (if not exactly regular living-rooms) with just three exterior locations (the exterior of Graham's house, the park and the country house setting of the final meeting of Mary and Greville). Though Adrian Johnston's score might be thought to lend a cinematic dimension to the piece, the music score by Poliakoff's regular collaborator is now familiar in television. It runs through the piece as underscore and is foregrounded for moments of high tension. Indeed, Johnston's score for *Capturing Mary* evokes the stirring of deep emotions while also capturing a ghost story chill enough to send shivers down the spine. Poliakoff also employs sound very effectively – the interruption of Mary's 'hallucination' in the park by the roar of a skateboard being a case in point. Thus, on a relatively low budget, Poliakoff, supported by his team, once again creates a hybrid vehicle which is highly suitable for the small screen but has the look of a film for cinema.

The achievement of the mix and the resonance, particularly of Maggie Smith's performance in the challenging role of old Mary, is a piece which may look like period drama for television but which fundamentally unsettles one of its key pleasures – indulgence in escapism to another time by way of the luxuriating in the bourgeois material settings. *Capturing Mary* brings out the literal point here. It is the unctuous Greville who stands for the refined pleasures of the English bourgeoisie – in this instance of the Edwardian period – a class which indulges its desires through eating rich foods, drinking fine wines, listening to refined music and finding sexual pleasure in ogling young women (possibly, in Greville's case, having sex with under-age girls), or even thrashing young boys. It sustains its sense of its own superiority by enacting its taste formation implicitly to affirm its colonialist values and its contempt for the industry of the under-classes exploited in the process of creating the wealth, whose superfluities it enjoys. Mary, 'the voice of youth', is the first sign of a cultural shift which historically sought to reject those values. Her downfall is having sufficient strength to refuse to be drawn into the inner circle but insufficient will overtly to resist them. She is ensnared at the cusp of an historical fault-line, unable to go back, nor able fully to cross it.

Where a more heritage approach to period dramas is taken (see Nelson 1997), nothing is allowed to puncture the illusion of a time when everybody was comfortable in knowing their place and a world in which the wealth of the rich (the bourgeoisie) appeared bountifully to cascade a share to all. In Poliakoff's treatment of the genre, however, a critical distance on society is at best afforded, as here, in *Capturing Mary*, through the palimpsest structure of the piece, but particularly also through the perspective of old Mary, who carries the pain of its victims. In a telling moment, Poliakoff turns to a favoured device of old photographic imagery, in this instance, Pathé newsreel footage from the late 1950s: '*the opening of Parliament, a movie première, the crowd gathering for Ascot in their ridiculous hats, debs queuing outside Buckingham Palace in readiness to make their curtsies before the Queen*' (2007: 145, s.d.). The viewer is thus confronted by actual history, the privileging in the news of high society, at precisely the point where old Mary is remembering 'thinking all these things he's [Greville's] told me are running underneath – underneath these events' (ibid.: 145). It is the optic of the double time-scale of *Capturing Mary*, and the double shock of recognition of what underlies a perhaps unquestioned British history by witnessing an enacted past from a present perspective, which affords 'complex seeing'. If *Capturing Mary* impacted on millions of television viewers in the manner described – and the potential is there in the principles of textual composition – it might have achieved a discomforting, and perhaps even political, awareness of which Brecht would have been proud.

Constraints of space prevent discussion of *A Real Summer*, a coda to *Capturing Mary* commissioned by the BBC's 'Culture Show' in which Ruth Wilson plays both young Mary and an apparently friendly debutante, Geraldine. Wilson's double performance is a *tour de force* and the themes – of change in the 1950s/1960s and of class duplicity – echo those in *Capturing Mary*. Thus roles for young women sit comfortably alongside the mature roles highlighted in the discussion above. The next chapter, however, returns largely to Poliakoff's theatre work and his strong interest in history.

7 HISTORIES/MEMORIES

In one sense, all Stephen Poliakoff's plays – even those explicitly set in 'the present' – might be considered 'history plays' since they are all at least in part concerned with socio-cultural trends. Thus plays which address cultural phenomena or issues pertinent to a particular moment aim to capture 'the present' in an awareness of change through time. In the later television work, as we have seen, the way in which the past is experienced in the lived present becomes a key feature of the treatment. There are some Poliakoff works, however, which relate overtly to specific moments and specific events of recognised histories: the First World War (*Clever Soldiers*); the 1917 October Revolution in Russia and the subsequent shooting of the Tsar and Romanov family in 1918 (*Breaking the Silence* and *The Lost Prince*); Munich 1938 (*Talk of the City*); appeasement (*Glorious 39*). With the exception of *The Lost Prince* and the most recent *Glorious 39* (discussed in Chapters 2 and 8 respectively), these are the 'histories' for consideration in this chapter. In addition, *Remember This* (1999) and *Joe's Palace* (2007) represent very different treatments of memory and serve to focus Poliakoff's interest in how we access the past.

Clever Soldiers (1974)

Clever Soldiers returns us to the beginnings of Poliakoff's career as a professional playwright when he was still drawing, as many writers do, on direct experience, but opening up imaginatively to other perspectives. Though the first half of the play is set in Oxford, the play was in fact written while Poliakoff was still a student of history at King's College, Cambridge. It is Oxford – one might say Oxbridge – and the historical context of the First World War which provides the locations of *Clever Soldiers*. The play's dramaturgy is direct, part of that 'commitment to visceral writing . . . to chart a character's change' (1997: ix). The character concerned is Teddy Rogers, whom we encounter in the opening scene on his last day at public school (redolent perhaps of Poliakoff's recent departure from Westminster). He is changing alone after a victory in a sports match, having opted not to join his team-mates, still in their muddy kit, on a drunken pub crawl. It is the first sign that Teddy is different from the rest since, particularly in comparison with Arnold who emerges from the shadows, he otherwise appears confident and successful.

An ethos of scarcely clandestine homosexuality is established since Arnold has sought the quiet of the changing rooms to say goodbye to his fag, Jenkins. The themes and characters established in this opening scene resurface both at Oxford and in the Great War in Act II. Teddy is struck by how he 'keep[s] seeing people . . . that [he] was at school with, and many others too, that are so alike' (ibid.: 11) and, writing to his tutor, David, from the front in Act II, he reports 'seeing people you knew at Oxford and school . . . Bright polished faces. They look exactly the same' (ibid.: 44). Indeed, Arnold subsequently turns up as an officer. Beyond the development of the character of Teddy, Poliakoff is tracing the well-trodden pathway to power of the English upper class.

At Oxford, Teddy's difference from the others is brought out by an unexpected sympathy with his tutor, David, who is of Welsh working-class origins, the two men sharing a sense of being outsiders. They resist the stagnancy and oppression of Oxford culture, represented on the one hand by Teddy's effete room-mate, H (Harold), and on the other by the surprisingly violent 'bloods'. The latter overtly echo Teddy's public school sportsmen in emerging from Christ's College, 'drunk as hell. Their wounds from the match all bandaged up' (ibid.: 19), to rampage through the city. In contrast, the character of H instances an early attempt at humour since, in H, Poliakoff sketches an Oscar Wildean character who draws attention to himself with rehearsed '*bons mots*' calculated to shock: 'As a nation we are far too tolerant of boredom don't you find Mr Jones – real boredom. We tolerate awful puddings and the Irish just because we consider Civil War an unsavoury alternative' (ibid.: 13).

The characteristic style of the play otherwise is strong, visceral images, some verbal and others graphically enacted. On his first encounter with H, for example, Teddy casually assaults him, pulling him down and sitting astride him in a gesture which is part sexual and part an assertion of power. In a verbal reminiscence, David relates how he 'killed a bull to get here' (ibid.: 25), as if he had to be 'blooded' equivalently to the upper-class entrants in order to be admitted. In trying further to explain to Teddy his sustained sense of class difference, however, he relates an incident when he was drunk by the river and encountered a group of drunken toffs dancing:

> We were all fantastically drunk. (*Loud.*) But the difference in our drunkenness! – you couldn't imagine it – we were a thousand miles apart . . .
>
> Everywhere you go, you can see them, grey, scabby, complacent faces. In this cage, crowding in front of me here, staring back, full of confidence, such a certainty of power . . . yes . . . and suffocating everything else around, saying this is how it is, the way we like it, and this is how it always will be. There is a complacency here that is totally savage. (ibid.: 26)

On a summer's day, Teddy and David are invited to H's picnic on a hill overlooking the city. Establishing what becomes a *leitmotiv* in Poliakoff's work, it is 'savagely hot' (ibid.: 30).[1] Teddy's intimacy with David irritates H as the pair share confidences in smiles and nods. When the conversation drifts to the topic of immortality, David proposes that, 'we all believe it, in our idiotic fashion, that we're actually going to do it. Achieve it [immortality]' (ibid.). Though such assurance is typically, as the play presents it, a matter of the self-confidence of the upper classes, David and Teddy privately share a sense of making a difference by way of a different possible historical trajectory which will undermine the establishment. They have come to believe that the imminent war will bring fundamental social change. The edginess of the occasion is marked by another curious visceral image when Arnold sucks a razor blade and Teddy just manages to prevent the sister, Sarah, from doing likewise. Sarah is the lone female character in *Clever Soldiers* whose world is dominated by men – that is, a certain kind of men. She is notable for being different. When she first visits Arnold, she is unconventionally dressed with short hair, eschews 'feminine' accomplishments (the piano), and has a readiness to question her brother and his friends which would have been rare at that time (see I.iv). When Teddy and Arnold leave to join their regiments, Sarah consciously begins to seduce Teddy on the station, partly as a means to shock but also to demonstrate the potential of her sexual power. Poliakoff, in short, has created a proto-feminist.

When war is declared, Teddy and David are excited, anticipating 'the end of all this, the chance of freedom for all' (ibid.: 34). They both intend to join up but David, having unaccountably been declared unfit when 'men twice [his] age [are] limping along to enlist and being accepted!' (ibid.: 40) is left behind with H. Act II of *Clever Soldiers* is set largely at the front, constituting Poliakoff's attempt viscerally to convey the feel of the trench experience. Though the mud, blood, cold and the pointlessness of it all are atmospherically drawn, the distinctiveness of Poliakoff's treatment is that Teddy's disillusion, shared with David by way of letters, is that the anticipated fundamental change does not materialise. Arnold – in spite of appearing a wimp in the face of the bloods' bullying (I.iv) – rises to the occasion of war and fulfils the public school–Oxford–officer trajectory quite successfully on those terms. He leads a platoon and takes responsibility when things go devastatingly wrong. Teddy is surprised to find how much of that habitus has become embodied in himself, and he is equally astonished at how the privates obey his orders. He finds himself conflicted between an enculturated drive to press on and a growing awareness that his goal of change through war is not being achieved.

When Teddy is back in Oxford on short leave, Sarah offers not only to fulfil the sexual favours she had tempted him with on his initial departure but to release him from the war by wounding him so that he is not fit to return. She has sustained her difference and anticipates social change post-war of the kind Teddy desires. Indeed, she is now working with a group of women to save '[p]eople like us . . . For what's about to happen, after this battle' (ibid.: 60). But Teddy finds he wants to go back to the front because, 'I love it there. I do. I really love it. I'm part of it' (ibid.: 61).

The parallel between games at public school and war games is explicitly drawn on Teddy's return to the front as he becomes increasingly delusionary and takes unnecessary risks in leading pointless advances:

> Look at the sun lying across the pitch. We are going to get there of course. Reach their touchline or at least their twenty-five line. (*He moves forward on the ground slightly.*) We're seeing something that nobody's ever seen before. Except we can't see it, we're buried in grey grass and slush and can only see a few red flowers. And if we lift our heads we get a ball quite quickly between our eyes. (*Nervous laugh.*) Balls in our head . . .
>
> I am part of this – yes (*Quiet.*) Across the pitch there is a red rain, quite strong, and it's very hot, and God, the smell when it gets into your clothes. (ibid.: 66–7)

Shortly after this visceral account of trench experience, he deliberately provokes a fight with a private, encouraging him to fight back, shouting:

> An order . . . (*catches hold of him*) You bastard, don't you see, it's going to make no difference at all, none of this. (*Close to him.*) England's untouched isn't it, it's too incredibly strong . . . isn't it? . . . you're mad you know, because afterwards you're going to get nothing you see! Because it's unbreakable isn't it? It's inside me – right through me and it just won't break . . . (ibid.: 68)

An intensely physical fight is engaged with Teddy inviting the private to 'break [his] face', saying, 'you're going to finish us, aren't you soldier? You have to. Don't you realise who you're really fighting?' (ibid.: 69). Ultimately Teddy stabs the private and, exhausted and defeated himself, dies next to him. A torrent of bells heralds a short coda scene between H and David, still at Oxford. H remarks, 'how lonely and beautiful it is. How like it's always been . . . It has been such an odd time recently' (ibid.).

The message of *Clever Soldiers* is clear in what Poliakoff, on reflection, sees as 'one of [his] most polemical plays' (ibid.: x). The parallels between public school and Oxford and between the social elite Bullingdon-style bloods and the officer class leading the troops in the Great War are both embedded in the structure of the play and overtly commented upon in the dialogue. The more oblique, multi-layered, metaphorical dramaturgy of Poliakoff's mature work is not yet evident but he does achieve a fluidity of action, the largely bare sets being lent atmosphere through sound and light and affording rapid changes of scene. In the graphic and verbal imagery, as illustrated, Poliakoff also achieves much of his aim of a visceral sense of the hot and heady days at Oxford in Act I and of the trench experience in Act II. He also brings his own take on the Great War, a field previously well-trodden in literature. Above all, in Teddy, he creates a complex character and, through a 'vivid, tactile, emotional theatre', seeks to draw the audience to see things directly through that character's experience. *Clever Soldiers* may not be Poliakoff's very best play but it marks a considerable accomplishment for a writer of twenty-two years, mixing as it does history and memory in an imaginative dramatic construct.

Breaking the Silence (1984)

Breaking the Silence at the RSC's Pit Theatre, Barbican, marks a moment when Poliakoff turned away from London and from the urban canyons which had brought his initial success in the 1970s and to his own family as source material for drama. The backstory to *Breaking the Silence* having already been recounted in Chapter 2, there is no need to unpack again here those extraordinary events in Russia in the early 1920s when Stephen Poliakoff's direct ancestors were saved from starvation by a chance meeting with one of Lenin's commissars. The outcome of that encounter – the summary designation of Poliakoff's grandfather as Telephone Examiner for the Northern Region – is, however, the starting-point of *Breaking the Silence*, on one level the most autobiographical of Poliakoff's plays. Attention here will initially be drawn, by way of a reminder, to the connections between the characters and Poliakoff's ancestors but thereafter the play will be treated as an independent dramatic construct. For *Breaking the Silence* goes beyond a family story to become a play of transformations – particularly for women – as the double-edged forces of modernisation mingle pain with advancement.

The setting for the play is *'a huge imperial-style railway carriage, filling the whole stage'* (1994: 1, s.d.) into which Polya and Sasha enter noisily in the opening moments. For the events of *Breaking the Silence* take place entirely on the equivalent train to that allocated to Poliakoff's grandfather. Still evidencing traces of imperial grandeur in its furniture and fittings, the carriage interior is somewhat run-down – indeed dusty, blood-smeared and littered with animal droppings. Teenage Sasha (master Alexander) is the equivalent of Poliakoff's father (also Alexander), and Polya is a thirtysomething dressed in the formal black attire of a maid. They are joined by Eugenia (the upper-middle-class equivalent of Poliakoff's grandmother), *'a fine-looking lady of forty . . . dressed in an exquisite and expensive long summer dress'* (ibid.: 8, s.d.), and shortly afterwards by the mercurial and working-class Verkoff, Commissar for Labour, whose fortunes are on the ascendant under the post-revolution Leninist regime, and Nikolai (the grandfather) *'an imposing figure in his late forties or early fifties, wearing a truly splendid fur coat'* (ibid.: 9, s.d.). The costumes of the family protagonists signify their pre-revolution status and indeed, when the main company is assembled, the image on-stage might be mistaken for a scene from a Chekhov play – *The Cherry Orchard* perhaps, with similar noises off of the movements of railway trains. As the play progresses, however, changes in clothes mark significant changes in circumstances.

A light and sometimes ironic humour is derived in the first half of the play from the fact that Nikolai Semonovich Pesiakoff refuses to acknowledge that anything has changed. Perhaps because his aristocratic and highly patriarchal authority is tempered by *'a very distinctive charm and lightness of touch'* (ibid.), he remains an engaging figure, though his arrogance and lack of perspective are extreme. Any negative audience reactions are also anticipated within the play, for example when Verkoff, now effectively Nikolai's employer, is drawn in exasperation to remark: 'Listen to him. My God, there have been people dying all along the line, whole households starving, wiped out, and he complains about being here' (ibid.: 12). There is a mordant humour in the treatment also in I.1 as the family members, in spite of their desperation for food, keep quiet when Nikolai magisterially declines Verkoff's offer of provisions. The tense joke is extended in I.4 when Verkoff is invited to dine in the railway carriage at a table set out in full finery with English silver but, when the meagre bird is served, Nikolai prattles on, a battle with the remnants of the White Russians raging outside, keeping everybody from eating by the sheer force of his etiquette. After this occasion, Verkoff remarks, 'He's got "made at the Ritz" stamped on his arse' (ibid.: 51). Nikolai is also afforded some witty remarks in the manner of H in *Clever Soldiers*, if less forced. He tells Verkoff, for example, 'Comrade – I thought you had a revolution so you would be able to dress like me – not I like you' (ibid.: 46–7). Though he risks his family's well-being by refusing to respond to letters from Moscow or to undertake his duties because he is preoccupied with his project to add soundtrack to film, he remains a dominant and broadly sympathetic figure.

It is the women, however, who prove more interesting precisely in their capacity to adapt to new circumstances. Gradually the maid, Polya, abandons her deference and speaks more directly, first to Sasha, then to Eugenia and ultimately to Nikolai. By the beginning of Act II she is telling him, 'You don't yell for it [tea] any more, remember, you wait for it now' (ibid.: 66) and calling Sasha a 'rude little bastard' (ibid.: 61). The change in her attitude, though not overtly revolutionary, is evidently afforded by the change of circumstances, not only through living in close quarters with the family in a railway carriage, but of the broader social environment beyond. Eugenia, too, throws off by stages an absolute obedience to her husband, in the first instance opening some letters from Moscow and filling in the ledger documenting railway progress, and ultimately in Act II, when the carriage is parked in a Moscow siding, by taking a job in the railway's offices, when she had previously remarked that Nikolai 'always found the idea of my working extremely unpleasant' (ibid.: 32). The shift is marked visually in costume changes from the formal elegance and expense at the outset: first she feels a sense of liberation in removing her stockings and finally she puts on '*a plain black skirt, a brown sweater and at the end a long great coat – she is totally transformed*' (ibid.: 58, s.d.). Both women continue to support Nikolai, with Polya assisting in the recording experiments, but they begin to think and act independently such that another accent of 'Breaking the Silence' – besides that denoting Nikolai's aim to put soundtrack on film – marks the beginnings of emancipation in another revolution at the start of the twentieth century: women finding a voice.

Sasha also grows from the spoilt child in a velvet suit at the beginning of the play, notably in the four-year gap between the two Acts. The first Act is set in 1920 and the second in 1924, the year of Lenin's death, as marked in the play by sounds of preparation for his funeral. His clothes have also changed and he now wants to be inconspicuous in Moscow by wearing, not his rich fur coat, but the standard grey woollen. He has come to see his father almost from the revolutionary point of view as a 'dilettante ... [whose] individualism destroys others' (1994: 64), a 'self-deluding old man' (ibid: 62) who 'has never done a proper day's work in his life' (ibid.). Sasha's independent decisions, however, prove less well-judged. Following Lenin's death, the climate in Moscow changes and Verkoff sends a note advising the family to leave Russia. Sasha knows that his father will not leave his 'work', the significance of which he has come to doubt. Again spending railway money without authority, Nikolai has ordered a crate of lenses from abroad to finalise his process, and Sasha decides that the only way to get his father to leave is to destroy them. In a moment of violence resonating with the noises of battle outside the carriage in the course of the play, Sasha smashes the lenses with a hammer, quickly masking his action by turning furniture upside down and pretending there has been an attack. On his return, Nikolai responds calmly at first in his old manner, but quickly becoming defiantly angry, vowing that he will still do it: 'This is both a promise and a warning and nothing can stop that now' (ibid.: 79). He refuses to leave the country but the women, with greater political astuteness, realise that getting to the border is their best chance. Though she could leave the family, Polya decides to go with them, at least to the border.

The final scene of the play, set in the railway carriage now at the border amid many others in the chaotic conditions of a mass exodus, involves a number of reversals and revelations. The two guards who deal with their papers, tetchy under the extreme pressure of the circumstances, turn out to be the very two they encountered in the deep north and whom Nikolai recommended for preferment. But they do not recognise him and, ironically, adjudge that a man looking like him could not possibly have worked on the railway. In searching the carriage, they find a bag of diamonds which, against the prudence of the women in abandoning items of wealth, Nikolai has casually brought along. As the situation is turning more grave, Eugenia discovers a missing letter sent by Verkoff which they hope might ease their passage. What it reveals, however, is that the Commissar knew all along that Nikolai would not do any railway work but, half believing in his invention, had consigned him to the railway posting as the best means of giving him the opportunity to prove himself. Verkoff has subsequently been amused by Eugenia and Polya's inventiveness in their forged ledgers. When the guards return, Nikolai is under arrest and – completing the pattern of changed clothes marking altered positions – he is stripped to '*his vest and trousers, barefoot, looking frail and vulnerable*' (ibid.: 94, s.d.). Polya is required to leave.

Nikolai tries to keep his dignity and there are even some comic moments when, reversing his earlier celebration of England, Nikolai observes, 'They're terribly slow the English . . . There is no energy of ideas, they instinctively distrust all ideas on sight' (ibid.: 97). Such observations, no doubt raising self-ironic laughter among the Pit Theatre audience, are a preamble, however, to more heartfelt revelations about the pain of leaving one's homeland. Nikolai admits to Eugenia: 'Nothing . . . in my life has prepared me for this shock, the sheer physical sensation when one is faced with leaving one's native land permanently – like you are being pulled away from a magnetic field and that everything will stop' (ibid.). To avoid any drift to sentimentality, the play has Eugenia, quietly but firmly, respond with an attack on patriarchy, questioning why Nikolai did not involve her in anything and, in a parallel heartfelt revelation, she shares with him what an oppressed and repressed life has been like for her: 'If I ever have to live through that again with me festering underneath (*Matter of fact*) beginning to scream and cry inside . . . (*Holding herself*) I felt there was so much in here . . . trapped in here . . . it was like burrowing out of a grave' (ibid.: 99). Emphasising how her life has fundamentally changed on the overall train journey, she tells him of her need for once to be open and honest since, in the event, this moment might be their last together. The parallel between tumultuous events within the confines of the railway carriage with those in the world outside is drawn, perhaps superfluously, by Nikolai: 'Large events, great events even, have happened just outside, and we've seen most of them – or heard most of them to be more accurate . . . And yet the energy generated in here, felt at times, if you will allow the slight exaggeration, felt it could flatten city walls' (ibid.: 100).

Now locked claustrophobically in the carriage, however, Nikolai has run out of ideas and, when the guards return, it is left to Eugenia to find a way out. When all seems lost, she suddenly comes up with a string of facts about railways in the Northern Region, about the delivery of locomotives and the opening of the new telephone exchange in Moscow, which she could only have gained from the experience of working on the railway. More or less convinced, the guards arrange for their train to leave the country, but the final images of Eugenia curled up in a foetal position crying in anguish offset a Pyrrhic victory with the pain of leaving, as the play concludes.

To those who know the backstory to the play, *Breaking the Silence* is evidently a family history and an *hommage* to the unrecognised achievement of Poliakoff's grandfather.[2] To any audience member who does not know it, however, the play stands independently as a dramatic construct relating through a specific family story the impact of events of world significance. It thus resonates particularly with the later television plays which, by means of telling a particular story with fascinating characters to draw the audience in, give a feeling for the times which official histories all too frequently fail to achieve. That visceral directness, evidenced in the discussion above of *Clever Soldiers*, continues to allow audiences to 'see the whole action through the eyes of the central characters' (1997: ix–x) but as part of a more sophisticated dramaturgy. Though *Breaking the Silence* has a point, it is less polemical and more layered than the early play. The broader implications of historical circumstances, largely carried by off-stage sound and lighting effects, ripple outwards to invite rather than to articulate insights into the implications of historical change. The specific shifts from subservience to independence of Eugenia and Polya resonate, by implication, with the more general modernist trajectory to emancipate women from an oppressive patriarchy. It is a less obvious revolution than that in Russia in 1917, but arguably has more far-reaching implications. But, even in this regard, the play is not unambiguous. In his monomania, Nikolai has conducted his own revolution, since he achieved an extraordinary modern invention which itself would, in due course, 'revolutionise popular entertainment' (1994: 67). Moreover, his sustained dignity is presented, partly through the lightly comic treatment, as having style and even a certain level of integrity. Early in the play, Eugenia remarks that 'we can only stand here and wait for what is coming' (ibid.: 34) where Nikolai summarises that they inhabit 'the farcical conditions in which history is being made' (ibid.: 68). But the play overall is less defeatist, exemplifying 'agency in structure' and standing ultimately as testimony to human ingenuity and survival in challenging times as, in very different circumstances, does the next play for discussion.

Talk of the City (1998)

Talk of the City is based on historical research into the BBC in the period leading up to the Munich agreement of September 1938, 'in an attempt to avert the crisis caused by Hitler's escalating demands'.[3] It marks the beginning of the infamous policy of 'appeasement', a moment in which British Prime Minister, Neville Chamberlain, joined by his French and Italian counterparts, signed an agreement with Hitler sanctioning Germany's annexation of the Sudetenland area of former Czechoslovakia, on the understanding that Hitler would refrain from further incursions, and that 'peace for our time', as

Chamberlain put it on his return, would be secured. It did not work out that way with the devastating consequences, particularly for Jews exterminated in *Kristallnacht* and the Holocaust, but for the whole of Europe, indeed the world, in the Second World War.[4] *Talk of the City* (*Talk*) is specifically concerned, however, with the culture of the BBC at this moment in history and, although the weighty events sketched here motivate the plot, it is the BBC's institutional response to their context, rather than the events themselves, which are the subject of the play, first produced at the RSC's Swan Theatre in 1998.

It might well have been a shock for audiences to be reminded that, in the early days of the BBC, radio was predominant and that television, in its infancy at Alexandra Palace, north London, was viewed from Broadcasting House in central London as a bit of a joke, operating at the outer limits and accessible only to the few thousand people who owned receivers. Precisely because the medium was not seen by BBC mandarins as important, however, television afforded a space for creativity and experiment which highly codified and policed radio had long since stifled. Early in the play Clive Lynn-Thomas, a Talks producer, observes: 'It's amazing, isn't it – the way this organisation behaves. It is only *fifteen* years old, and yet it has become an instant cathedral of broadcasting, managed to create all this sham venerability' (ibid.: 26). In contrast 'Honker' (aka Harry Wallace) introduces Alexandra Palace as a breath of fresh air: 'there *are* freedoms here. Other freedoms I like to think. Our show "Trafalgar Square" . . . has real people' (ibid.: 18).

In introducing up-and-coming radio entertainer, Robbie Penacourt, to television, Poliakoff is able in *Talk* to exploit the different protocols of the two media in respect of both creative potential and a nascent democratic tendency in television, inclined to speak to the mass of people, in contrast with radio which, as institutionalised by Lord Reith, was disposed to be buttoned-up and highbrow.[5] Indeed, within BBC Radio, as the play illustrates, there was a stark division between the Talks Department and Light Entertainment, the former occupying the high ground and, as Presbyterian Scot, Reith, might have put it, 'ne'er the twain shall meet'. But in *Talk*, the two are brought together when Clive, against the grain of his schooling in

BBC tradition, is impressed by Robbie's disposition to experiment with form and even to improvise.

Poliakoff brings colour and fun to *Talk* by exploiting the many ironies of the early BBC context. Following the news summary delivered in the plummy tones and 'received pronunciation' of the 'BBC voice', the play's opening scene intercuts the continuing news in voice-over, with the moments of final preparation before Robbie's 'Friday Night at Eight' radio show goes on air. Robbie, as BBC Radio protocols required, is in full evening dress and the dancers appear in full showgirl costumes, in spite of the fact that they will not be seen. The irony of the situation is emphasised when producer, Daphne, who is strict about keeping to the script, complains that the suitcase Mabs has brought on as a prop for his detective story spot is yellow and not blue as the script dictates. Daphne tersely remarks, 'I don't like wireless lies, you know that' (ibid.: 7). Ironically, however, when Robbie and his entourage visit Alexandra Palace in scene 2, excited by the opportunity of having their finest show costumes seen at last, they are informed by Honker (he of the creative freedoms) that 'we cannot allow wireless costumes on television . . . I know I know it's senseless. But there's trouble for me if I break these regulations' (ibid.: 17).

The light-hearted treatment of the stuffiness of the BBC is interspersed with greater seriousness as the play progresses and specifically when Clive tries to interest Robbie in a project which challenges two BBC bastions. In the first instance, the project proposed is innovative in its challenge both to medium forms and to enshrined BBC protocols, but the content might be as bland as the proposed 'English apples'. The aim simply is to: 'use somebody from the variety side, from Light Entertainment, in a "Talk". Somebody who can sing and play many parts – to help both dramatise and document the world we live in' (ibid.: 29). That person, in Clive's view, is Robbie and, though he recognises the proposal as 'revolutionary' (ibid.: 30), Robbie's instincts for free-flow and improvisation are excited by it. BBC Head of Programmes, Arnold (known behind his back as Arnos) Grove is predictably cautious, however. He asks: 'What would one call it? It's a very complicated idea for the listener to grasp, they could get confused between what is proper fact and what is entertainment' (ibid.: 33). In satirising 'Arnos Grove', Poliakoff is no doubt venting some of his own frustrations at the repressive caution of BBC executives and their under-estimation of the capacity of audiences to accept both formal innovation and a seriousness of content which informs the backstory to *Shooting the Past*.

Indeed, Clive's project ultimately is to embrace in an accessible, because entertaining, form some serious content, in that he is increasingly concerned about what he has learned of the plight of Jews in Germany and at the conservative caution – if not outright prejudice – informing the BBC's playing down of the situation. He proposes that Robbie take the role of a real Jewish man (with a changed name) whose 'normal day' they would follow in the manner of what has since become a 'day-in-the-life of . . .' drama-documentary but at the time was unconscionable as a hybrid form. As Clive tells Robbie, 'At the end of the day he is arrested. His liberty is taken away. You will portray this man and sing his songs' (ibid.: 39). Both are excited by the idea but realise it must remain a secret since it will not be easy to convince the BBC hierarchy. Isabel, a market researcher lover of Clive's, and producer Daphne, are the only two others included in the secret development programme.

In addition to the plight of the Jews being intermittently reported, if under-played, in voice-over BBC news announcements throughout *Talk of the City*, a personalised human dimension is introduced through an intimate relationship between bisexual Robbie and Bernard (aka Baron von Freier von Brandis) who, like many others, has assumed a title to mask his Jewish identity in an attempt to flee Hitler's Germany. Robbie directly asks him, 'How difficult are things for Jewish people in Germany now?' but Bernard finds it 'a difficult question to answer in this country. Because a few people ask you . . . and you start to tell them – and you quickly realise they really don't want to know' (ibid.: 43). It seems as if the evasion of the reality of Hitler's Germany runs through the populace, up through the BBC hierarchy to the Prime Minister in his policy of appeasement. An emotional response to the Jewish predicament is elicited, however, in a poignant moment of parting in II.6, when Bernard must return to Germany, supposedly briefly, but all concerned know he may not be allowed to return. Thus the urgency of Clive's plan is intensified.

Encouraged by Clive's interest in innovation, Robbie takes more risks with his radio show, though not yet aspiring fully to documentary revelations. He invents a new, wacky, detective, Inspector Curioso, and, under the guise of fantasy, begins to introduce a commentary on current affairs, including some remarks based on Bernard's 'foreign observation' (ibid.: 71). Though some audience response reveals an element of shock, many people go with it and Robbie's caricature of Hitler passes unnoticed. The approach is broadly well received by the BBC hierarchy and Robbie is delighted when 'Friday Night at Eight' is awarded the weekly link-up with America, usually reserved for the prime-time Monday-night programme. Even Daphne accepts that Robbie is licensed to 'deviate [from the script] . . . in moderation' (ibid.: 63). Walt Disney on a clandestine visit shows some interest in Robbie because he 'speak[s] to the child in people' (ibid.: 79), but he is well aware of the commercial potential of 'Inspector Curioso', not as the subversive device under development by Clive and Robbie, but as a cartoon figure. Disney's visit thus opens up an additional question about the function of broadcasting and the reinforcement of the divide within the BBC between Talks and Light Entertainment. Robbie, like others on his team, is confronted with a choice between commercial success, with a mass entertainment audience and career advancement to stardom, and the use of popular means to give access to more serious considerations in the everyday world.

The development of the latter, in the form of Clive and Robbie's subversive docu-drama project, suffers a setback in II.3 when it transpires that one of the gang of four has leaked the details of their secret to Arnold Grove. Clive tries to persuade him not only of the inherent worth of the project but of how it might be presented amid other documentaries to solve the BBC's 'question of balance' (ibid.: 82). But Grove is ahead of him, claiming that they have already commissioned a talk on each of the parallel topics Clive proposes. Grove assumes the haughty, paternalistic stance of the lingering Reithian ethos at the time in which executives assumed that their view of the world was the only fair view. He justifies the tacit policy of avoidance of a more direct address of Jews in Germany by arguing that 'it is undeniable that there is anti-Semitism in the mass of the population' (ibid.: 83–4). When Isabel informs him that in the audience research in which she has been involved, 'the degree of prejudice reported is quite mild in fact' (ibid.: 84), Grove refers to over-statement of claims about 'the Hun bayoneting babies' (ibid.) in the First World War, and to the allegation that 'Jewish people are prone to exaggerate' (ibid.: 85).[6]

Realising he has been both betrayed and outflanked and will be obstructed by Grove's insistence on 'hard evidence' (ibid.: 86), Clive becomes increasingly angry but sustains his determination to air 'a hugely urgent story that has to be told' (ibid.). He informs Robbie of the betrayal of their secret and tries to persuade him to take the opportunity of his imminent big show 'to do something in this broadcast', but Robbie is unconvinced: 'That would be a crazy thing for me to attempt. If I start blurting out political messages, in the middle of my show – Doubly idiotic with this audience of bishops and all the senior figures – Mr Disney too!' (ibid.: 91). Though he has not abandoned his commitment to the project, he is now somewhat torn between it and his rising stardom. In preparing for the show, he indicates it may be edgy by warning colleagues that this 'may be a slightly rough ride' (ibid.: 92). Some colleagues, singer Milly in particular, say that they do not want to rock any boats since they want to capitalise on this opportunity for exposure in America, the home of the entertainment industry.

In the event, Robbie is edgy, breaking taboos by using sexual innuendo and making the sound of kissing on air, by not wearing a dinner-jacket, and by singing one of his own compositions – all against BBC rules. He goes so far, under the guise of Curioso, to attack 'hypocrites who say one thing in public and love something else totally different in private' and '*betrayal* yes, oh yes, by people so close to Curioso . . . people right next to him . . .' (ibid.: 95). Daphne, at whom some of the *double entendre* was aimed, is angry and shows her true allegiances in referring upwards to Mr Grove, who will hold a post-mortem on the broadcast. Pressed by Robbie, she acknowledges that 'Of course I passed on everything I knew to management – that was my job' (ibid.: 97). Arnold Grove, however, is untroubled by the show because 'NRD thoroughly enjoyed himself' (ibid.: 99) and the audience approved. Clive, however, is furious at the wasted opportunity, accusing Robbie of abusing the chance to speak home 'with the world on the very edge of an abyss . . . for settling private scores' (ibid.), and 'resorting to a piece of self-promotion of the most shameless kind [because] you think you've been tapped on the shoulder by America' (ibid.: 100). In Clive's view, Robbie copped out at the vital moment refusing 'to connect with the real world' (ibid.).

In *Talk*, Poliakoff has thus constructed in the broadcasting world an equivalent of appeasement on the political front and, through Clive, he points to a sense, evident in other work, of conservative Britain's inward-looking isolation from Europe. In response to Groves's claim that audiences are 'already complaining there's far too much news from abroad', Clive retorts: 'It's so close, for God's sake, Europe, where this is happening – *Europe*, that filthy word – you know how near it is? . . . It's not some dark primitive continent a million miles away. If we could walk across the sea, it would be almost a brisk stroll to where all this is going on' (ibid.: 101).

Clive departs to undertake research in Germany, returning for the last scene of the play with a box of hard evidence which informs Robbie's final broadcast. In the interim, Robbie has more fully understood the power of radio, having learned from the impact of the broadcast of *War of the Worlds* in America.[7] He recognises that he really did miss an opportunity in his broadcast with a USA link. He has fallen under a cloud, however, and where everybody suddenly wanted to be on his show, they are now cancelling. Even Milly is demanding conditions of work set in writing. But informed by Clive's evidence, Robbie takes the microphone at the end of the play to: 'do a song written by a Jewish man who lived in Munich until very recently . . . Hearing the song will be a comfort – because it's a beautiful song – but it's not meant to be a comfort.

He sings for a moment. Then stops. Quiet, simple.

It will reassure – but I promise you, it shouldn't reassure . . .'

Both Robbie Penacourt and Poliakoff have found a means of mixing entertainment and seriousness in work intended not to appease but to dislocate and mobilise a more complex seeing. *Talk* is dialogue-led and follows a traditional linear narrative trajectory, but its mode of presentation – involving several 'live' radio broadcasts with dancing girls in full costume and other variety acts – draws also upon a popular theatre tradition. Though it is informative about the BBC historically. in its attitudes to appeasement and the Jewish question, it also uses historical distance, as Brecht frequently did in his plays, to afford insight from a critical distance into a current political situation. Though by 1998, Britain was a long-term member of the European Union, a deep Euro-scepticism had dogged the Thatcher years and may have been a factor in the Conservatives losing the 1997 election to Labour. The strong message in *Talk* about the perils of Britain pretending events in continental Europe are not a matter for them, was thus as relevant in 1998 in respect of contemporary politics as it was revealing about a major British institution's attitudes historically.

Remember This (1999)

Remember This concerns the experience of a middle-aged London man, Rick Peck. Recovering from an apparent heart attack on the verge of his second marriage, Rick's enforced convalescence leads him to sift the clutter of his past and to stumble upon a new insight into the non-durability of image on video-tape. Ironically this revelation partly fulfils a life-long ambition by making him briefly an interna-tional celebrity, but it does not make him rich. The play intertwines a family story with a serious reflection on media technologies, but it is not self-serious in tone. Comedy is afforded by a clash of disparate characters. There are three women in Rick's life: life-long buddy, Margaret; wife-to-be Victoria who 'floats through everything [like] a posh mist' (1999: 8); and her contrasting sister, Hannah, a business consultant with a postmodern entrepreneurial dynamism – a version of Rick's life-long 'eye for the main chance' which has, until now, brought him only grief. Progressively through the play we learn that he was the first with a video camera, the first to make a wedding video and the first to offer a stretch-limousine service. But these ventures all came to nothing. Rick's real hope for a socially progressive family trajectory has rested in the educational achievement of his son, Jimmy (from a former marriage), who is a PhD candidate on the topic of George Gissing.

More fully than in *Blinded by the Sun*, a double perspective is invoked by the use of a narrative device and other 'Brechtian' strategies identified by Williams in respect of 'complex seeing'. *Remember This (RT)* opens at the height of Rick's new-found fame with Rick being summoned to record a home television interview conducted by Margaret. Rick appears from the shadows rock-star-style in dark glasses with a cigarette and a pint of beer in hand. The situation and dialogue, though they convey a slight sense of self-irony, establish that Rick's story deserves to be preserved for posterity. The lights, camera set-up and the building background music (*'Seventies music – classic tracks'*, ibid.: 3, s.d.) afford a sense of an event. In effect, however, the play has a double time-scheme: direct address to the audience in the here and now relates events which comprise a replay of the (partly video) recorded events of Rick's life. Such a sophisticated dramaturgical device prefigures the double time-scheme and direct address to a tape recorder (and to camera) by Oswald in introducing *Shooting the Past*. In *RT* the devices serve to draw attention to the themes of time passing, recording technologies and memory. In the second Act particularly, characters take turns at confiding in the audience through a video diary. This device, along with the double time-scheme, elicits 'complex seeing' by creating a tension between the audience's partial insights into the individual characters' perspectives in the here and now, and the overall narrative-driven experience. The audience wants to know what will happen to Rick and his discovery, although they partly know the outcome by means of the framing strategy through which the play opens well into the sequence of the narrative events recounted.

As he begins to clear out a store-room full of apparent junk (visually very evident in a cluttered set), Rick plays back some of his old videos. When he tries to play for Jimmy a video of his first wedding, Rick discovers that the image has mysteriously disappeared, leaving just the sound. Rick tries another tape, identifying from the soundtrack that it was a barbecue – 'they were new things in England barbecues –' (ibid.: 34), but again there is no image. Rick reminisces, recalling himself dancing, and notes the irony that he is both there and not there, given the absence of image. They try more tapes, some to comic effect revealing Rick's past lusts, while others are more sombre, conveying 'the sounds of the factory where Margaret and [Rick] met' (ibid.: 36). Margaret appears as a string of obscenities resounds from her younger self: 'who the fuck do you think I am? Audrey fuckin' Hepburn . . . ? Put that away at once' (ibid.: 37).

The juxtaposition of an ageing Margaret in the present against her dynamic and exuberant younger voice reinforces the now complex time-scheme the play has set up. It makes Margaret reflective and she suggests that they try to find the first tape with images to mark the period where the image has been effaced. Against the intensified sound of Beethoven's Seventh Symphony and a darkened stage, an image of Rick's father, *'A man in his mid-fifties, working class, strong accent, chain-smoking'* (ibid.: 38) gradually emerges on the screen. In *RT*, soundtrack is an integral part of the action as the video images fade and it is left to the soundtrack to convey the events of personal history – which they do to great effect, particularly in the latter part of the play.

In earlier plays, Poliakoff drew upon pop music to catch the feel of the times and this approach is subsequently augmented by the functional usage of sound to mark changes of scene, sometimes accompanied in the theatre by lighting dissolves (or cross-fades) as in television, to mark either the passage of time or, indeed, a change of scene (as in Jimmy's art installation below). Poliakoff's usage extends to symbolic reference such as the use of Beethoven to accompany the introduction of Rick's father (who reappears in the play's appendix).

Rick evokes a strong sense of actual family history in commenting affectionately on his 'cheeky chappie' dad who was 'always so nervous of the world' (ibid.: 39) such that a fleeting, but unmistakable, sense of an upwardly mobile trajectory through Rick and on to doctoral scholar, Jimmy, is conveyed. When the tape is switched off, Margaret deduces that the tapes were durable from 1982 and Rick and Margaret, with that London 'eye for the main chance', sense that there might be a business opportunity here. Hannah, however, is ahead of them with an international ambition. She arrives accompanied by Sergei, a curator from a media archive in Geneva whom she has interested in Rick's discovery.

Rick's story and its dramatic presentation thus manifest a number of Poliakovian traits: an interest in the history of material culture, and new technologies in particular, but with some ambivalence about their worth. That element of conservative scepticism about mass media technologies (non-stop radio and muzak), seen in the 1970s plays to resonate with the Frankfurt School of media critique (see Chapter 3), recurs here. Jimmy, for example, isolates himself by use of a Walkman, the muffled sound of which, Rick remarks, is 'the worst sound in the world – the half-heard personal stereo' (ibid.: 10). But consideration of media technologies broadens as the play progresses to amount to an almost existential commentary on memory as an analogue of media storage capacity and the necessity but unavoidable transience of both in contemporary life.

Having identified the period of image effacement, the assembled 'family', along with Sergei, gathers around a pyramid of encased, old televisions – 'a job lot from a business [Rick] tried once' (ibid.: 52) – constructed for a showing. The scene, an ironic reconstruction of the traditional image of the television family, is ironised by a construction reminiscent of Nam June Paik's 1980s TV installations. By now Rick has advertised, 'via the internet and on local media' for other tapes of the vintage of his own effaced collection, and proposes to show a selection of what has 'arrived from all over the world' (ibid.). They begin with the sound from behind the closed doors of the encased televisions of children's birthday parties, a sound which swells when Margaret, on Rick's instruction, opens the doors to screens which show flashes of light but no clear image. The second showing of tapes, from 'the early eighties, when ordinary people began to get hold of video cameras' (ibid.: 53), yields the sounds from various family holidays, prompting the assembled company to speculate as to the images missing. Contrary to Hannah's sense that Rick is a wily and thrusting entrepreneur, Rick draws a political conclusion from what they are experiencing:

I'll tell you what it shows us – it's the best example yet of the techno rich and the techno poor.

All those people with cheap video cameras, camcorders, thought they were preserving their weddings . . . their new houses . . . their young families . . . giving a shape to their progress, something lasting in a changing world – able to show their grandchildren.

Well it's not there, is it!

While the rich, of course, have got the money to get all their tapes transferred really quickly, digital tapes, digital cameras, they can catch their memories before they lose them! (ibid.: 54)

Ironically, Hannah reads in this *cri de coeur* a 'terrific pitch, that's a great pitch, Rick!' (ibid.). The final example clinches the emotional impact on several different levels. It is the faded recording of the birth of a baby. For reasons of her own, Victoria is touched while Rick is ambivalent, articulating the sadness of his discovery but unable to resist a trick. Sergei asks sceptically about the research sample (which turns out to be just fifty-three tapes submitted out of potentially millions) but he acknowledges that, if Rick is right against all probability of a non-professional making such a discovery, he has stumbled upon an unknown phenomenon. Hannah believes Rick is, knowingly or otherwise, part of a conspiracy to tackle 'the great question of the age . . . How on earth to keep moving the consumer on'. The question, she says, is, 'how to coax the average punter to keep up? The market depends upon it! To make them keep upgrading their possessions' (ibid.: 58).

The second Act of the play broadens the implications of Rick's discovery and begins to bear out the publicity claim made for *RT* that, 'Poliakoff's provocative play is a story of intense rivalry between the generations in a world that seems to record everything and remember nothing as it hurtles into the next century'.[8] Called urgently to Switzerland by Sergei, Rick, Margaret and Hannah, along with the theatre audience, see disappear not just the personal, domestic narratives of Act I, but major historical events. Though their research is at its early stages, Sergei and his colleague, Chain, at the Swiss archive have found disintegration on footage of some major historical land-marks: the fall of the Berlin Wall in 1989; the G7 summit of 1990, featuring Margaret Thatcher, Chancellor Kohl, President Mitterrand and George Bush among others; Margaret Thatcher's 1989 speech to the Conservative Party. With each projected tape, the image breaks up and the soundtrack peters out with a grunt which Margaret describes as 'a sort of fart into oblivion!' (ibid.: 70). Presidents of America, Ronald Reagan and Bill Clinton, suffer the same ignominy as the tapes fade. Poliakoff is, of course, effectively using the degeneration of video-tape as a device to signify postmodern culture in which history and memory collapse into the spatialisation of time and only that which is stored in media technologies is remembered. It is an instance, in Baudrillard's term, of 'the implosion of the real'.[9]

The generational conflict noted in the publishing blurb is manifest in the marked difference between Victoria and Hannah, who are contrasting representatives of the new generation, and Rick, who despite his entrepreneurial spirit, has a strong and even sentimental regard for the past and the actual history of his family and friends. The video diary device affords Victoria an opportunity to acknowl-edge to the camera – and, of course, the theatre audience in direct address – that she is aware that she and Rick appear to be completely different people and that she might appear 'utterly brainless'. She admits that she has 'NO IDEA, no it's true! Nearly every day I hear something and I have *no idea* what people are talking about' (ibid.: 63). She thus comes to represent in the play a generation of people who are completely preoccupied by their personal concerns: shop-ping, a new house, perhaps family, without any sense of a broader historical context. Throughout Rick's convalescence, she has continued to engage solely in such activities. Hannah, in contrast, is a jet-setter, working in three other countries on the day she joins Rick and Margaret in Switzerland. She is networked into a range of experts available at the ends of mobile phones to give instant advice. Her interest in Rick's discovery is not in the implications of the effacement of history, but in the business opportunity his discovery might represent.

Yet another perspective is afforded by Rick's medical consultant, a self-confessed luddite, who is delighted on learning of Rick's discovery that new media technologies might be called in question. Though he acknowledges that Rick's impending success might be good for his stress, he proposes an angiogram test. The lights change and, highlighted, Rick prepares for the operation. The image from the camera passing up through Rick's body is projected on the back wall of the stage, but Rick prefers not to watch, preferring to give way to the floating sensation of the drugs. He begins imaginatively to prefigure his announcement and its impact:

> People will look up the last period of the twentieth century and will have to tell what it was like from Hollywood movies . . . ! (*He looks at us for a moment.*)
>
> No letters to read either because all those e-mails have gone . . .
>
> So there will be no alternative except to try to remember . . . The end of short-term memory . . . yes!
>
> (*He smiles.*) Even school kids may get interested in the recent past, because it is suddenly an endangered species . . .
>
> It will become fashionable to remember . . . ! (ibid.: 83)

As if to contest his father's insight, Jimmy arrives in a new rock-style image to announce that he's ditched his PhD. Having realised that he is the 'first video child' (ibid.: 94), Jimmy has retrieved the tapes featuring his childhood and used them in an art installation. He leads his father through it as the scene cross-fades. In effect it is a sound installation of Rick's paternal voices documenting Jimmy's life and, to his father's astonishment, Jimmy relates that people are queuing up for the experience of 'My Smudged Life' in which he melts the CD containing his thesis in boiling water and sets fire to it. The rationale is: 'There isn't time to put the work in any more. If you want to be there, be really successful, and we all do if we're honest – Fuck the preparation, fuck the accumulation of knowledge. Nobody cares about that now. Do it in one leap if you possibly can –' (ibid.: 100).

Rick is genuinely appalled at what he is hearing; the play has emphasised throughout his pride in his son's educational achievements as a key to his success but, once Jimmy has left, Rick's initial depression lifts when the consultant tells him he is in good shape and free to leave. Suddenly energised, Rick declares he is 'not going to be plagiarised by [his] own son' and that he is 'going to get out of there – and beat the shit out of him' (ibid.: 103).

The action of the play concludes, however, at Rick and Victoria's postponed wedding.[10] Victoria calls Rick away from his camera ironically documenting events, and for the first time, she asks what he is thinking.

RICK   I was thinking . . . I'm a little scared . . .

(*He grins*.) I don't know, for instance, how long I'll be alive . . . !

I don't know a lot of things . . .

VICTORIA   Just like me . . . you see . . . You have no idea.

Fade (ibid.: 114)

Though this dialogue and the fading of the lights mark the end of the play with an apparent capitulation and regression on Rick's part, the script includes an appendix, a video of Rick's father (with Rick off-camera) in a rambling monologue.[11] Rick has taken him to hear music he purportedly likes in a concert in a park, but his father denies knowing the music and muses, in the manner of somebody suffering from dementia, a past meeting with a German general and, finally, on how he has called a radio phone-in to talk about fishing. The content is unimportant in its detail but it records an affectionate portrait of a human being, real despite his selective memory and thus throws into relief a number of aspects of *RT*.

In ultimately privileging a humanist celebration of ordinary individual experience over a postmodern, post-human (or inhuman) corporate identity, *RT* again prefigures *Shooting the Past*, but with a difference. Ultimately, for Rick – like Oswald – the embodied experience of being human, the mnemonic power of the human mind and the individual and collective memories which inform cultural identity, are of utmost importance. Hannah, the postmodern businesswoman in *RT*, notably remains a discontented figure chasing shadows around the world, in contrast to Anderson in *StP*, who discovers a new identity through the revelations from recorded images about his past.

Poliakoff uses technological disintegration as a metaphor for a culture disposed to efface history and live in a de-contextualised present. In *RT*, the point is made explicitly: 'Everyone was so busy correcting their computers for a simple mechanical oversight, they missed the fact that our recent history was written on sand, and is being washed away . . .' (ibid.: 83).

Further, Poliakoff seems concerned about the value shift in contemporary culture which denigrates traditional, if obscure, knowledge in favour of what will sell fast in the marketplace. The issue is figured broadly in *StP* in the contest between the fusty, old photographic archive and the dynamic and progressive, 'American school for Business for the 21st century'. In *RT*, the value conflict figures directly in Jimmy's abandonment of his PhD on George Gissing to make a fast buck out of his 'Smudged Life'. As he tells his father, his PhD thesis on which he has worked for years is:

> of no worth because unless there is a headline, nobody gives a shit. Where was it going to get me if I finished it? Do you think the world wants to know about a Victorian loser – of course not – unless I can prove he was Jack the Ripper or something. Hissing Gissing . . . ! There's no space any more for such quiet things. (ibid.: 101)

Though his position is more liberal humanist than Marxist, Poliakoff makes an oblique connection in his critique of the erosions of society by capitalist impulse.[12] The ultimate difference between Hannah and Rick, who at one point almost come together in *RT*, lies in Rick's more solid grounding in actual experience in contrast with Hannah's imbrication within the corporate business world to the extent that she can see things only in terms of business opportunities:

> Think about it Rick, what better way to get to the public, than saying 'Hey everyone you're losing your memories . . .! You're

losing your children, can't just wind back and see them as babies any more – because it will all have evaporated!'

So, hurry, hurry! Get the new technology . . . transfer everything! . . . Buy now . . . buy the latest . . . get down there . . . get modern! And all will be fine . . . !

That's fantastic, it's breathtaking . . . It's so cynical, it becomes magical.

(ibid.: 59)

Hannah is a member of the postmodern, service industry generation, where Rick and Margaret's foundations are on the factory floor. To Hannah the manipulation of the signifier is dislocated from any referent in the real, whereas Rick cannot ultimately dissociate his discovery from his memories of actual experience. *RT* obliquely associates the effacement of history with the drive of capitalism in Hannah's suggestion that the greatest question of the age is: 'in a world of permanent revolution how to coax the average punter to keep up? The market depends upon it! To make them keep upgrading their possessions' (ibid.: 58). The purpose of life, in Hannah's view, is to keep people buying or, in Marx and Engels's words, 'the bourgeoisie cannot exist without constantly revolutionizing the instruments of production, and with them the whole relations of society' (Taylor 1969: 83).

The end of the play sees Rick settling for a kind of quietism rather than becoming a political revolutionary, though his decision to abandon his entrepreneurial quest marks a choice of an alternative lifestyle. It is perhaps unfortunate that this is achieved through a marriage to Victoria, whom the play has indelibly established as so mindless that it is hard to accept an attempted redemption in the final moments. But, precisely because the ending is somewhat inconclusive and unsatisfactory, the audience is left with the challenge of negotiating the multiple perspectives the play has directly offered and the position Rick finally adopts. Accordingly, I see *RT* as the most Brechtian of Poliakoff's plays. Tactics of narrative perspective, direct address, complex time-scheme and dramatic reversal serve throughout, as noted, as a kind of Brechtian 'interruptus' to shock members of the audience into critical thought. Poliakoff does not deliver the clear resolution which Brecht bemoaned (Willetts 1987 [1964]: 37) in what he termed the 'dramatic theatre'; instead he leaves the audience to work out their own course within the given parameters of the play's concerns. Though Poliakoff's lean to humanism might not have been entirely favoured by Brecht, the implicit critique of capitalism might well have been.

Joe's Palace (2007)

Ten years on in *Joe's Palace* Poliakoff most strongly realises his sense that history informs the present since the uninhabited west London house in which it is set seems haunted by the past. However, far from affording frames and interruptions such that lessons from history might be pointed up, a pervading sense is conveyed of the protagonists being stuck, encumbered by the weight of history to the point of inertia. In *Joe's Palace*, Poliakoff revives the more visceral dramaturgy of his early theatre work but evokes in moving images an atmosphere of visually beautiful, though gloomy, stasis. The patterning of the piece sets in parallel the two protagonists, Elliot Graham (Michael Gambon), the multi-millionaire owner of the house, and Joe Dix (Danny Lee Wynter), the mixed-race son of one of the cleaners who takes the job of concierge. Though they come from opposite ends of the socio-economic spectrum they are *doppel-gängers* in isolation, unable to engage with the outside world, the one, Joe, in search of the family he lacks and the other, Mr Graham, in search of the dark secret of his family's wealth. Both are observers. When Joe is figured in the high-rise flat he shares with his mother, he is typically on the balcony looking down on the groups of youths on the street.[13] When employed, he is frequently framed in the sliding front-door panel or in the panels of the Georgian windows of the house looking across to Mr Graham equivalently framed in an iterative trope. Joe is invited to eat with Mr Graham improvised lunches of cold meats and cheeses Joe fetches on account from the local delicatessen. As a bond is formed between the pair, Joe is entrusted to run messages. In one humorous sequence he nonchalantly takes some valuable objects (two bejewelled animal snuff-boxes from the Prussian court and a Fabergé cigar case) to television's *Antiques Road Show* on Graham's behalf, though, unlike most participants, neither is interested in the very great commercial value of the objects, as ironically marked by Joe's 'thumbs up' to camera.

Visually, the fine house which Mr Graham retains in top condition and bedecked with fresh flowers (as in *Capturing Mary*), holds attention through Poliakoff's interest in architecture, colour and texture supported by Danny Cohen's cinematography, as the camera roams with Joe through its many rooms and up and down its central staircase. The main characters, too, are intriguing and sustain interest through strong performances. Joe is taciturn but relaxed, seemingly unfazed by his new role and comfortable not only in the house but eating lobster at a local restaurant to which Mr Graham takes him. Though he appears well-mannered and self-effacingly gentle, Elliot Graham might, it is hinted, be unpredictably menacing. On his appointment as concierge, Joe is informed by the outgoing Dave, that Mr Graham 'was in the Army . . . Special Unit. Killed people with his bare hands' (2007: 15). Since he lives across the road, Mr Graham might, it is implied, appear at any time, and, indeed, one evening when, alone in the house and tentatively making an exploration, Joe opens a door, he is confronted by the bulk of Mr Graham in the basement shadows. The very idea of Graham as a menacing killer is ultimately a MacGuffin, however, and this sequence, and the atmosphere of the house in general, might be seen in part as an *hommage* to Hitchcock.[14]

Such action as takes place in the house involves the sexual affair between Richard Reece (Rupert Penry-Jones), the youngest member of the cabinet, and Charlotte (Kelly Reilly), a former parliament lobbyist and now mother of two. Both are married but the sexual indulgence in opulent surroundings – to which Mr Graham agrees since he thinks it good to bring life to the house – initially suits them both. Over half a dozen summer visits which lend a rhythm to the middle section of *Joe's Palace*, auburn-haired Charlotte appears in a sequence of colourful print dresses and is beautifully framed against doorways and staircases, juxtaposing her elegance with that of the house. The sexual encounters, when Richard arrives, are passionate and explicitly shot with a range of full-body shots and facial reactions in close-up. Indeed, the last of a sequence of close-ups on Charlotte's face marks the moment when sadness comes to sour the affair. To Joe's displeasure, Richard subsequently brings another young woman, Patricia (Michelle MacErlean) to the house.

Though there is a given narrative logic as to why Richard and Charlotte find the use of the house convenient, and the visual presentation of the affair brings dynamism, warmth and colour to offset the gloom and stasis of Mr Graham, the repetition of the sexual encounters is perhaps a touch indulgent. Joe's increasing anticipation of the visits, evident in his thoughtful preparations, and his growing attraction to Charlotte – not so much sexually but as a surrogate mother – indicate his pleasure at filling 'his' house with a 'friend's family'. His own alternative attempt to do so – again under Mr Graham's licence – proves unsuccessful, first when Tina (Rebecca Hall), the young woman from the deli, turns down Joe's invitation and, secondly, when he picks up a young man living rough who ultimately threatens him with a knife. It is as if everything associated with Graham is destined to stasis, if not destruction. In the contrast of two secret worlds, the younger generation, represented by Richard and Charlotte, is seen as unfettered by moral inhibitions about their affair, in contrast with the paralysis through soul-searching of the older generation represented by Mr Graham. Even Charlotte, who attacks Graham as an impotent voyeur, is ultimately overcome by sadness when she visits the house alone after the affair with Richard has ended.

Poliakoff initially offers a choice of points of identification between an older generation weighed down with history and memory, and a younger generation, successfully unfettered by responsibilities, at least in Joe's idealised view of Richard and Charlotte. Ultimately, however, it is Mr Graham who is liberated, if not ennobled, by taking the much harder route of confronting reality, while Richard remains restless and Charlotte has fallen into ennui and sadness.[15] She reappears to meet Joe again at the very end of the piece to claim that, unlike the reinvigorated Graham, she is unable to move on. Since she has earlier remarked on her extreme good fortune, it is hard to feel sympathy. Beyond the weight of the house's atmosphere which did not seem initially to affect her, there is no objective correlative for her misery, particularly when set against the experience of Jewish women in Berlin as recounted in unravelling Mr Graham's mystery.

Unable to act because he is overwhelmed by a sense of guilt and distrust about the origins of his vast wealth, Graham has employed professional historians to sift his father's papers. But until Tina from the deli, an amateur historian, gets on the case, nothing dubious has come to light. Tina, however, opens a pack of papers marked 'country walks' which reveal Mr Graham's father to have been not only complicit with the Nazi regime in respect of doing business, but witness to a particular event in a Berlin park in which Jews were casually humiliated by Hitler's storm-troopers. The men were rounded up and made to crawl naked across the park while the women were made to climb into trees and tweet like birds. These scenes are graphically presented as envisaged in Mr Graham's visions, which he shares with Joe in a rowing boat on the moat of a castle given him as a present by his father when he was a boy. Shortly afterwards, he leaves Joe and walks off with a pistol in his hand.

Joe lands the boat and chases Graham, physically tackling him before he can fire the gun. An explosive noise heralds a crane shot in which Mr Graham and Joe are figured lying on the ground looking up at the rooks as they wheel above the castle battlements. This shot echoes several others in which Joe has been framed from the top of the house's stairwell, as well as of Richard and Charlotte side by side on the bed after sex. This coming together of the pair in natural surroundings at a moment of crisis under winter skies marks the bottoming of their introversion and affords the basis for a new future. The final sequence of the piece shows the pair joined by Tina having a picnic in the courtyard of the house, with Joe remarking, 'when we've finished this meal, but not before, we are going to move on' (ibid.: 108). But unlike similar remarks ending some of Poliakoff's earlier plays, the resolution of *Joe's Palace* suggest this remark is not ironic.

Joe's Palace is a distinctively Poliakovian piece in that many elements from his now recognisable palette are in the mix. The built environment predominates; the story is told from the perspective of an adolescent boy; the visual aesthetic is full of rich colour and texture; the protagonists are quirky and intriguing; the weight of totalitarian European history grounds the piece. There is a home cinema showing of old film sequences of 'phantom rides' through London traffic to which Mr Graham has had sound added, drawing upon Poliakoff's family history.[16] There is a set-piece scene (particularly resonant here through Gambon's performance with that in *Perfect Strangers*) in which Graham, attending against his better judgement a photo-shoot of the country's richest men, finds himself making a speech berating his peers and suggesting that they hold up placards saying 'Tax us! Tax us! Tax us!' (ibid.: 66). There is patterning in the narrative. For example, a scene of couples dancing in a London park for the sheer pleasure of it prefigures the degrading separation of couples in the Berlin park. In another layering, Mr Graham and Joe share a fondness for animals. Joe has a picture of a wombat on his bedroom wall and befriends a cat, while Graham has only ever been happy as a farmer. These affections resonate with the animal-shaped snuff-boxes which turn out to have been stolen from their Jewish owners to whom Graham returns them after discovering the truth about his father. There is patterning, too, in the cinematography with characters framed in doorways, windows and on staircases, as well as corridor and 'tunnel' long-shots. There is even a trademark red London bus 'wipe' at the end of the piece. There is Poliakovian usage of strong noise to mask cuts and the understated, but typically effective, soundtrack is by Adrian Johnston.

Joe's Palace emphatically deals with the idea of the past informing the present but, because Poliakoff was also interested in exploring loneliness, the major historical events involved impact very particularly, rather than illuminating broader concerns in the contemporary as they do in other works. The downside of an atmospheric piece in which there is little dynamic action – as remarked by critics of Poliakoff's early plays – is the lack of narrative drive and resolution. However, in the early atmospheric plays, Poliakoff compellingly captured the spirit of the times, as he does again in much of his later television work. But *Joe's Palace* lacks the political commentary of

Friends and Crocodiles or *Gideon's Daughter*. In art cinema, a sense of enigma might be created by intriguing characters and mesmeric atmosphere alone, as Poliakoff attempts in *Joe's Palace*, eschewing the surprising revelations of character and the crafted story-telling which motivates other pieces made at this time in his career. But in popular moving picture media – and particularly on television – audiences still require a level of plausibility which *Joe's Palace* does not fully afford. Despite its various functions, the protracted sequence of visits of Richard and Charlotte comes to feel as filler to pass time in an empty space awaiting the unlocking of Mr Graham's stasis. Ironies such as Tina from the deli proving a more thorough investigative historian than the professionals seem forced in this context, rather than aspects of an integral, if irregular, pattern. If anything, the tying up of loose ends in short sequences under Joe's voice-over at the end appears heavy-handed because some aspects of the piece seem not quite to fit.

Poliakoff takes as a minor triumph the fact that he persuaded BBC schedulers to move the evening news to accommodate the non-standard length of *Joe's Palace* when it was first transmitted on a Sunday evening in November 2007. Tensions between the demands of different moving media on a writer-director with a free spirit will be part of the considerations of the next chapter.

8 MEDIUM BOUNDARIES
FEATURE FILMS AND FILMS FOR TELEVISION

In *Soft Targets*, the Russian agent Alexei Varyov (Ian Holm) wistfully remarks: 'What I really want to be is – a naive fantasy of many men of my generation – I wish to be a film director . . . I have an eye for things, I'm like a camera lens, as one of your directors said, and it may just be coming possible.' This observation may well apply to Stephen Poliakoff himself, who refers to all his moving image work as 'film', irrespective of the medium of the work's distribution.[1] His first feature film as a screen writer, *Runners* (1983) led shortly to a move to direct his own feature, *Hidden City* (1988), followed by what might be seen as the high point to date of his cinema career, *Close My Eyes* (1991) and *Century* (1994). Thereafter, however, *Food of Love* (1997) was a relatively lightweight romantic comedy and *The Tribe* (1998), which returned Poliakoff to more familiar 'urban canyon' territory, was ultimately released in the BBC film slot, 'Screen Two', in the absence of a cinema distribution deal. A decade would pass before Poliakoff returned to feature film with *Glorious 39* (2009). In the interim he achieved his best 'cinematic' work in the medium of television. Poliakoff has explained his move away from cinema just at the time when his career in film appeared to be taking off in terms of 'the distribution situation for British films in this country which got particularly bad in the 1990s'.[2] For a prestigious theatre writer advised early in his career to 'write first for the theatre and only then try TV and movies',[3] and who had accordingly moved successfully from the theatre into television screenplays prior to his feature film debut, this halting film career trajectory might seem something of a disappointment, notwithstanding the huge success in 'films' for television. A further exploration of why things turned out this way is illuminating.

Poliakoff is by disposition an auteur. He likes to write from his own imagination and experience – albeit with an awareness both of history and of the broad social currents of the times. Once he has scripted his creative vision, he wants it to be realised as exactly as possible. As Adrian Hodges (1982) has noted, 'unusually for a writer in the [film] industry, his involvement is total throughout all stages of production'. In this respect, when he moves outside the theatre, he is destined to be at odds with the motion picture industries. Moreover, in cinema, the writer's vision scarcely figures historically in the production processes of Hollywood feature movies and is, at best, relegated to a minority interest in art-house film and, more recently to independent production houses.[4] Poliakoff's contemporary, Trevor Griffiths, who also, as Poole and Wyver (1984: 123) remark, 'fought vigorously for control over his own scripts', learned from the bitter experience of his first brush with Hollywood that the writer's vision can be distorted in a painful industrial process. Though ultimately accredited as co-author with Warren Beatty on the film *Reds* (1981), Griffiths reflected that it 'is only 35 per cent mine' (ibid.: 127). It is hard to imagine Poliakoff working in such circumstances and thus unsurprising that various approaches from Hollywood over the years have not come to fruition. In television in the 1990s, it was Poliakoff's vociferous resistance to the drift of the British industry towards fast-paced, formulaic series which ironically resulted in a decade of success under TV3 in the late 1990s (see Chapter 2).

In respect of feature film, the costs of production typically make executives wary of originality and innovation, preferring to build upon what has been successful in the past. Even in the relatively independent, low-budget sector of feature film, and to a lesser extent in films for television, the pull of genre remains significant.[5] Indeed, my argument is that even an independently minded auteur such as Poliakoff cannot entirely ignore the industrial forces in play when working in film and television. Though he may make strenuous efforts to retain total creative control, there are inevitable negotiations – compromises even – in the complex process of making a film requiring the skills of many people beyond the writer and/or director for its realisation.

Accordingly, this chapter reviews Poliakoff's film career through the lens of genre and the shifting differences between the media of film and television, if only to observe how he has both deployed and deviated from medium-, or genre-specific, forces. The key examples for discussion are: a film for television, *Soft Targets* (1982) directed by Charles Sturridge and transmitted in the BBC's celebrated 'Play for Today' slot;[6] Poliakoff's first feature film, *Runners* (1983), also directed by Sturridge;[7] and three films written and directed by Poliakoff himself, *Hidden City* (1988), *Food of Love* (1997) and *Glorious 39* (2009). Respectively they afford examples of reworkings of the Cold War Spy genre, a missing person drama, an art film, a romantic comedy and a historical drama. Poliakoff's other feature films, *Close My Eyes* and *Century*, are discussed in Chapter 5, but the examples chosen here best illustrate his engagements with generic film forms and tropes, as he made a career move from theatre and television plays into films for television and feature films.

There is ultimately considerable porosity between the boundaries of Poliakoff's theatre, television and film work. Charles Sturridge, among others, has remarked that Poliakoff's theatre writing is cinematic, and his interest in the built environment and socio-historical contexts lends itself particularly to setting character and action against a broad backdrop in a manner traditionally considered to be the province of film rather than television.[8] Well-honed dialogue with sub-textual implications moves readily from theatre work to television screenplays though typically it has a lesser place in film. Poliakoff does not draw a sharp distinction between feature film and 'film' for television: 'The most obvious thing is the size of the image. TV demands swift close-ups and a lot of emphasis. You can give far more information in cinema, especially in a two-shot for example, where you can include much more detail. But I think other differences are arguable' (Hodges 1982: 12).

Soft Targets (1982)

Soft Targets is a Cold War spy movie resonating on television with *Smiley's People* (1982) in the wake of *Tinker Tailor Soldier Spy* (BBC 1979) and *Reilly – Ace of Spies* (ITV 1983). In developing the script,

Poliakoff cannot have been unaware that he was working in the territory of an established, and topical, genre. Auteurist Dennis Potter, to whose distinctive work for television Poliakoff's *oeuvre* has been likened,[9] had also essayed spy dramas with *Traitor* (BBC 1971) and *Blade on the Feather* (BBC 1980). This may have helped draw Poliakoff into the territory and, indeed, Kenith Trodd, the legendary producer of much of Potter's work, produced *Soft Targets*. As might be anticipated from this team, *Soft Targets* is not a standard Cold War spy movie, but instead combines a spoof of such movies' conventions with a Poliakovian study of outsiders.

The structuring principle of the piece is one of bathos, namely the setting up of generic expectations, only to deflate them. Poliakoff's script, well realised by Sturridge's astute direction and ably supported by the telling soundtrack specially composed by Geoffrey Burgon, draws upon trope after trope of the Cold War spy movie while gradually revealing that agent Alexei Varyov is not an important spy at all. But the trick is that even he does not know it, and Holm plays the role superbly in a low-key, clipped, but precisely accented, 'Russian' English and with a conviction that any moment he might be grabbed by either MI5 – or indeed Russian – operatives. Early in the piece when the young Foreign Office official, Harman (Nigel Havers) intercepts Alexei at the airport, it is almost possible to believe that a world of Cold War intrigue is being entered. Having caused him to miss the bus back to his accommodation, Harman obliges Alexei to accept a lift and proceeds to drive at spy car-chase speed down the ramps of a multi-storey car park. It is then, almost ten minutes into the film, that viewers are sure this is a spoof.

Soft Targets offers a double pleasure, however, of the possibility of murky political complications for the protagonist and the enjoyment of awareness of the conventions in play. Once the cover of the spy dimension is truly blown, a complex experience remains nevertheless on offer in that there is greater awareness of the sheer fun to be had in making a spoof spy movie, but tempered by the narrative of the isolated outsider. Alexei Varyov is the obvious outsider and his viewpoint is used to throw British mores into relief, particularly at a society wedding in the Sussex countryside to which he drives friends of

Harman, Frances (Celia Gregory) and Celia (Helen Mirren). Amid the forced dancing and background arguments typical of weddings, the bride's mother expresses the hope that Alexei will find something he can eat from the buffet. One boorish Brit asks if he does anything 'under cover' while another suggests he might send a postcard when 'they're about to start dropping the big one'. It is the common myth that because Alexei is a Russian he must be a spy – or at least ideology must control everything he does – that the film aims to explore and explode. As Alexei departs across the grounds, a group of drunken, overgrown public schoolboys gathers below an upstairs window to heckle the bride and sing lewd rugby songs. All this is seen from the perspective of Alexei's outsider position, reinforced by his framing of moments through the lens of his stills camera, an action which in itself ironically sustains the possibility that he might actually be spying.

The complex patterning which is a marker of Poliakoff's maturing work creates in *Soft Targets* another outsider to parallel Alexei, and even to outstrip him in respect of angst in isolation. Indeed, this is where the Poliakovian vision subverts the Cold War spy movie beyond the mere spoof of its generic tropes. Alexei first meets Celia at a party in London and a loose friendship begins to develop, but she is evasive. Alexei seeks her out by following Harman's car which drops her off at a London hotel, only to find that nothing mysterious is going on. She simply works there as a waitress. Finding themselves driving aimlessly around London, Alexei offers to show Celia the Russian Embassy hostel where he lives. Seemingly lonely and unsure of herself, Celia asks if she can stay the night. Two days later, she fails to turn up in the cafe where she proposed to meet Alexei and it transpires that she is in hospital, having attempted suicide. After visiting, Alexei leaves the hospital with Celia's mother (Margery Mason), his remark under a sad piano refrain accompanied by sombre strings bringing out the parallel between him and Celia: 'I suppose we've both been kinds of exiles – me and your daughter. To be alien and a stranger in a foreign city is bad, but to be a stranger in your own city must be very frightening.' Celia, it seems, has been in a claustrophobic relationship with Frances, a woman of the chattering classes, when Celia herself is of humble origins. Just as much as Alexei, she is an outsider looking in on British upper-middle-class society, which she now seeks to escape.

The parallel between Alexei and Celia is further extended through a depiction from their points of view of behaviour which is by turns raucous and depressive in both the Russian and British contexts. The bleakness of Alexei's hostel is interrupted by the effusive behaviour of some of his colleagues who raid his room in his absence to borrow video-tapes of the football. Frances appears equally as manic on losing control when a number of guests cancel invitations to a dinner party. Many images are repeated as part of the visual patterning of the piece. Celia's locker at the hotel holds no mysteries just as Alexei's post box at the Russian embassy is always empty. The sparse corridors of the hospital at the end of the piece echo those at the airport in the beginning. Throughout the lighting levels are low, and shadowy faces are repeatedly framed through gridded windows. Several car and bus journeys afford opportunities to explore a range of London locations, again – as in the precincts of *Hitting Town* – largely unpeopled.

It is in the exploration of urban London locations, and in particular the visit to the Sussex estate, that *Soft Targets* moves beyond the studio constraints of cheaper television products of the time towards a more cinematic scope and imagery which is extended in Poliakoff's subsequent work.[10] Nevertheless, utilising the shot-range said to typify the intimate screen of the television medium, *Soft Targets* is dominated by close-ups and mid-shots and the scale of its drama is ultimately intimate in comparison with the international and exotic locations of, say, a James Bond movie.[11] The potential for Poliakoff's screenplays to be 'cinematic' is evident but the piece is limited as a film by the constraints of the 'Play for Today' slot in its period. It is a significant achievement, however, to have both used and subverted the conventions of a major genre, putting an individual stamp on it by foregrounding the alienation of outsiders, some of whom might happen to be spies.

Runners (1983)

Runners takes up the theme of outsiders within their own country when Tom Lindsay (James Fox) is dislocated from his English Midlands roots and drawn into 1980s London to search for his missing daughter. Though there is an element of mystery to drive the narrative – Rachel, aged eleven, has simply abandoned her bike and 'done a runner' without contacting her parents at all – the film's focus is less on the motives and experience of the 'runners' (young people who unaccountably leave home) than on the experience of parents under such circumstances. The context, however, is a dysfunctional Britain under the Tories: 'TEBBIT', for example, is scrawled in big letters among the graffiti on a hostel wall.[12] Litter, in the form of plastic bags blowing in the wind, characterises the environment from the film's opening shots to its last. Uncollected black bags of rubbish accumulate in piles on London street corners, and rail strikes prevent even the prostitutes on Victoria Station from working. Furthermore, bombs might be placed almost anywhere in urban environments by activists in the 'struggles' over Northern Ireland. It is evidently a moment of socio-cultural unrest and change. Jobs are hard to come by for new entrants to the labour market, and those of people like Tom Lindsay, in apparently secure employment, are under threat. At the end of the film, when Tom ultimately finds his daughter after two years, she appears to have imbibed not illicit drugs but a work ethic, sustaining herself by handing out leaflets for a car-hire company. Thus a need to work and a fear that work might not be available is a possible explanation, in the absence of any other, why Rachel has left an apparently stable family home at such a tender age.

The lack of explanation of Rachel's motives is less acceptable in a film which adheres considerably to narrative realism, indeed quite closely to social realism, than in the more expressionistic *Bloody Kids* or *Hidden City*. The loose plotting in these films mobilises an exploration of environment contributing to the very feel of dislocation and arbitrariness. In *Runners*, in contrast, the more realistic treatment borders on psychological horror, but Poliakoff subverts this tendency when resolution is formally achieved by a tentative reconciliation between daughter and father on Victoria Station. Having been kidnapped by her father and locked up in his hotel room, Rachel has sedulously refused to come home. But when she witnesses her father's breakdown into tears on phoning his wife, she softens and – in a rare moment of sentimentality in Poliakoff's work – she is partially reconciled to him. Framed by separate 'cages' as the phone call is being made, they drift together from different angles to meet in front of a fast-food outlet which has just opened in the early morning.

The body of the film is concerned, however, with the experience of parents and here the realist approach affords the gnawing anxieties to be portrayed with conviction. Indeed, as producer Barry Hanson remarked, *Runners* 'gets very near to the nervous system, that special feeling of horror ... that people feel about possible assault and murder of kids'.[13] Uncharacteristically James Fox plays a northern lower-middle-class father with some credibility and an acceptable, if imprecise, accent.[14] It is he, rather than Rachel's mother, who manifests a Poliakovian obsession with solving the mystery of his daughter's disappearance. He scours the house for clues, and nervously awaits the ring of the phone by night and day. When, after two years, his wife has come to accept what she sees as the inevitable, Tom travels to London on the advice of a well-meaning but disorganised support group who, as Helen (Jane Asher), a mother in a similar situation to Tom, observes, has at least 'shown an interest' in their predicament. Helen ultimately joins Tom at the Victoria Station hotel to search for her missing twelve-year-old son, Andrew. The pairing is bonded by their common experience and cause and, although Helen announces over dinner that she is not going to sleep with Tom, the possibility of a romance is opened up.

Panoramic views of London emphasise the scale of the location to be searched by Tom and Helen and its density is affirmed by overviews of the Victoria Station concourse, bustling with commuters. Details of brutalist architecture are contrasted with faded Victorian grandeur, conveying a sense of a temporal shift to less confident and comfortable spaces. Imagery of tunnels and long corridors, much favoured by Poliakoff, serve here to suggest a labyrinthine environment in which it is difficult to discern things and from which it is almost impossible to find a way out. Such corridors are figured in Rachel's school, in the hotel, in a hostel dormitory, on the underground railway escalators, on a train, and in the serried ranks of lockers to which Helen and Tom are lured by a hoax phone caller. The soundscape, composed and conducted by George Fenton, affords a mix of strident staccato strings to convey suspense, plaintive brass to carry deep emotion, and the refrain of a single acoustic guitar which, while typically nagging and quizzical, can be augmented by a beat to create a sense of urgency. In this, his first feature film, Poliakoff begins to benefit from the advantage film has over theatre and television, in affording opportunity visually and sonically to construct an environment which goes beyond the mere space in which the characters and action are set to become an integral part of the vision of the work.

Two key 'theatrical' scenes, however, assist in locating agency in structure to convey the depths of despair to which parents plummet in the circumstances of a completely unexplained absence of their children. From the hotel window, Helen thinks she spots Andrew on the station concourse. With Tom not even fully dressed, the couple set off in pursuit, ignoring closed barriers and aghast station officials to board the train on which 'Andrew' has embarked. Unmindful of the figures they cut as they run from carriage to carriage in their search, barging over the ticket collector in the process, they finally catch up with the boy, who is not Andrew at all. Momentarily abandoning realist logic for a theatrical – indeed, almost melodramatic – moment, the film has Helen fall on her knees in her despair to hug the unsuspecting youth. In her performance, however, Jane Asher manages genuinely to convey the power of conflicting emotions. Her tears of anguish and frustration here are echoed by Tom's when he phones his wife at the end of the film to report that, although he has found Rachel, he cannot persuade her to return home. However, the conflicted nature of his feelings has already been revealed in the sequence in the hotel bedroom where he is holding Rachel against her will.

Rachel is sitting on the floor in the corner of the bathroom as far away as possible from her father, but face to face with him as he is reclined on the bed. In a controlled voice he says: 'All the time I was looking for you, I thought it would be like a police series on tele – finding you being held by a mad axe-man or something. I wish it was true.' Attention is drawn here to the fresh and realistic vision of *Runners* in comparison with the more sensationalist accounts of formulaic television police drama. Having inadvertently dozed off, Tom jumps up later that night fearing Rachel may have escaped again. Now looking menacing from a low-angle shot from Rachel's point of view, he demands that she talk to him. Rachel moves away from him as he says: 'You may well look like that. At this moment I could easily kill you. That would be a story, wouldn't it? A man searches for his daughter for two years, prepared to forgive her anything – drug addiction, becoming a prostitute – and when he finds her, she makes him so angry . . . he kills her.' Though this scene, which continues for some time in a virtual monologue, is effective in conveying the conflicted nature of Tom's feelings, Poliakoff has fallen back on a theatrical strategy to achieve it. In telling his daughter of the impact her disappearance has had on his life, Tom articulates unnecessarily what the audience has already understood:

You don't know what worry means do you? You have no conception, have you? My whole life's been torn apart because of you. I've probably lost my job because of you. I met a woman I would never have met who's had an effect on me, and on your mother. I dedicated my whole life to finding you, to rescuing you from whatever it was.

But as much as he is trying to get Rachel to understand the anguish she has caused the family he is forced also to come to terms with the misplaced nature of his concern, as she might see it. Rachel is unharmed and surviving adequately in London with no need or wish to return home. The Poliakovian twist on a realist investigation of street kids in *Runners* would appear to be that they are simply dealing with new socio-cultural circumstances which their parents have not yet caught up with. The point is perhaps laboured at the end of the film when, after the partial reconciliation with Rachel, her father tells her: 'Well. At least I saw the city the way you see it a bit. It's falling to bits. But you survived it.' The final word, however, is Rachel's. To attract her dad's attention from the distance she has walked away, she shouts 'Hey!', adopting the refrain Helen has taught Tom to use to make kids in the street turn round so their faces might be seen. The tables are turned. The mystery of Rachel's disappearance has not been resolved but her alternative point of view has been accommodated.

Hidden City (1988)

Though the narrative of *Hidden City*, Poliakoff's first feature as a writer-director, is also driven by a significant element of mystery, it is more a pretext for exploration of the subterranean depths of the city of London and its urban inhabitants than an enigma in search of a resolution. Like the earlier 'cinematic' television piece *Bloody Kids*, *Hidden City* follows, in picaresque mode, the meanderings through London of its '*flâneur*' protagonists, seeking to capture the feel of the times with an expressionistic treatment. Besides exploring London life, the film also features several other Poliakovian preoccupations, namely past secrets preserved on celluloid, obsessive behaviour, a disposition in young people to break free from orthodoxy, and an interest in the social impact of new media technologies. There are also passing jibes at elements of entropy in 1980s British culture, from the failure to fix a leak in a school building to a lack of energy and enterprise in business.

Under a liquid electronic soundtrack (composed by Michael Storey) the titles sequence leads the eye close above the River Thames and adjacent waterways in a sparse industrial landscape. The imagery is evocative in being almost black and white as buildings are silhouetted against the sky and the roving camera moves under bridges and through tunnels. The narrative proper, announced by an urgent, synthesised beat, opens with a mildly disturbing, wide-angle shot of serried ranks of schoolchildren, each child glued to a television monitor in what appears to be a cinema-size laboratory. Briefly evoking a world redolent of *Nineteen Eighty-Four*, the sequence turns out to be an experiment by protagonist James Richards (Charles

Dance), an educational statistician seeking to test a hypothesis. On the basis, revealed later in the film, that, in the age of television, children can no longer retain information from the printed page, Richards is exploring the potential of the moving image as a learning medium. Tellingly in the overall context of *Hidden City*, the film supplier has once again sent the wrong film, incurring the wrath of Richards and leading to the sacking of the second protagonist, Sharon Newton (Cassie Stuart). In the first of the film's uncanny coincidences, Sharon is seen stalking Richards until she jumps out on him as he is on his way to work, tearing his jacket sleeve.

In one of many jobs, in spite of her youth, held by Sharon, she has briefly been a film librarian. In viewing some old Government Information film footage, she has spotted an incident of apparent abduction but is unable to follow up a clue to an explanatory sequel because the second film concerned is classified by the Home Office and stored by the Ministry of Defence. Sharon wants Richards, whom she has never met before, to use his influence to help her track down and secure it. Though apparently wealthy and famous for a piece of research on children's knowledge of sex, Richards is notoriously unproductive, having written just one book and with a childless marriage on the point of disintegration. He does have cultural capital and connections, but he is drawn to Sharon's cause against his scientific-rational disposition as a man who interprets the world through numbers. He remarks to others that she is certifiable but is inexplicably drawn to follow her bidding. The pursuit of the elusive film across London through several stages of intrigue affords Poliakoff the opportunity expressionistically to explore the urban environment.

That Poliakoff aspired to art film is indicated by his engagement of Witold Stok, a cinematographer previously associated with the eminent Polish director, Krzysztof Kieslowski, in what turned out to be the first of three collaborations.[15] Commentators have noted also distinct resonances between *Hidden City* and Antonioni's first English-language film *Blowup* (1966) which won the Cannes Grand Prix in 1967 and became influential on subsequent cinema. As Mike Sutton has remarked, an influence on *Hidden City* is evident 'not only in its conspiracy plot but also in its portrayal of London as almost a foreign country'.[16] Bosley Crowther of the *New York Times* wrote of *Blowup* that it is:

> a fascinating picture, which has something real to say about the matter of personal involvement and emotional commitment in a jazzed-up, media-hooked-in world so cluttered with synthetic stimulations that natural feelings are overwhelmed . . . a stunning picture – beautifully built up with glowing images and color compositions that get us into the feelings of our man and into the characteristics of the mod world in which he dwells.[17]

These words might also be applied to *Hidden City*, at least in so far as the hunt for lost film footage to make sense of an enigma – similar to the search for the mysterious body in the grass in the stills taken by fashion photographer Thomas (David Hemmings) in *Blowup* – is primarily a means to explore the mood of a culture and environment at a specific historical moment.

The cinematic explorations of 1980s London in *Hidden City* take us not through the familiar surface landmarks (though we see a number of iconic Routemaster buses) but into the dark underbelly of the city, visually articulating the repressed unconscious of an instrumental culture also manifest in Richards's dreams of his schooldays. Unlike Antonioni's pastel colours to reflect 1960s London in *Blowup*, *Hidden City*, in keeping with Richards's observation that in the 1980s 'it's the blandest city in the world', the predominant tones are soft greys and browns. Visual interest is sustained, however, by the unusual locations and angles. The camera travels progressively with James and Sharon through parts of London not often seen on feature film. Spectators are taken into run-down, back-street cafes opposite nondescript doorways through which Masons disappear clutching their distinctive but mysterious cases. We are led into the seemingly endless labyrinth of underground tunnels beneath Holborn and a chasm running under Oxford Street used for storage of the relics of forgotten histories.[18] We visit the vast wasteland of an open refuse tip (an environment similar to that evocatively used by Antonioni in *The Red Desert*, 1964), and on to the incineration plant in the Edmonton suburb where Richards climbs into a vast skip of refuse to retrieve a film can which turns out not to contain 'The Hedgerows of England', the sought-for film.

In conversation they walk across Hampstead Heath, their search having apparently reached a dead end, and Sharon questions the value of Richards's research and points to its redundancy when she notes he has drawn the conclusions before the research has finished. It is at this point in the film that the anomie of London in the 1980s is more overtly associated with Richards's personal lack of direction. In a reflective flashback, his schoolmaster, Mr Jackson, chides him for not achieving his potential, a charge which his adult life appears to have borne out. In another of the film's uncanny coincidences in defiance of statistical predictions, Richards literally bumps into his former schoolmaster the next day in London, only to hear his only published book being criticised for not making the most of the data. Sharon, meanwhile, though she suspects she is being followed, chases up a new lead at another film repository.

Richards is once again lured into unfamiliar territory by her phone call announcing that she's found the lost footage. This time the assignation is a Halloween party at the film distribution company where Sharon once worked. Perhaps predictably in a basement, the party's heady atmosphere of loud music, projected film and intertwined couples is to be relatively short-lived in comparison with 1960s parties in that, more typical of the 1980s, Bruce, the company boss, ends his parties promptly at 1 a.m., 'worried about the loss of valuable working time'. Sharon, whose image is once again completely transformed, is disappointed that the video download of her footage is very dark and the image unclear, but it points to another sequel, 'Hop Pickers in Kent'.

Bruce admits to Richards that he seems unable to watch a film right through because endings depress him with their sense of completeness, and that he even wishes he could fast-forward the news. He claims, however, to have developed a technique for recording his dreams as he sleeps and, when Richards shows an interest, he gives him a tape of one of his own dreams – another intervention of the uncanny into *Hidden City*. The dream sequence vivifies a fantasy much explored in Poliakoff's work that photographs and moving image technology might make available to us forgotten, or repressed, pasts which might inform the present, if not, in some instances, therapeutically redress its injuries.

In *Hidden City*'s present, however, the consequences of retrieving old footage appear to be at once actual and surreal. Sharon's flat has been turned over and Richards is attacked in the street by two mysterious men while a third takes his car. When he returns home, his flat has also been turned upside down, though it seems the searchers are not after the film footage but the medical records Richards casually removed from the London refuse tip. Ultimately, however, the outcome of the mystery, as indicated at the outset, is of secondary importance to *Hidden City*'s cinematic evocation of a time and place. The mix of soundtrack, visual imagery and screenplay marks an impressive film feature debut in which Poliakoff inscribes his distinctive signature of thematic concerns and outsider viewpoints.

Food of Love (1997)

Though *Food of Love* evidences some characteristics of Poliakoff's work, this feature film does not mark his finest hour. Indeed Demetrios Matheou's review suggests that the plot moves forward, 'as if drawn by a magic marker'.[19] It shows little of the tight structuring and complex patterning of the 'cinematic' television work which began shortly after this film, and thus it invites only brief analysis. Opening in a Poliakovian London building-site landscape, the plot concerns Alex (Richard E. Grant), a City banker who is so disaffected by the mindless pursuit of money that he runs a drama group with inner-city kids in his spare time. Somewhat stage-struck, it occurs to him that, by way of escape, he might host a reunion of the student group with whom he performed Shakespeare's *Twelfth Night*, directing the play again and taking the role of Orsino. This is the prime mover for a Poliakovian summer party, a gathering in a twee English village of a group of people who have not seen each other for years, and some of whom are former lovers. In the mix is also a selection of inner-city youths from Alex's drama group, notably Jessica (Holly Davidson) and Alice (Tameka Empson – a rare black performer in Poliakoff).

After various disasters, including a death and the loss of a key actor through gallstones, the troupe eventually confronts an audience of hostile, elderly locals who have only come because of rumours of exposed flesh. This audience talks noisily, unlike the attentive and highly appreciative audience at their preview in a local prison, until Alex berates them in a magisterial manner. He echoes Poliakoff, perhaps, in suggesting that, if they would only listen as the prisoners did, they might benefit. Alex has already managed one educational achievement in tutoring Jessica to abandon her estuary vowels and speak the verse intelligently. But besides pedagogy, the value proselytised is love, as the film's title (a line, of course, from *Twelfth Night*) suggests. Alex and Michèle make love, as do Sam (Joe McGann) and Madeleine (Juliet Aubrey), reviving their former passion. Untypically in Poliakoff, however, the characters are little more than stereotypes, giving a quality cast little to work with. Richard E. Grant dominates the film, animating Alex's obsessive drive to fulfil his ambition. When he just about does so, Jessica tells him he should become a drama teacher. Though it is an attempt at romantic comedy, there is little of the pastoral or, indeed, the humour, of which there are many instances in other Poliakoff work.

Glorious 39 (2009)

Glorious 39, in contrast, marks the culmination of a highly acclaimed and prolific period of exclusively moving image work since 1999, with Poliakoff's return to 'features'. In this more proscribed industrial context, it is not surprising that the film is more evidently generic than Poliakoff's pieces for television. Despite his view that there was 'no point making something that was like something else' (2009: viii), he takes on in *Glorious 39* the challenge of crafting a 'suspenseful thriller' (ibid.: vii) while aiming also to retain something of his distinctive vision, again revisiting history through a family story.

Glorious 39 investigates the context of appeasement in 1939, a moment when the English establishment sought to make an accommodation with Hitler to avoid involvement in a war it felt it could not win, and the loss of which might undermine its dominance of the socio-political hierarchy. Indeed, the terms in which patriarch Alexander Keyes (Bill Nighy) explains the perceived need for appeasement to his adopted daughter, Anne (Romola Garai), in *Glorious 39* betray the fact that fractional class interests masqueraded as universal human interests. He tells her: 'everything we believe in, everything *I* believe in, democracy, culture, art – (*He smiles.*) all those sorts of things, civilisation itself in fact, my dear, will be destroyed if we get involved in this ruinous war . . . Everything we value most will have gone' (ibid.: 115).

Although it is specifically a person of Romany origins who finds herself excluded from the rhetorical 'we' of this assertion, Poliakoff's typical concern in his work with the plight of Jews is evident in the hinterland of the implications of the moment of – and motives for – appeasement. Thus a suspense-thriller is moulded to embrace an alternative view of the English ruling class, exposing its duplicities and self-interests, and using the murder mystery dimension vividly to illustrate the lengths to which supposedly 'civilised' and 'cultured' people will go.

Glorious 39 shares key features with Poliakoff's most 'cinematic' television work. The narrative is patterned and layered, with colour and repeated image forms used to link and contrast parallel environments and events. This feature extends to the use of landscape with beautifully lit skies, both in mid-afternoon and evening, shot in wide angle across open, flat, Norfolk terrain to bring out the carefree, leisured lifestyle that the upper class enjoys. A range of Poliakovian parties and picnics are located in the Keyeses' country estate under the gloriously hot summer of 1939 from which the film takes its multiply accented title.[20] In an early sequence, Anne, an actress with excellent organisational skills, has organised a family party to celebrate her father's birthday. Set in the garden of the fine house – complete with a ruined abbey in which the Keyes siblings, Anne, Ralph (Eddie Redmayne) and Celia (Juno Temple) are featured running freely – a party of family and friends is assembled for the celebratory dinner in full evening dress, a symbol of one mode of 'civilisation'. It is on this occasion that Alexander's apparently genteel patriarchy is established, where the mysterious Mr Balcombe (Jeremy Northam) is encountered, and when Hector (David Tennant) is fatally outspoken. These sunny landscape and party sequences contrast with dark and desolate environments when the warring factions, both international and familial, take hold. Two sequences, the first disturbing and the second increasingly distressing, will serve to illustrate the gathering murkiness.

It is at a family picnic that, for Anne particularly, disturbing things happen. Again, it is a beautiful day, the green of the grass contrasting with the golden corn and sun. Having worn red at the beginning of the film, Anne looks striking in a bright yellow dress and, in memory flashbacks, she recalls fleeting moments of passion stolen with her lover Lawrence (Charlie Cox) before his work with the Foreign Office has taken him abroad. The idyll is punctured when Anne, who has volunteered to stay with baby cousin Oliver while learning her lines, awakes from her daydreams to discover him gone. In seeking Oliver, Anne encounters first his older brother, Walter, lurking suspiciously, and then an isolated baby shoe. The alarm having been raised, the picnic party returns hurriedly and it is Balcombe who leads Anne back down a path she has already investigated to discover Oliver safe in his pram. Though the panic is over, Anne feels for the first time an outsider from the family, as if they are constructing her as an irresponsible 'actress', the term being used on a number of occasions to indicate at least a disposition to emotional excess. Back at the family's London house, the sense of estrangement is reinforced when Ralph pointedly offers to find out Anne's true parentage.

The narrative rhythm of *Glorious 39* is punctuated by three suspected murders and a series of escape attempts by Anne from death threats. First, Hector, a young MP committed to replacing Prime Minister Chamberlain with Churchill, is found dead, having aired his views too publicly. Secondly, Anne's fellow-actor, Gilbert (Hugh Bonneville) who has assisted her understanding of some mysterious 78 sound recordings, is found dead at the film studio, the murder again having been arranged to appear a suicide. Thirdly, Anne's lover,

Lawrence, is found by her amid slaughtered animal carcases hung in an outbuilding, his throat having been cut. All the deaths touch Anne deeply and contribute to her increasing sense of isolation as all those she loves and trusts appear to be meeting gruesome ends.

Suspense is thus steadily cranked up through major narrative incidents such as the picnic and mysterious deaths, and by 'everyday normality veering into the sinister in the manner of *Thirty-Nine Steps*', as Jonathan Romney puts it.[21] Anne's increasing isolation is compounded by her growing awareness that all is not as it seems. Finding a moment apart again to play the suspect 78 recording, Anne discovers her brother's complicity in 'Thin Men Dancing', a conspiracy to destroy opposition to the policy of appeasement, the name of which is an ironic distortion of the children's game Anne devised with her siblings called 'Fat Men Dancing' (ibid.: 12). Shocked and appalled, she is now put in a position of performing surface normality while she plans her escape, since, despite the announcement of war, her Aunt Elizabeth (Julie Christie) remains apparently preoccupied with social events and taking tea.[22] Indeed, Anne's escape attempts augment the murders informing the narrative rhythm of *Glorious 39* and lead to the second, harrowing and dislocating sequence.

Arrested by the army for lack of ID when driving out of Norfolk, Anne appears to be rescued by her close family and taken to a party at the Foreign Office. But, by this two-thirds point in the film, the game of cat and mouse is fully engaged. Looking conspicuously stunning in that Poliakovian red dress, Anne is drawn from a gala event into the 'downstairs' (ibid.: 89) party for embassy children. In a labyrinthine basement, a party game is suffused with the whiff of nationalism as Ralph sings British traditional songs before revealing to his adopted sister her true identity, 'your parents were gypsies' (ibid.: 95). Now genuinely fearing Ralph, Anne tries for a second time to escape, again encountering Walter lurking in the labyrinth, and mysteriously (but truthfully as it turns out) mouthing 'they don't love you' (ibid.: 96).

A third escape attempt is urgently required following the most viscerally horrific sequence at the vets in the suburban fringes of London to which Anne, on instruction, has taken the family cats to be put down. The chaos of the external environment – with bonfires of carcases and children roaming wild – contrasts powerfully with the summer light, and the greens and gold of earlier landscapes. The experience at the vet's, presented from Anne's point of view, is at first mildly disturbing but moves swiftly to become overtly dislocating, the large figure of the vet (Richard Cordery) shot from low angles seeming particularly threatening in his unctuous reassurances. The unheralded arrival of Alexander to collect Anne cues the final family confrontation, but drugs in the flask proffered to Anne by her father prevent her from hearing any answer to her question about his involvement in 'Thin Men Dancing'.

The final escape from enforced incarceration by her family comes readily when her mother, Maud (Jenny Agutter) – who, until now, has done nothing but garden – unlocks the door. But not before a direct confrontation with her father and siblings after which Ralph threatens simply to facilitate her demise by depriving her of water. In between these moments a sequence of high-angle shots depicting Anne as a vulnerable figure in isolation is interspersed with close-ups of Anne's haunted, red-eyed face under a soundtrack mixing the typically affective Adrian Johnston soundtrack with air-raid sirens and the bells of St Paul's. Passing Walter – now offering to hail a taxi – Anne finally gets away, as her family plays games with children in the park.

The body of *Glorious 39* is framed by a device in which, at the outset of the film, seventeen-year-old Michael, the grandson of Celia, seeks out his now ancient cousins Walter (Christopher Lee) and Oliver (Corin Redgrave), in their old-fashioned residence near St Paul's. At the end of the film, the framing device returns us to a present in which Michael draws his cousins outside to meet an old lady in a wheelchair. They at first mistake the figure for Aunt Elizabeth and fear she is bearing down in revenge on them for finally revealing the family's dark past to Michael. But the figure in the chair is, in fact, an elderly Anne Keyes, who has survived against all expectation. The final twist, then, is that Michael, our guide as it were into the family history, knew the story all along but just 'wanted to hear it from [their, Walter and Oliver's] own lips' (ibid.: 126).

Apart from being a bit confusing to some viewers in that the relationships between these characters is not entirely clear,[23] the framing device, rather than inviting 'complex seeing', reinforces the sentimentality of Anne's escape in the first place. It is not fully plausible that the ruthless defenders of appeasement and the status quo would have allowed Anne to get away. But, once again, Poliakoff sacrifices plausibility to mobilise a more metaphorical discourse. Consonant with his increasing disposition to humanism as evident in the post-1999 television pieces, he ends *Glorious 39* with the triumph of hope over experience. Walter and Oliver are trapped in a time-warp indicated particularly by their collection of old radios. It takes Michael's intervention to offer a way out of stasis. Those who resist in Poliakoff's work, however mildly and however much against insuperable odds, tend to survive.

In spite of shouldering the weight of Jewish history and being fully aware of the might of destructive forces in supposedly civilised, let alone totalitarian, cultures, Poliakoff ultimately commits to the durability of the human spirit and celebrates the achievement of those individuals who find the courage and strength to stand against corruption and evil for what they perceive to be right. The point is made explicitly in *Glorious 39* when Ralph tells Anne: 'Don't you realise we want people to feel defeated?! To feel there's no hope?! That way we can do our deal with the Germans' (ibid.: 110). Anne's response is unequivocal despite the risks: 'You think you can scare me into silence, you fucking bastards . . . I am not afraid of you' (ibid.: 118).

Sentimental ending or not, *Glorious 39* invites us to see Anne Keyes as one such resistant individual, but it also, and much more clear-sightedly, suggests that the veneer of a particular kind of civilised culture might well mask a disposition to violence in defence of fractional class interests. Seen this way, Poliakoff has successfully moulded his long-standing concerns with the need to be watchful and attuned to the complexity of things to an established generic form.

Glorious 39 bears the hallmarks of Poliakoff's mature screen work, featuring a stellar collection of British actors. Bill Nighy is effectively cast against 'nice guy' type, and Romola Garai has been praised for being 'believable in every aspect of the character's journey from unsuspecting innocent to horrified, unhinged victim'.[24] Tropes which are now familiar Poliakovian signatures – underground corridors, shots up staircases, sumptuous interiors, outdoor summer parties, picnics, red dresses, garden flowers (Maud's in this instance), children living wild – all feature in *Glorious 39*. In particular savvy cats are an iterated figure, Michael (Toby Regbo) being observed by a cat as he wanders through the streets by St Paul's echoing Joe's encounter in *Joe's Palace* (Poliakoff 2007: 84). Some critics were not fully convinced by *Glorious 39* but, acknowledging the mix of history and the thriller genre, a Cambridge historian adjudged that the work 'filled a gap in the way that the culture has handled these questions'.[25]

9 THE 'POLIAKOVIAN' REVIEWED

The stated aim of this book is to review the works of Stephen Poliakoff and to afford a critical framework for the evaluation of his *oeuvre* over a forty-year career. This has not been an easy matter, precisely because he has ranged across the media of theatre, film and television, the audiences for which are not co-terminous, and the criteria for the evaluation of which vary within the media, let alone between them. There are some things about which we might be clear: Poliakoff is patently not a postmodern, intermedial deviser of contemporary theatre; he is not a Hollywood blockbuster movie maker; and he is not a team writer for mainstream television. Though it might be productive to ask why not (and this book has offered a contextual and biographical account of Poliakoff's disposition), an interrogation of his motives is ultimately a matter for the psychoanalyst, not a critical reviewer.

It has been observed that Poliakoff's work seems to polarise audience members into those who absolutely love it and those who hate it.[1] There is, of course, an element of taste formation in such a division. If segments of the audience prefer action-adventure, or are comforted by linear dramatic narrative with stereotypical characters and a clear beginning, middle and end, they are unlikely to favour Poliakoff. Those, in contrast, who like the challenge of oblique storytelling with complex characters who may turn out to be quite other than they first seem, and those who are lured by the texture of colour, sound and pattern, wanting to be drawn into a sustained dramatic exploration, will be more appreciative, particularly of the film and later television work. In Pierre Bourdieu's seminal account (1992: 11–18), taste formation is significantly a matter of class, a disposition to realism being attributed to the working class and an 'aesthetic disposition' to the middle class. While subsequent studies, embracing social mobility and education, see the matter as more complex, it

214

might be acknowledged that Poliakoff's work is more likely to appeal to an elite fragment (as Bourdieu might put it) of the overall potential audience. Poliakoff's early aspiration to prestigious 'establishment' venues (NT and RSC) as outlets for his plays linked him early with predominantly middle-class audiences. But he has always wanted his work to be seen by as many people as possible – indeed he now requires that television repeats are written into the contracts for his work in that medium – and always believed in the potential of the strong stories at the core of his work to reach out. Indeed, the achievement of viewing figures in excess of eight million for *The Lost Prince* on television suggests the potential of a broader audience appeal and Poliakoff is most pleased by audience research which suggests that viewers stay with his work when they discover it.

To break down a crude binary division of love/hate, a range of more particular critiques might helpfully be summarised. To begin with some negative perspectives, Poliakoff was challenged, particularly in the early days, with a lack of political engagement. From the point of view of avowed Marxists in the early 1970s, Poliakoff's plays were seen to lack a framework for political analysis in comparison with those of Brenton, Bond or Griffiths. Poliakoff's critique of popular culture is ambivalent in that it is not always clear whether he attributes social failings to the individual youths or to the harsh environment which the economic and social structures afford them. His 'expressive realism' leads him sometimes to overlook plausibility of both character and plot. In contrast in respect of 'complex seeing' his early dramaturgy may convey a visceral sense of the worlds he constructs, but does not consistently afford a critical distance on those experiences.

Another feature needing acknowledgement is Poliakoff's exclusivity, resulting from a strong emphasis upon white male European experience. This critique is particularly telling in respect of his assumed role as chronicler of London. Despite his wide-ranging coverage of the built environment, there is little sense of multicultural London in Poliakoff's work, and very few people of colour. Where they appear, with the exception of Joe (in *Joe's Palace* and *Capturing Mary*), they are typically in very minor, non-speaking roles (Waveney in *Coming in to Land* perhaps being the exception that proves the rule). Even Joe has been criticised for being culturally 'white' and, given the general absence of black youth from environments such as south London in *The Tribe*, multiculturalism and black urban youth may have to be acknowledged as a blind-spot. The intense focus on core characters and the foreground of the built environment tends on occasion to isolate individuals in non-places rather than intermingling them with the broader society. To some extent this might be accounted for by limited budgets in the early plays. In *Hitting Town*, for example, the precinct is perhaps empty because additional actors are expensive, but the absence of presence is felt also in the television adaptation, where the budget was larger. Even where there is a social hinterland, focus on the individual leaves an impression of a disconnect from broader society.

In respect of women, Poliakoff's apparent penchant for beautiful young females has been acknowledged, but the dominant feature – particularly in the later film and television work – of images of naked or scantily clad women (and on occasion, men) invites address of the question of the integrity of sex and nude scenes to the drama. Poliakoff is on record in admiring *West Wing* among American 'quality TV' series for avoiding sex after Episode One.[2] He takes a particular satisfaction himself in grabbing and holding an audience without resorting to the over-worn tropes of sex, or even romance, as we have seen in respect, for example, of *Shooting the Past*. In the context of *Perfect Strangers*, the overt sexual relationship between Rebecca and Daniel is justified as a modern counterpart to the former physical passion of Daniel's grandfather and Henrietta. But the repeated presentation of the sexual exploits of Richard (Rupert Penry-Jones) and Charlotte (Kelly Reilly) in *Joe's Palace* may not be strictly necessary, though it has its dramatic functions as discussed. While in *Friends and Crocodiles* the overall hedonist atmosphere and readiness for distraction of Paul needs to be established, the camera roves perhaps a little too frequently over the bare torsos of the women in Paul's bed or as they take the sun in the garden. For the record, it should be noted here that Poliakoff's interest in non-normative sexual relations does not extend to the inclusion of today's lesbian, gay, bisexual and transgendered communities. By way of balance, however, it should be acknowledged that Poliakoff has created a wide range of unorthodox characters, including a number of complex and compelling female roles, both young and more mature.

Poliakoff's narrative forms may extend a predominantly masculine dramatic tradition. Even where, in *Coming in to Land*, he deals with the outsider in the form of a female European immigrant, the enlightenment gained in the dénouement, as Una Chaudhuri has argued, is at least as much that of the male British protagonist, Neville, as the female Polish immigrant, Halina, notionally the subject of the play. Chaudhuri argues that:

> [t]he remapping accomplished by *Coming in to Land* is restricted to the consciousness of Neville; it is not shared by Halina, Waveney, Andrew or Peirce ... The remapping, after all, does not tell us – or, more importantly, challenge us to or invite us to imagine something new in the way of the politics of location. Instead it invites us to participate ritualistically – as witnesses as celebrants – in the self-discovery of the Hero. (1997: 190)

A narrative trajectory from male blindness into enlightenment, as Chaudhuri notes, marks the tradition since *Oedipus* at the inception of established Western drama. The insights in all Poliakoff's plays, however, are not always afforded only to male protagonists in this way – Frau Messner, Harriet, Lilian and Mary stand as counter-examples. But it may be that Poliakoff's humanism is located in a tradition of universalism and the 'brotherhood of man' which makes him less sensitive than he might be in the early twenty-first century to the relative perspectivism of plural culture. A reading from a postcolonial perspective such as Chaudhuri's, however, does not allow for the variable readings of texts aesthetically, as the 'complex seeing' which Poliakoff's various dramaturgical devices, at best, invites.

It is evident that Poliakoff can be professionally contrary and resistant to the temper of the times. In the early 1970s, he resisted the strong energy to work outside established theatre buildings in an overtly political theatre. He espoused a Frankfurt School critique of popular culture at precisely the time when cultural studies was asserting its value. He resisted writing collaboratively in his early theatre career. Subsequently, in the medium of contemporary television, where even 'names' such as Paul Abbott work in teams, Poliakoff has again stood, and spoken against, the practice. In his strategy of 'slow television', he has resisted the current tendency to a fast-pace, high-energy drama. These resistances might be constructed – as I have done in respect of *Shooting the Past* – as counter-cultural strategies. Such stances have, however, led some people to read Poliakoff as reactionary, conservative even, but, like his character Oswald in *StP*, Poliakoff is a modern man acutely aware of contemporary developments, particularly in media technologies. In a media-saturated world, he is tuned in to the need to make his work visible through the various publicity channels such that he is now habitually introduced as 'the award-winning Stephen Poliakoff'.

On a professional level, Poliakoff may not be easy to work with. He is an individualist, proud that his work is self-generated, and an obsessive, driven by his ambition to do great work. In an industry based in collaborative practices, his insistence upon having overall creative control can be very demanding of others in his intense energy, not only to create the piece, but to assist in publicity on its completion.[3] At worst, he may appear arrogant. But, many of Britain's major actors, and other production personnel, have not only opted to work with him but, in many instances, have returned to repeat the experience. Indeed, partly because his process typically affords them an unusual amount of rehearsal time, actors have relished the opportunity to work on a Poliakoff project.[4] Directors (Ron Daniels, Charles Sturridge), composers (Adrian Johnston), cinematographers (Witold Stok, Danny Cohen), editors (Clare Douglas), have sustained productive working relationships with Poliakoff over several projects. It would seem that professional colleagues tolerate Poliakoff's idiosyncrasies out of respect for what he achieves, and what he leads them to achieve. Moreover, personally, he is often boyishly genial.

The crunch question about Poliakoff, then, is: 'Does the quality of the work achieved pale all other considerations into insignificance?' My answer would be resoundingly affirmative, notwithstanding some fair comment in the points above. To turn to the positives, in the best pieces as I have reviewed them in this book, his mature dramaturgy extends the notion of variable perspectives to create 'complex seeing' (*Remember This*) into a 'complex seeing-feeling' (*Perfect Strangers*), using character and camera as participant observer. By locating memorable individuals in layered narratives, he sets 'agency in structure'. Above all, his work affords an aesthetic experience unlike any other, certainly in the medium of television.

In respect of political impact, Poliakoff's move into television might be embraced by Griffiths's concept of 'strategic penetration' which accepts some compromises in order to reach a broad audience. The idea is that socialist playwrights should negotiate the requirements of working in institutions motivated by commercial profit in order to reach a much larger audience than even a long run in the theatre could secure.[5] Not only has Poliakoff achieved 'penetration' by sustaining high visibility in television, he has made an impact on the institution itself. Poliakoff typically writes 'human condition' rather than 'state of the nation' pieces. His critique of unhappy socio-political circumstances is refracted through his disposition to humanism, as evident in the later television, rather than in more radical political analysis. Taking the long view, consonant with Poliakoff's historian perspective, it may even be that to have asserted human concerns, to have chipped away over decades against the sedimentation of the instrumental forces of monetarism and individual consumerism which dominated the 1980s, 1990s and noughties, Poliakoff's political drama strategy is as effective in promoting resistance as any other.[6]

Where many of the more overtly political writers among his contemporaries have, for good or ill, become marginalised, he has flourished in 'a second starburst'.[7] There is scarcely another dramatist of Poliakoff's generation who has consistently sustained an output averaging roughly a major piece each year in prestigious venues from the NT and RSC to the BBC and Channel 4. Moreover, the range of media in which Poliakoff has achieved success marks him as exceptional.[8] Though there have been some relative failures (*The Summer Party*, *Food of Love*, *The Tribe*), the standard of work generally has been consistently high and, in some instances, exceptional.

Though not wishing to denigrate the theatre and feature film work, in my judgement it is the recent television work that marks the pinnacle of Poliakoff's achievement since all his talents came together to seize the moment of 'high-end' contemporary TV drama. The work has been recognised as 'event drama' in this context,[9] but it makes a particular contribution to the medium by offering an alternative approach to the dominant American model, refashioning the idea of the 'authored television drama', not simply reviving a lost tradition. This is an extraordinary achievement, particularly for a single, and singular, individual. Proposing that he is 'TV's foremost writer', Gerard Gilbert suggests that Poliakoff has 'inherited Dennis Potter's crown'.[10] Though the work of the two dramatists is different, the justice of the comparison is clear in so far as both men have something of a fractious relationship with the television medium but ultimately undermine their predictions about the inexorable diminution of its drama output by producing extraordinary work of a singular character. The comparison rests otherwise in the idea of a distinctive vision and thus, in drawing to a conclusion, I propose briefly to revisit the Poliakovian.

In Chapter 3, I sketched a number of characteristics, the evidence for which is traced throughout the book. In respect of cultural trends, Poliakoff ambitiously aims in *Friends and Crocodiles* to chart decades of modern British history where, in the earliest plays, he restricts himself to the 'feel' of various cultural moments of the early 1970s. Amid an array of fascinating characters, there are iterated types: the quirky strong women recounted, and men of individual – and frequently thwarted – ambition. Those recalling Poliakoff's grandfather and father include: Nikolai Pesiakoff, Bill Galpin, Paul Reisner, and – the female exception who proves the rule – Lizzie. A specific interest in the impact of new technologies is manifest in repeated observations in the dialogue of the plays and usage of gramophones, telephones, mobile phones, computers and video projection in works as diverse as *Breaking the Silence, Coming in to Land, Remember This* and *Shooting the Past*.

In respect of themes and tropes, as Sarah Cardwell has observed, 'the use of repetition, patterning and rhythm is characteristically present in Stephen Poliakoff's dialogue . . . [and he] intensified them as his work developed' (2005b: 68, n. 11). Repeated visual tropes include a range of landmark buildings and the concealed corners and subterranean tunnels of London's dark under-belly. As a sub-set of the London environment, red buses feature, either directly in the plot (*Friends and Crocodiles*), as an occasional means of transport (*Perfect Strangers*, *She's Been Away*), as metonymic signifier (*Hitting Town*), or simply as a technical 'wipe' (*Joe's Palace*). Summer days, parties and picnics afford scenarios in many pieces and travel by bus and train is a feature. It is interesting that Poliakoff himself enjoys bus and train travel for the dynamic of the moving image observed through the window.

The overview of Poliakoff's *oeuvre* confirms also his strong interest in European (especially Jewish) history, with a felt sense of how the past informs, even haunts, the present. Again, the thread weaves through more works than might be listed but is a particular feature of *Century* and the more recent 'film' works, *Shooting the Past*, *Perfect Strangers*, *Joe's Palace* and *Glorious 39*. The perspective of 'the outsider' indeed its use not only as a principle of dramatic composition but as a critical strategy – is manifest in pieces ranging from *Shout Across the River*, *Stronger than the Sun* and *Coming in to Land* through to Johnnie's point of view in *The Lost Prince*. The treatment of family stories becomes very evident in respect of kinship ties in *Perfect Strangers*, but is manifest also in the 'work family' in the library of *Shooting the Past* and elsewhere. Familial relationships, particularly those between fathers and sons or daughters, resonate from *Shout Across the River* through *Breaking the Silence* to *Playing with Trains* and on to *Perfect Strangers* and *Gideon's Daughter*.

Whether this makes Stephen Poliakoff a rare 'auteur' depends upon the conception of that term. There are undoubtedly distinctive tropes, evident through repetition in his work, which reflect his experience, his preoccupations and, to some extent, his personality (tunnels, corridors, cages; hot summer days, parties and picnics; Routemaster buses and cats). But the work is very diverse and these preoccupations alone may not suffice. In a weak sense of the term, Poliakoff qualifies, particularly in respect of his post-1998 television work, since a Poliakovian piece might be identified from a glance at the screen in respect of the characteristics noted above. If, however, a stricter sense of 'auteur' as more typically used in film studies is at issue, it is a matter of the detailed patterning and layering of images in visual storytelling in such a way that repeated tropes are identifiable both within individual works and across the range of work. As my analysis suggests, I find *Perfect Strangers* and *The Lost Prince* to be contenders on the level of internal patterning, and a range of tropes might be identified across the 'film' work: large-scale banquets are covered by 'staging in depth'; long-shots and cameras travelling down tunnels of various construction figure; staircases are frequently shot from both low and high angles; characters are framed in doorways and in other geometries.

Ultimately, however, such an approach begins to ascribe 'authorship' to the writer-director when this book, while celebrating Poliakoff's distinction, has been at pains to set agency in structure, including acknowledging the input of others to the work. Many other people – producers, cinematographers, designers, music composers, and, of course, actors – have contributed to what is inexorably a collaborative process of production. Though Poliakoff strives hard to get his vision on the stage or screen, he remains dependent on the professional and creative contributions of others to achieve his ends.

In sum, Stephen Poliakoff's achievement over a forty-year career is remarkable and distinctive. The best work in each of the media of stage and screen, as awards attest, is of a very high order. I coin the term 'Poliakovian' to mark his distinction in theatre, film and television in respect of characteristics recognised through their resurfacing and reworking across a prolific and diverse output. I look forward to future feature films and to his planned return to theatre after a decade's absence, with his new play *My City* scheduled for the Almeida in September 2011. But most of all, I hope the various pressures on contemporary British television production will not close down the space for distinctive drama work which, almost single-handedly, Stephen Poliakoff prised open in the late 1990s and early noughties.[11]

APPENDIX A
THE WORKS OF STEPHEN POLIAKOFF

Granny, 1969 (unpublished)

Bambi Ramm, 1970, London (unpublished)

A Day with My Sister, 1971, Edinburgh Traverse (unpublished)

[*Lay-by*, with Hare *et al.*, 1971, Edinburgh Traverse]

Pretty Boy, 1972, Royal Court Theatre, London (unpublished)

Berlin Days, 1973, Little Theatre, London (unpublished)

Clever Soldiers, 1974, Hampstead Theatre Club, London

Sad Beat Up, 1974, Little Theatre, London (unpublished)

The Carnation Gang, 1974, Bush Theatre, London (unpublished)

Hitting Town, 1975, Bush Theatre, London

Hitting Town, 1976 (TV adaptation) Thames Television for ITV, tx 27/4/1976

Heroes, 1975, Royal Court Theatre, London (unpublished)

City Sugar, 1975, Bush Theatre, London (1976, revived Comedy Theatre, London)

City Sugar, 1978 (TV adaptation) Scottish TV and Film Enterprises for ITV, tx 6/8/1978

Strawberry Fields, 1977, Cottesloe Theatre, NT, London

Stronger than the Sun, 1977, BBC (dir. Michael Apted)

Shout Across the River, 1978 (Donmar) Warehouse, London

American Days, 1979, ICA, London

Bloody Kids, 1979 (dir. Stephen Frears, Black Lion Films)

The Summer Party, 1980, Crucible Theatre, Sheffield

Caught on a Train, 1980, BBC (dir. Peter Duffell)

Favourite Nights, 1981, Lyric Theatre, London

Soft Targets, 1982, BBC 'Play for Today', 1970–1984 (dir. Charles Sturridge)

Runners, 1983, first feature film (dir. Charles Sturridge, Goldcrest Films with Hanstoll Enterprises)

Breaking the Silence, 1984, Pit Theatre, RSC Barbican, London (transferred to Mermaid Theatre)

Coming in to Land, 1987, Lyttelton Theatre, NT

Hidden City, 1988 (feature film, dir. Poliakoff, Film4 Productions for Channel 4)

Playing with Trains, 1989, Pit Theatre, RSC Barbican, London

She's Been Away, 1989, BBC (dir. Peter Hall)

Close My Eyes, 1991(feature film, dir. Poliakoff, Beambright with FilmFour International)

Sienna Red, 1992, Liverpool Playhouse (then touring)

Century, 1994, BBC (feature film, dir. Poliakoff, BBC, Beambright Productions)

Blinded by the Sun, 1996, Cottesloe Theatre, NT, London

Sweet Panic, 1996, Hampstead Theatre, London (revived Duke of York's Theatre, 2003)

Food of Love, 1997 (feature film, dir. Poliakoff, MP Productions with FilmFour International for Channel 4)

The Tribe, 1998 (feature film, dir. Poliakoff, BBC Films, Screen Two)

Talk of the City, 1998, Swan Theatre, RSC, Stratford (and Young Vic, 1999)

Shooting the Past, 1999, BBC (dir. Poliakoff)

Remember This, 1999, Lyttelton, NT, London

Perfect Strangers, 2001, BBC (dir. Poliakoff)

The Lost Prince, 2003, BBC1 (dir. Poliakoff)

Friends and Crocodiles, 2006, BBC (dir. Poliakoff)

Gideon's Daughter, 2006 (dir. Poliakoff)

Joe's Palace, 2007, BBC (dir. Poliakoff)

Capturing Mary, 2007 BBC (dir. Poliakoff)

A Real Summer, 2007 BBC (dir. Poliakoff)

Glorious 39, 2009 (feature film, dir. Poliakoff, UK Film Council, talkback thames, Magic Light Pictures, BBC Films)

APPENDIX B
THEATRE PLAYS – VENUES AND CASTS OF FIRST PRODUCTIONS

Clever Soldiers Hampstead Theatre Club, November 1974, dir. Vivian Matalon
Cast:

Teddy	Simon Ward
David	Michael Byrne
Harold	Michael Feast
Sarah	Sheila Ruskin
Fag	Sean Bury
Private One	Bruce Bould
Private Two	Duncan Preston
Arnold	Roger Davenport

Hitting Town Bush Theatre, London, April 1975, dir. Tim Flywell
Cast:

Clare	Judy Monahan
Ralph	James Aubrey
Nicola	Lynne Miller

City Sugar Bush Theatre, London, 9 October, 1975, dir. Hugh Thomas
Cast:

Leonard Brazil	John Shrapnel
Rex	Leon Vitali
Nicola Davies	Lynne Miller
Susan	Natasha Pyne
Big John	James Beattie
Jane	Hilary Gasson

Strawberry Fields Cottesloe, NT, March 1977, dir. Michael Apted
Cast:

Kevin	Stephen Rea
Charlotte	Jane Asher
Nick	Kenneth Cranham
Mrs Roberts	Ann Leon
Taylor	Frederick Warder

Cleaner	Maya Kemp
Kid	Peter Hugo

Shout Across the River RSC (Donmar) Warehouse Theatre, London, 21 September 1978, dir. Bill Alexander
Cast:

Mrs Forsythe	Lynn Farleigh
Christine	Gwyneth Strong
Martin	Andrew Paul
Lawson	Nigel Terry
Mike	David Threlfall

American Days ICA, 12 June 1979, dir. John Chapman and Tim Fywell
Cast:

Tallulah	Toyah Willcox
Gary	Phil Daniels
Lorraine	Caroline Embling
Ian	Jack Elliot
Sherman	Antony Sher
Murray	Mel Smith

The Summer Party Sheffield Crucible, 12 March 1980, dir. Peter James
Cast:

Kramer	Brian Cox
Caroline	Patti Love
Louise	Hayley Mills
Nigel	Alan Rickman
Ken	Peter Schofield
John	Roger Lloyd-Pack
Stephen	Mark Drewry
David	Dexter Fletcher
Kid	Patrick Murray

Favourite Nights Lyric Theatre, Hammersmith, 2 November 1981, dir. Peter James
Cast:

Catherine	Susan Tracy
Langer	Pete Postlethwaite
Sarah	Gwyneth Strong
Mr Michaels	Martin Friend
Alan	John Duttine
Girl	Marion Bailey
American	Peter Banks

Breaking the Silence RSC, Pit, Barbican Theatre, 31 October 1984, dir. Ron Daniels
Cast:

Polya	Juliet Stevenson
Master Alexander (Sasha)	Jason Lake
Eugenia Pesiakoff	Gemma Jones
Alexei Verkoff	John Kane
Nikolia Pesiakoff	Daniel Massey
Guard 1	Richard Garnett
Guard 2	Campbell Morrison

Coming in to Land National Theatre London, 18 December 1987, dir. Peter Hall
Cast:

Halina	Maggie Smith
Neville	Anthony Andrews
Andrew	Andrew C. Wadsworth
Peirce	Tim Pigott-Smith
Booth	Michael Carter
Waveney	Ella Wilder
Turkish woman	Nezahat Hasan

Playing with Trains RSC, 29 November 1989, dir. Ron Daniels
Cast:

Bill Galpin	Michael Pennington
Roxanna Galpin	Lesley Sharp
Danny Galpin	Simon Russell Beale
Gant	Ralph Fiennes
Frances	Lesley Dunlop
Mick	Mark Lewis Jones
QC	William Chubb
Judge}	
Vernon Boyce}	Robert Demeger

Sienna Red Liverpool Playhouse, 15 April 1992, dir. Bill Kenwright
Cast:

Harry	Martin Shaw
Cecelia	Francesca Annis
Anatasia	Robin Weaver
Drew	Struan Rodger
Reeder	David Ryall
Leo	Colin Tierney
Kathy	Polly Kemp
Martinson	William Abney

Blinded by the Sun Cottesloe, NT, 28 August 1996, dir. Ron Daniels
Cast:

Al	Douglas Hodge
Elinor	Frances de la Tour
Christopher	Duncan Bell
Joanna	Indra Ové
Professor	Graham Crowden
Ghislane	Orla Brady
Barbara	Hermione Norris
Charlie	Walter Sparrow

Sweet Panic Hampstead Theatre, 1 February 1996, dir. Stephen Poliakoff
Cast:

Clare	Harriet Walter
Mrs Trevel	Saskia Reeves
Martin	Mark Tandy
Richard	Rupert Penry-Jones
Gina	Kate Issitt
Mr Boulton	Philip Bird

Talk of the City RSC, Swan Theatre, Stratford-upon-Avon, 22 April 1998, dir. Stephen Poliakoff
Cast:

Robbie	David Westhead
Daphne	Diana Kent
Milly Dews	Sian Reeves
Clive	Angus Wright
Honker	Tom Goodman-Hill
Bernard	Mark Hadfield
Arnos	John Normington

Remember This Lyttelton, NT, 8 October 1999, dir. Ron Daniels
Cast:

Rick	Stanley Townsend
Hannah	Geraldine Somerville
Margaret	Serena Evans
Victoria	Annabelle Simpson
Jimmy	Tam Williams
Sergei	Colin Hurley
Chain	James Duke
Consultant	Seymour Matthews

REFERENCES

Books and Articles

Barthes, Roland (1977) 'The Death of the Author' and 'From Work to Text', in *Image, Music, Text* (London: Fontana)

Bourdieu, Pierre (1992) 'The Aristocracy of Culture', in *Distinction*, trans. Richard Nice (London and New York: Routledge)

Brandt, George (1981) *British Television Drama* (Cambridge: Cambridge University Press)

— (1993) *British Television Drama in the 1980s* (Cambridge: Cambridge University Press)

Brenton, Howard (1975) 'Petrol Bombs Through the Proscenium Arch', *Theatre Quarterly*, Vol. 5, no. 17

Bull, John (1984) *New British Political Dramatists* (Basingstoke: Macmillan)

—— (1994) 'Poliakoff, Stephen', in Mark Hawkins-Dady (ed.), *International Dictionary of Theatre Playwrights* (London, Detroit, MI and Washington, DC: St James Press)

Butler, Robert (2001) 'Stephen Poliakoff: Obsessive Teller of Awkward Truths', *Independent*, 6 May

Caldwell, John Thornton (1995) *Televisuality* (New Jersey: Rutgers University Press)

Cardwell, Sarah (2005a) 'Style, Mood and Engagement in *Perfect Strangers*', in J. Gibbs and D. Pye (eds), *Style and Meaning in the Detailed Analysis of Film* (Manchester: Manchester University Press), pp. 179–94

—— (2005b) *Andrew Davies* (Manchester: Manchester University Press)

Carroll, Noel (2003) *Engaging the Moving Image* (New Haven, CT and London: Yale University Press)

Caughie, John (1981) *Theories of Authorship* (London: BFI/Routledge)

— (2007) *Edge of Darkness* ((London: BFI)

Chaudhuri, Una (1997) *Staging Place: The Geography of Modern Drama* (Michigan: University of Michigan Press)

Cooke, Lez (2003) *British Television Drama: A History* (London: BFI)

Craig, Sandy (1980) *Dreams and Deconstructions: Alternative Theatre in Britain* (Amber Lane: Ambergates)

Creeber, Glen (1998) *Dennis Potter: Between Two Worlds: A Critical Reassessment* (Basingstoke: Macmillan)

—— (2004) *Serial Television* (London: BFI)

Demastes, W. W. (ed.) (1996) *British Playwrights, 1956–1995: A Research and Production Sourcebook* (Westport, CT: Greenwood)

Edgar, David (1979) 'Ten Years of Political Theatre, 1968–78', *Theatre Quarterly*, Vol. 8, no. 32, pp. 25–33

Enzensberger, Hans Magnus (1988) 'Das Nullmedium oder warum alle Klagen über das Fernsehen gegenstandlos sind', *Mittelmass und Wahn* (Frankfurt am Main: Suhrkamp Verlag)

Foucault, Michel (1979) 'What is an Author?', reprinted in Paul Rabinov (ed.) (1991) *The Foucault Reader* (London: Penguin Books)

Freedland, Jonathan (2004) 'Out of the Box', 10 February, http://www.guardian.co.uk/g2/0.3604,1144522,00.html

Gardner, Lyn (1987) 'Coming of Age + An Interview with Stephen Poliakoff', *Drama* (163), pp. 19–20

Giddens, Anthony (1984) *The Constitution of Society* (Cambridge: Polity Press)

—— (1987) *Social Theory and Modern Sociology* (Cambridge: Polity Press)

Gilbert, Gerard (2006) 'Stephen Poliakoff: TV's Foremost Writer', *Independent*, 6 January, http://news.independent.co.uk/people/profiles/article336705.ece

Hayman, Ronald (1979) *British Theatre Since 1955: A Reassessment* (Oxford: Oxford University Press)

Hodges, Adrian (1982) 'Portraying Dark Visions of Today', *Screen International* (375), 25 December

Hogg, Christopher (2010) 'Reevaluating the Archive in Stephen Poliakoff's *Shooting the Past*', *Journal of British Cinema and Television*, Vol. 16, no. 3, pp. 437–51

Holdsworth, Amy (2006) '"Slow Television" and Stephen Poliakoff's *Shooting the Past*', *Journal of British Cinema and Television*, Vol. 3, no. 1, pp. 128–33

Itzin, Catherine (1982) *Stages in the Revolution: Political Theatre in Britain Since 1948* (London: Eyre Methuen)

Jacobs, Jason (2000) *The Intimate Screen: Early British Television Drama* (Oxford: Oxford University Press)

Jencks, Charles (1989) *What is Post-Modernism?* (London: Academy Editions/St Martin's Press)

Kelleher, Joe (2009) *Theatre and Politics* ((Basingstoke: Macmillan)

Kerensky, Oleg (1969) 'Review: *Granny*', *The Times*, 28 July

—— (1977) *The New British Drama: Fourteen Playwrights Since Osborne and Pinter* (London: Hamish Hamilton)

Kershaw, Baz (1999) *The Radical in Performance* (London and New York: Routledge)

Knox, Simone (2008) '"Muito boa qualidade, de facto": *Shooting the Past* e o caso das séries dramáticas de qualidade da televisão britânica na era da televisão de qualidade americana', trans. S. Tico ['"Rather Good Quality, in Fact": *Shooting the Past* and the Case of British Quality Television Drama in the Age of AQTV'], in G. Borges and V. Reia-Baptista (eds), *Discursos e Práticas de Qualidade na Televisão* (Lisboa: Livros Horizonte), pp. 271–86

MacGowan, Ken (1955) 'The Coming of Sound to Screen', *Quarterly of Film, Radio and Television*, Winter

Marlow, Janet (2006) 'Shooting the Future', *Broadcast*, 17 February, pp. 16–17

Martin, Matthew (1993) 'Stephen Poliakoff's Drama for the Post-Scientific Age', *Theatre Journal*, Vol. 45, no. 2, May, pp. 197–211

McCabe, Janet and Kim Akass (2007) *Quality TV* (London and New York: I. B. Tauris)

McGrath, John (1981) *A Good Night Out: Popular Theatre: Audience, Class and Form* (London: Methuen)

McKechnie, K. (2007) *Alan Bennett* (Manchester: Manchester University Press)

Meszaros, Beth (2005) 'Infernal Sound Cues: Aural Geographies and the Politics of Noise', *Modern Drama*, Vol. 48, no. 1, Spring, pp. 118–31

Middeke, Martin (1994) *Stephen Poliakoff: Drama und Dramaturgue in der Abstrakten Gesellschaft* (Paderborn, Munich, Vienna, Zurich: Ferdinand Schöningh)

Nelson, Robin (1977) *TV Drama in Transition* (Basingstoke: Macmillan)

—— (2006) 'Locating Poliakoff: An Auteur in Contemporary TV Drama', *Journal of British Cinema and Television*, Vol. 3, May, pp. 122–7

—— (2007) *State of Play: Contemporary 'High-End' TV Drama* (Manchester: Manchester University Press)

—— (forthcoming 2011) '"Author(is)ing Chase": Questions of Worth in Valorizing *The Sopranos*', in David Lavery, Douglas Howard and Paul Levinson (eds), *The Essential Sopranos Reader* (Lexington: University Press of Kentucky)

Patterson, Michael (2003) *Strategies of Political Theatre: Post-War British Playwrights* (Cambridge: Cambridge University Press)

Peacock, D. Keith (1984) 'The Fascination of Fascism: The Plays of Stephen Poliakoff', *Modern Drama*, Vol. 27, no. 4, pp. 494–505

Poliakoff, Alexander with Deborah Sacks (1996) *The Silver Samovar: Reminiscences of the Russian Revolution* (Nottingham: Atlantida Press)

Poliakoff, Stephen (1977) *Strawberry Fields* (London: Methuen New Theatrescripts No. 8)

—— (1984) 'Getting My Words on Screen'

—— (1986) *Coming in to Land* (London: Methuen Modern Plays)

—— (1989 [1976]) *Plays: One* (London: Methuen)

—— (1994) *Plays: 2* (London: Methuen)

—— (1996) *Blinded by the Sun* (London: Methuen Modern Plays)

—— (1997 [1989]) *Plays: 1* (reissued in a new series London: Methuen Contemporary Dramatists)

—— (1997a [1994]) *Plays: 2* (reissued in a new series London: Methuen Contemporary Dramatists)

—— (1998) *Plays: 3* (London: Methuen)

—— (1999) *Remember This* (London: Methuen)

—— (2003) *The Lost Prince* (London: Methuen)

—— (2005) *Friends and Crocodiles* and *Gideon's Daughter* (London: Methuen)

—— (2007) *Joe's Palace* and *Capturing Mary* (London: Methuen)

—— (2008) 'Ringside at the Revolution', *Guardian*, 28 May

—— (2009) *Glorious 39* (London: Methuen)

Poole, Mike and John Wyver (1984) *Powerplays: Trevor Griffiths in Television* (London: BFI)

Poster, Mark (ed.) (1989) *Jean Baudrillard: Selected Writings* (Oxford: Blackwell)

Rabey, David Ian (1986) *British and Irish Political Drama in the Twentieth Century: Implicating the Audience* (New York: St Martin's Press)

Rabinov, Paul (ed.) (1984) *The Foucault Reader* (Harmondsworth: Penguin Books)

Ritchie, Rob (1987) *The Joint Stock Book: The Making of a Theatre Collective* (London: Methuen)

Romney, Jonathan (2009) 'Review: *Glorious 39*', *Sight and Sound*, Vol. 19, no. 2, p. 57

Shepherd, Simon (2009) *The Cambridge Introduction to Modern British Theatre* (Cambridge: Cambridge University Press)

Taylor, A. J. P. (ed.) (1969) *The Communist Manifesto* (Harmondsworth: Pelican)

Wardle, Irving (1981) 'Review: *Favourite Nights*', *The Times*, 3 November

Watts, Janet (1977) 'Profile: Stephen Poliakoff', *Guardian*, 4 April

Willetts, John (1987 [1964]) *Brecht on Theatre* (London: Methuen)

Williams, Raymond (1974) *Television, Technology and Cultural Form* (London: Fontana)

—— (1980) 'Social Environment and Theatrical Environment: The Case of English Naturalism', in *Problems in Materialism and Culture* (London: Verso), pp. 125–47

—— (1981 [1968]) *Drama from Ibsen to Brecht* (Harmondsworth: Penguin Books)

Woollacott, Janet (1982) 'Messages and Meanings', in Michael Gurevitch et al. (eds), *Culture, Society and the Media* (London: Routledge)

Television Broadcasts and DVD Recordings with Special Features

Shooting the Present (BBC2, 4/12/01)

Stephen Poliakoff: A Culture Show Special (BBC2, 13/9/07)

Bloody Kids, Granada Ventures

Close My Eyes, FilmFour4 DVD

The Tribe, Tango DVD

Shooting the Past, BBC DVD

Perfect Strangers, BBC DVD

The Lost Prince, BBC DVD

Friends and Crocodiles, BBC DVD

Gideon's Daughter, BBC DVD

Joe's Palace, BBC DVD

Capturing Mary, BBC DVD

A Real Summer, BBC DVD

Glorious 39, BBC DVD

Websites

http://links97.blog.lu/archives/1049/20100329
http://www.bbc.co.uk/drama/lostprince/stephen poliakoff.sthml

http://news.independent.co.uk/people/profiles/article336705.ece
http://www.bbc.co.uk/bbcfour/audiointerviews/profilepages/poliakoffs1.shtml
http://www.screenonline.org.uk/film/id/494649/index.html
http://www.screenonline.org.uk/tv/id/523306/index.html
http://www.screenonline.org.uk/film/id/523323/index.html
http://www.screenonline.org.uk/tv/id/510865/
http://www.screenonline.org.uk/tv/id/969924/
http://www.matthew-macfadyen.co.uk/press3.htm
http://.www.bbc.co.uk/poliakoff.friendsandcrocodiles/youreviews.htm
http://www.siliconvalleyhistorical.org/home/the_bubble_bursts
http://www.britishtheatreguide.info/articles/200904.htm
http://www.guardian.co.uk/g2/0.3604,1144522,00.html
http://www.acblack.com/drama/article.aspx?id+36.
http://www.thestage.co.uk/features/feature.php/9680.
http://en.wikipedia.org/wiki/Blowup.
http://www.bfi.org.uk/sightandsound/review/267

Press Reviews and Articles (Many Unattributed)

Broadcast, 2 November 200
Broadcast, 17 February 2006
ScreenDaily.com, 15 September 2009
Daily Express, 19 August 1976
Daily Telegraph, 5 June 1972
Daily Telegraph, 20 November 1974
Guardian, 4 April 1977
Guardian, 15 March 1980
Guardian, 3 May 2001
Guardian, 27 January 2003
Guardian, 28 May 2008
Guardian, 14 November 2009
Independent, 6 May 2001
Independent, 6 January 2006
Independent, 22 March 2007
The Times, 28 July 1969
The Times, 22 September 1978
The Times, 17 March 1980
The Times, 30 December 1993
The Sunday Times, 6 July 1975
The Sunday Times, 11 November 2007

Other Journal Articles (Unattributed)

Circuit, May 1985
Plays and Players, November 1978
Screen International LFF Supplement 3, 9 November 1993
Sight and Sound, 1991, Vol. 1, no. 5
ScreenDaily.com

NOTES

Introduction

1. In line with German tradition, Martin Middeke's doctoral thesis, a substantial study of Poliakoff's early plays, was published in book form (Middeke 1994).
2. There are book-length studies, for example, of the work of David Hare, Howard Brenton, Trevor Griffiths, Alan Bennett.
3. Keith Peacock (1984: 494) remarked that 'Poliakoff has received scant critical attention and this situation has begun to change only recently with critical responses to the 1999–2009 moving image work.'
4. It does not address, other than in passing, the unpublished *Granny* (1969), *Bambi Ramm* (1970), *A Day with My Sister* (1971), *Lay-by* (1971), *Pretty Boy* (1972), *Berlin Days* (1973), *Sad Beat Up* (1974) and *The Carnation Gang* (1974). Summary accounts of these plays are accessible in Kerensky (1977: 247–57). Accounts of *Heroes* are given in Itzin (1982) and in Peacock (1984)
5. The book does not address, other than in passing, radio adaptations of Poliakoff's theatre plays.
6. There are three collections, *Stephen Poliakoff: Plays 1*, *Plays 2* and *Plays 3*, and other plays were published separately, some in the 'Methuen New Theatrescripts' series and others in the 'Methuen Modern Plays' series. Most are reasonably accessible, though some are rare and available only in major libraries such as the British Library.
7. He has observed, for example, that '[f]ilm is a much more controlled medium [whereas] in theatre it is easier to do two or three things at the same time – for something to have different levels of meaning' ('Getting My Words on Screen': 30). Poliakoff's words are taken from a transcript of a Q & A in the author's possession, for which there are no bibliographic details. It probably dates from 1984 and an event at the National Film Theatre, South Bank, London.
8. This remark is made in a documentary on Poliakoff, *Shooting the Present* (BBC2 2001, directed by Louise Turley).
9. Although questions have been raised about the extent to which early television drama was little more than theatre plays recorded with a multi-camera set-up (see Jacobs 2000), there can be little dispute about British TV drama's roots in theatre.

1 Poliakoff: A Life on Stage and Screen

1. See, for example, Janet Watts profile (*Guardian*, 4 April 1977) and Gerard Gilbert (*Independent*, 6 January 2006).
2. In an interview with Robin Nelson at the offices of Talkback Thames, Newman Street, London, 11 November 2009.
3. Respectively Barthes (1977: 143) and Rabinov, ed. (1984: 119).
4. The 'intentional fallacy' involves reading the author's intended meaning through the work as if it were fixed in the inscription producing a singular, universal reading.
5. 1977: 160. 'Filiation' implies that 'the author is reputed the father and the owner of his work', the origins and propriety of which Barthes questions.
6. The first remark is made in 'Getting My Words on Screen' (Poliakoff 1984: 30), and the second in a television documentary on Poliakoff, *Shooting the Present* (BBC2 2001).
7. The notion of 'auteurism' has a complex and contested history. It is used here initially in a weak sense to mark Poliakoff's own view of the originality of a 'writer's vision' but a stronger sense of distinctive patterning in the signature of the moving image work will subsequently be explored.
8. In the context of 'American Quality TV', writer-producers such as David Chase have recently been hailed as auteurs (see Nelson 2007 and forthcoming 2011). For a discussion of the history of the writer in British television drama, see Brandt (1981, 1993) and Cooke (2003).
9. For a seminal discussion of authorship and auteurism, see Caughie 1981.
10. Cited in Brandt (1981: 56–7).
11. Cited in Gerard Gilbert, 'Stephen Poliakoff: TV's foremost writer', *Independent*, 6 January 2006, accessed online 22 March 2007.
12. There are other 'named' television writers, some of whom have also worked in theatre and/or film – for example, Alan Bleasdale, Peter Flannery, Mike Leigh, Jimmy McGovern, Lynda LaPlante – but few, if any, have sustained an output across media over forty years.
13. Cited in *Circuit*, May 1985.
14. See Stephen Poliakoff, 'Ringside at the Revolution', *Guardian*, 28 May 2008.
15. Lenin was in favour of the telephone as part of the organisation of industry on the basis of modern, advanced technology; Trotsky, in contrast, was against new technological developments.
16. Introduction to the Methuen edition of *Joe's Palace* and *Capturing Mary* (2007: vii).
17. In 2007, *The Sunday Times* discovered and revealed this information; see http://links97.blog.lu/archives/1049/20100329.
18. Alexander Poliakoff published his memoirs, with Deborah Sacks, as *The Silver Samovar*.
19. Stephen Poliakoff interviewed by Robin Nelson, 11 August 2010.
20. All four children are Cambridge-educated. Stephen's brother, Martyn (CBE, FRS),

became Professor of Chemistry at the University of Nottingham in 1991 and also Honorary Professor of Chemistry at Moscow State University. One sister, Lucinda (aka Polly), is a medical practitioner in East Anglia and the other, Miranda, is curator of the Fulham Palace Museum, having set it up in 1992.

21. Stephen Poliakoff interviewed by Robin Nelson, 22 November 2010. Poliakoff recalls little of his maternal grandmother (who died when he was eight) and her plays, other than that one apparently featured Edith Evans. His cousin, Ivor Montagu, co-wrote the screenplay for *Scott of the Antarctic* (1948).

22. http://www.bbc.co.uk/bbcfour/audiointerviews/profilepages/poliakoffs1.shtml, 3 August 1983, accessed 26 March 2007.

23. Poliakoff had previously co-written another play 'in collaboration with a friend' (Kerensky 1977: 247).

24. Stephen's mother was ultimately much more supportive than this remark might suggest. The biographical information and quotations here are drawn from a number of sources, including several conversations between Stephen Poliakoff and Robin Nelson. A recent printed source is Gerard Gilbert's interview with Poliakoff first published 6 January 2006 and reprinted in the Independent Online, 22 March 2007, http://news.independent.co.uk/people/profiles/article336705.ece, 1–3.

25. For a further account of Poliakoff's response to Cambridge, see Kerensky (1977: 245–6).

26. Michael Rudman was director of the Edinburgh Traverse from 1970–73 before moving to the Hampstead Theatre, 1973–78, and on to the National Theatre where he was director of the Lyttelton, 1979–82 and associate until 1988. Nigel Planer is perhaps best well-known as an actor in *The Young Ones* (BBC 1982) but he is also a comedian, novelist and playwright.

27. According to Robert Butler (2001), 'At their first meeting Ramsay said that Poliakoff's script was badly photocopied and the page numbers were muddled up. Poliakoff said she must have read the wrong script. Ramsay liked his composure.'

28. The other award of £1,500 per annum went to John Morris.

29. Though a very different writer from Poliakoff, his contemporary Trevor Griffiths famously remarked that his best work *Apricots* and *Thermidor* played to a handful of people at Soho Poly while his television plays attracted an audience of millions (see Poole and Wyver 1984: 1–9).

30. First televised on ITV on 23 March 1980.

31. Charles Sturridge came to prominence through his direction for Granada television of eleven episodes of a serialisation of *Brideshead Revisited* (1981), taking over when the original director, Michael Lindsay-Hogg (five episodes) had to withdraw.

32. *Guardian*, 15 March 1980.

33. *The Times*, 17 March 1980.

34. Poliakoff's television work is typically transmitted only on the American public service channel, which has a very limited audience.

35. *Guardian*, 14 November 2009.

36. http://www.bbc.co.uk/drama/lostprince/stephen_poliakoff.sthml, accessed 22 October 2004.
37. As actor Matthew McFadyen relates, Poliakoff was accustomed to playing with and sucking biro pens until an actor suggested that drinking straws might avoid the unfortunate consequences of ink stains. Since then he has always carried straws to accommodate his nervous tic (*Shooting the Present*, documentary, BBC 2001).
38. Following Cambridge, Poliakoff returned to London, where a decade later he married Sandy Welch in 1983. They live in Hammersmith with their two children, Laura and Alexei.
39. Bauman's position as succinctly summarised in the *Guardian* (Society, 3 November 2010, p. 3) by Randeep Ramesh, but see also Giddens's notion of 'practical consciousness' (1984: 535).
40. This study makes no claim to a psychoanalytic analysis of the motives in Poliakoff's writing.

2 A Second Starburst: TV Mini-series 1999–2007

1. See Marlow (2006: 16–17). The trilogy became two, two-part mini-series with *Joe's Palace* and *Capturing Mary* the second pairing.
2. For a discussion of contemporary 'serial television', see Creeber 2004.
3. For an explication of the idea of the 'cinematic' in contemporary television, see Nelson (2007: 9–11).
4. For discussions of 'US Quality TV', see McCabe and Akass (2007).
5. For a discussion of 'Least Objectionable Programming' strategy and 'the network era', see Nelson 2007.
6. Peter Lennon, *Guardian*, 3 May 2001, http://www.matthew-macfadyen.co.uk/press3.html, accessed 31 October 2006.
7. Interview with Robin Nelson, 11 August 2010.
8. The viewing figures for the output under discussion vary between 2.5 and 8.9 million (for *The Lost Prince*). They are substantial figures in this market context and much appreciated by industry mandarins, as evident in follow-up commissions. The figures and insights are courtesy of Poliakoff in an interview with Robin Nelson, 22 November 2010.
9. Poliakoff's remark is made in an interview with Jonathan Freedland (2004) and Lindsay Duncan makes the second point in an interview for *Shooting the Present* (BBC 2001), accessed 23 January 2005.
10. Voice-over or address to camera is used, for example, in *Sex and the City* (HBO) and *Desperate Housewives* (ABC).
11. See Enzensberger (1988: 89–106) for an argument suggesting that, when postmodernism appropriates formerly critical devices, it may be necessary to cut to black to make an impact. In Poliakoff's case, slow television may be an equivalent strategy.

12. On his first encounter with American television, Raymond Williams experienced it in this manner and coined what became the seminal concept of 'flow'. See Williams 1974.

13. *Shooting the Present*, BBC 2001.

14. I am indebted in this section, particularly, to the insight of Sarah Cardwell, with whom I share a sense that television is not ontologically constrained to be a poor second to art film.

15. Barthes (1977: 163–4) distinguishes between the more everyday 'pleasure of consumption', *plaisir*, and the higher order pleasure of '*jouissance*'.

16. For an account of Poliakoff's findings, see 2003: vii–viii.

17. As a means of sustaining audience for long-form dramas when research suggests audiences fall away if viewers miss an episode, the two-part drama shown on consecutive nights, established by Lynda LaPlante's *Trial and Retribution*, has become favoured for appropriately intense narratives.

18. Online audience responses accredited respectively to Joao Paulo N. Cota, Mitcham and Lee Galeozzi, Merthyr Tydfil, http://.www.bbc.co.uk/poliakoff.friendsandcrocodiles/youreviews.html, accessed 19 February 2007, p. 2

19. For an account of the timeline of the dot.com boom and bust, see http://www.siliconvalleyhistorical.org/home/the_bubble_bursts, accessed 23 October 2010.

20. See Rachel Alborn of Darlington, http://.www.bbc.co.uk/poliakoff.friendsandcrocodiles/youreviews.html, accessed 19 February 2007, p. 8.

21. Paul Worthington, Abergavenny, http://.www.bbc.co.uk/poliakoff.friendsandcrocodiles/youreviews.html, accessed 19 February 2007, p. 6.

22. In my initial visual reading, the louche lifestyle of the first main phase struck me as redolent of the 1960s (apart from the clothes and hairstyles) partly because, in other works, a summer party is Poliakoff's metaphor for the 1960s.

23. James Callaghan was previously Labour Prime Minister, 1976–79, and, after Margaret Thatcher, John Major was Prime Minister from 1990–97.

24. Mark Wellby reported that for him, 'the production did not hang together', http://.www.bbc.co.uk/poliakoff.friendsandcrocodiles/youreviews.html, accessed 19 February 2007, p. 9.

25. Amanda of Reading remarks that, 'the characters are interesting but simply not believable'; Sara Latham of Norfolk found that 'the characters were two-dimensional'; K. Williams of Surrey reported, 'I kept waiting to be engaged by any of the characters, or plot line, but was kept at arm's length throughout', http://.www.bbc.co.uk/poliakoff.friendsandcrocodiles/youreviews.html, accessed 19 February 2007, pp. 7, 6, 6, respectively.

26. http://.www.bbc.co.uk/poliakoff.friendsandcrocodiles/youreviews.html, accessed 19 February 2007, p. 8 both.

27. Simon Peacock of Dorset, http://.www.bbc.co.uk/poliakoff.friendsandcrocodiles/youreviews.html, accessed 19 February 2007, p. 3.

28. Poliakoff wrote *Gideon's Daughter* just when his own daughter, Laura, had left home for university, causing a personal wrench for him.

29. Umberto Eco has described this irony as double coding: 'I think of the postmodern attitude as that of a man who loves a very cultivated woman and knows he cannot say to her "I love you madly", because he knows (and she knows that he knows) that these words have already been written by Barbara Cartland. Still there is a solution. He can say, "As Barbara Cartland would have put it, I love you madly"' (in Jencks 1989: 16).

30. *Guardian*, 27 January 2003.

31. Simone Knox (2008) argues that Poliakoff's work justifies the British model of television production against the American.

3 Developing a Dramaturgy: Finding a Framework for Critical Review

1. British theatre history has witnessed: the eviction of medieval morality plays from the church precincts; supervision of court entertainment by the Master of the Revels under the Lord Chamberlain (1494); the closure of the theatres by the Puritans under Parliamentary Ordinance (1642–60); direct censorship by the Lord Chamberlain's office after the Restoration (1660–1968).

2. For recent discussions of politics and theatre, see Kershaw 1999 and Kelleher 2009.

3. For agit-prop theatre and a broad account of 'Stages in the Revolution', see Itzin 1982.

4. For a succinct account of Joint Stock's collective approach, see Shepherd (2009: 72–3), and for a detailed account, see Ritchie 1987.

5. At the Edinburgh Traverse, directed by Michael Rudman.

6. Hayman 1979: 93–4. For a fuller account of *Lay-by*, see Bull (1984: 39–41).

7. For a discussion of the strategies and tactics of political theatre of this kind, see McGrath 1981.

8. For a substantial account of the various companies and their different political affiliations and approaches to theatre, see Itzin 1982.

9. Acknowledged in interview with Robin Nelson, 22 November 2010.

10. In interview on 23 November 2010, Poliakoff was not consciously aware of the Frankfurt School.

11. 20 September 2004: http://www.britishtheatreguide.info/articles/200904.htm, accessed October 2010.

12. Cited in *Circuit*, May 1985.

13. Poliakoff may have drawn upon Stephen Frears's camera treatment in *Hitting Town*.

4 'Meteoric Rise' (1970s): Urban Youth on Stage and Screen

1. This term is believed to have been coined by Matthew Martin (1993).
2. See Appendix B for cast list.
3. The television adaptation in the 'Plays for Britain' anthology was transmitted by ITV (Thames) on 27 April 1976.
4. This change to a pop-singer/actor did not prove a success.
5. Scottish TV for ITV, 6 July 1978.
6. *The Times*, 22 September 1978.
7. Ibid.
8. *Daily Express*, 19 August 1976.
9. *Daily Telegraph*, 5 June 1972.
10. *Daily Telegraph*, 20 November 1974.
11. *The Sunday Times*, July 1975.
12. *Plays and Players*, November 1978.
13. See, for example, Shepherd (2009: 14–17, 36–7).
14. Janet Watts profile, *Guardian*, 4 April 1977.
15. BFI Screenonline, *Bloody Kids*, http://www.screenonline.org.uk/tv/id/510865/, accessed 11 October 2010.
16. Producer Barry Hanson confirmed, in a telephone interview with Robin Nelson (8 September 2010), that the project was led by the script, first called *Red Saturday*.
17. BFI Screenonline, op. cit.
18. *The Sweeney* (Euston Films/Thames for ITV, 1975–78), a classic television police series, is parodied in the first series of *Life on Mars* (Kudos Film & TV/BBC Wales, 2006–07).
19. BFI Screenonline, *The Tribe*, http://www.screenonline.org.uk/tv/id/969924/, accessed 12 October 2010.

5 Issue Pieces

1. Interview, *Drama*, Vol. 1, 1987, p. 19.
2. For a discussion of the move of political theatre writers from small- to large-scale, see Shepherd (2009: 14–16, 46).
3. *Strawberry Fields* was written in the exceptionally hot summer of 1976. See author's introduction (Poliakoff 1997: xiv).
4. *Easy Rider* (1969) is a cult road movie expressing late-1960s freedoms as Peter Fonda and Dennis Hopper ride motorcycles across the USA.
5. 'Strawberry Fields' is the title of a Beatle song written by John Lennon and recorded in 1966.

6. David Edgar in conversation with Robin Nelson and Richard Pinner at Birmingham Rep., 6 July 2010.

7. The Calder Hall (CH) Magnox (180MW) reactors entered service in the late 1950s with a dual purpose of producing both weapons-grade plutonium and electricity. Weapons-grade plutonium production appears to have taken place in the late 1970s following an upgrade to 240MW in the 1960s.

8. For a full account of *Edge of Darkness*, see Caughie 2007.

9. Poliakoff in an interview with Gerard Gilbert, *Independent*, 6 January 2006.

10. *Broadcast*, 2 November 2007.

11. *Sight and Sound*, Vol. 1, no. 5, p. 37.

12. Ibid.

13. Screenonline: http://www.screenonline.org.uk/film/id/494649/index.html.

14. *Screen International*, 9 November 1993, p. 5.

15. *The Times*, 30 December 1993.

16. Ethical issues in science are explored again by Poliakoff in *Blinded by the Sun* (1996).

17. Eugenics was espoused even by eminent 'progressive' intellectuals such as H. G. Wells, John Maynard Keynes and George Bernard Shaw; by American presidents, Woodrow Wilson and Theodore Roosevelt; and by medical pioneers such as Margaret Sanger and Marie Stopes.

18. Crystal Palace in Sydenham, where the second Great Exhibition was moved in 1854 from the original 1851 site in Hyde Park (and much enlarged, using twice as much glass), is one of Poliakoff's favourite London fringe sites, even though the grand edifice has long been destroyed. The site features in *The Tribe*.

19. Poliakoff has remarked that his 'grandfather was shocked to see couples necking openly in Green Park', *Screen International*, op. cit.

20. Ibid.

21. I.3 finds the protagonists in a shopping mall, for Elinor's birthday celebration. They are to experience flying through a virtual reality (VR) headset, in part to address Elinor's fear of flying. As in earlier Poliakoff plays, 'shopping-mall muzak' (1996: 21, s.d.) plays in the background of the scene accompanied by the 'sound of money pouring out of arcade machines (ibid.: 23, s.d.).

6 Quirky Strong Women

1. Richardson was nominated for BAFTA Best Actress and the Golden Globe Award for Best Actress in a Miniseries or Motion Picture Made for Television.

2. Richardson was nominated for the Satellite Award as Best Actress in a Miniseries or Television Film.

3. Since Poland is now a member of the EU and its citizens have rights to seek work in other member states under European law, the play is now dated in its details. But its concern with the question of 'landing' is relevant since immigration

remains a sensitive issue, flaring up from time to time particularly in relation to rises in unemployment. The broader political context of Cold War tensions, with hints on several occasions that Halina's fate will hang on 'world events . . . [t]he recent sudden squall of East West tensions' (1986: 5), no longer applies.

4. The business is faring very badly with no customers even in the run-up to Christmas. Picking up on a Poliakovian theme, Waveney explains the lack of custom in terms of a critique of an overblown consumer culture 'too many shops selling this stuff . . . Nine in this street alone. Soon be eating each other' (ibid.: 23).

5. Though the international sleeper train known as the Orient Express has changed its route several times in its history, the most famous Paris–Istanbul route ceased in 1977. The 'Orient Express' has become synonymous with intrigue and luxury travel,

6. As is well documented (see Poliakoff 1997: ix), Poliakoff himself suffered something of the encounter with a formidable Viennese woman central to the action of *Caught on a Train*.

7. See Screenonline, BFI, http://www.screenonline.org.uk/tv/id/523306/index.html.

8. Ibid.

9. In an interview with Poliakoff, for a 'Culture Show Special' (BBC2, 10 November 2007).

7 Histories/Memories

1. A very hot summer's day informs the tensions of *Strawberry Fields* and *A Summer Party* and, in the later film and television work, there are picnics and lavish outdoor parties in *Close My Eyes* and *Friends and Crocodiles*. In some instances the summer party image seems to resonate with the late 1960s and Woodstock, while in others, as here, it serves to intensify an atmosphere of heavy oppression. It would be less remarkable if England were noted for hot summers.

2. To anybody who knows the Poliakoffs' family story, there are numerous details, beyond the narrative of the invention of printing sound on film, referenced in *Breaking the Silence*: the image of grandfather 'looking as if he's stepped out of the last century' (48) and his love of things English (23); an inherited compulsion to achieve (27); the near starvation being relieved by a handful of dried millett (18); the Moscow apartment (23); Poliakoff's father's memories of hearing the noise of events of the revolution from the apartment as a boy (43); constantly being 'on the edge of great events' (55); the automated telephone exchange in Moscow to which grandfather contributed; the rarity of Jews achieving status in Moscow society (33); concealed diamonds (88) (all refs to the 1994 edition).

3. Introductory notes to the Methuen publication of the play (1998: xiv) which acknowledge sources and Harriet St Johnson as researcher (ibid.: xxix).

4. Poliakoff revisits this historical moment of appeasement in *Glorious 39* (see Chapter 8).

5. The fiercely moral John Reith (1889–1971) was the founder of the BBC. He was its first general manager when it was set up as the British Broadcasting Company in 1922; and he was its first director general when it became a public corporation in 1927, ultimately resigning in 1938 just before the events of *Talk of the City*.

6. See research notes (1998: xxviii) for evidence of this view among BBC executives at the time.

7. As the research notes to *Talk of the City* relate, 'the broadcast on 30 October of an adaptation of H. G. Wells's *The War of the Worlds* by Orson Welles's Mercury Theatre of the Air created panic across America' (ibid.: xiv).

8. Cover note of Methuen 1999 edition.

9. See 'Simulations and Simulacra' in Poster (1989: 166–84).

10. Set at Fulham Palace where Poliakoff's sister is curator.

11. In an interview on 23 November 2010, Poliakoff acknowledged that he wrote this subsequent to the initial playscript and performance.

12. As famously identified by Marx in the 'All that is solid melts into air' passage of *The Communist Manifesto*.

13. Joe's mother departs early in the film to live with her new partner in Spain.

14. In Hitchcock's own words, the MacGuffin is 'the device, the gimmick, if you will, or the papers the spies are after ... The only thing that really matters is that in the picture the plans, documents or secrets must seem to be of vital importance to the characters.' Hitchcock didn't invent the MacGuffin, but he made it his own, employing it time and again throughout his career such that when it is used by others it is often seen as homage (adapted from BFI Screenonline, Hitchcock and the MacGuffin).

15. See Poliakoff's Introduction (2007: viii).

16. Besides the oblique reference to his grandfather and to Poliakoff's own preference for thinking while in transit, Graham tells Joe during the cinema showing that he is watching the landscape of his father's youth evoking a starting-point for *Joe's Palace* in the drives around London Poliakoff took with his father looking at houses (see ibid.: vi).

8 Medium Boundaries: Feature Films and Films for Television

1. 'Stephen Poliakoff has always wanted to be a film director', *Screen International*, 9 November 1993, p. 5.

2. Author Profile: http://www.acblack.com/drama/article.aspx?id+36.

3. Interview with Richard Brooks, *The Stage*, 16 September 2005, see http://www.thestage.co.uk/features/feature.php/9680.

4. Poole and Wyver observe that 'the writer within the Hollywood system has traditionally been treated as little more than a technician' (1984: 123).

5. A disposition on the part of production executives in the early 1990s to produce an element of novelty only by combining aspects of different genres which had previously found success is satirised by Robert Altman in *The Player* (1992).

6. *Soft Targets* was the first play, of seventeen, in the thirteenth series: BBC1, October 1982–May 1983.

7. Sturridge's career took a big step forward when he directed the acclaimed *Brideshead Revisited* (1981) for Granada television, taking over from the original choice of Michael Lindsay-Hogg who had other commitments by the time a strike at Granada had ended.

8. See, for example, Carroll (2003: 270) for a comparative table of the allegedly distinctive features of the film and television media which, Carroll notes, are becoming increasingly blurred.

9. See Gerard Gilbert, 'Stephen Poliakoff: TV's foremost writer', *Independent*, 6 January 2006.

10. For an account of the developments of drama in British television history, see Cooke (2003).

11. For an account of early British television drama and the idea of the intimate screen, see Jacobs (2000).

12. Norman Tebbit, MP for Chingford at the time, was a senior member of Prime Minister, Margaret Thatcher's cabinet, widely regarded as a henchman implementing harsh social and economic measures.

13. Telephone interview with Robin Nelson, 7 September 2010.

14 The Lindsay family home is in Nottingham, though Tom tells Helen he hails from Stockport.

15. Stok was also to be cinematographer on *Close My Eyes* and *Century*. He had worked with Kieslowski on *Personnel* as early as 1975, subsequently building a distinguished career in Poland and the UK.

16. BFI Screenonline: http://www.screenonline.org.uk/film/id/523323/index.html.

17. *New York Times*, 19 December 1966, accessed 25 August 2010 at http://en.wikipedia.org/wiki/Blowup.

18. These underground tunnels feature also in the stage play, *Sweet Panic* and in *The Tribe*.

19. http://www.bfi.org.uk/sightandsound/review/267, accessed 22 August 2010.

20. See 2009: x–xii: 'Glorious' is Anne's nickname; the weather was exceptionally good in 1939; the summer was marked by the ball in Blenheim Palace and other grand parties.

21. *Sight & Sound* review. The Hitchcock tradition has been acknowledged by Poliakoff as an influence (2009: viii).

22. Some critics – see, for example Romney in *Sight & Sound*, 19(2) – have identified as implausible the continuation of the Tory vendetta once war had broken out. Poliakoff, here as elsewhere, is more concerned with metaphor and the broader implications of his work.

23. Kathleen, Alexander's considerably younger sister, is mother to Walter and Oliver and though she appears in the film (played by Jane Fowler), the role is not developed,

indeed it is virtually non-speaking. Thus, although the identity of Walter and Oliver in old age might be grasped, the relations between them and the women are opaque. This matters, of course, only if it attracts attention but, in a more classic realist film such as *Glorious 39* where plot and plausibility are more foregrounded, viewers may well notice such things.

24. Allen Hunter, 15 September 2009, *ScreenDaily.com*.
25. Ibid.

9 The 'Poliakovian' Reviewed

1. See A. A. Gill, 'Driven to Boredom by Stephen Poliakoff', *Sunday Times*, 11 November 2007.
2. In interview with Robin Nelson, 11 November 2009.
3. See Clive Owen, *Independent*, 19 April 1998.
4. See the commentaries on the various BBC-published DVDs where, for example, Timothy Spall and Lindsay Duncan report positively on the process.
5. For a summary account of 'strategic penetration', see Shepherd (2009: 46–7).
6. Indeed, where such companies as Red Ladder have endured, their policy has shifted away from hard left politics to more specific social issues: the ecology, for example.
7. Edward Bond, for example, is less visible nowadays, while David Edgar is perhaps better known now as a journalist than as a dramatist. Other writers such as Howard Brenton have made the 'strategic penetration' move into television.
8. The output, for example of Peter Flannery, a close contemporary with a not dissimilar disposition and career path, has been intermittent since *Our Friends in the North* (RSC 1982; BBC2 1996).
9. By Richard Brooks in *The Stage*, 16 September 2005, online at http://www.thestage. co.uk/features/feature.php/9680, accessed 26 March 2007.
10. *Independent*, 6 January 20006, accessed online at http://news.independent.co.uk/ peole/profiles/article336705.ece, accessed 22 March 2007.
11. In celebrating Poliakoff, it should not be overlooked that writers such as Jimmy McGovern, Tony Marchant, Lynda LaPlante, Paul Abbott, Russell T. Davies and Shane Meadows have all made contributions to the development of British television drama over the past decade, though none perhaps manifests a sustained and distinctive vision such as Poliakoff's.

INDEX

Note: The abbreviation SP in the index refers to Stephen Poliakoff. Page references *in italics* indicate venues and casts of first productions of plays.

Works by Stephen Poliakoff published by Methuen Drama

Plays and screenplays

Friends & Crocodiles *and* Gideon's Daughter
Glorious 39
Joe's Palace *and* Capturing Mary
The Lost Prince
Perfect Strangers
Remember This
Shooting The Past
Sienna Red
Sweet Panic
Sweet Panic *and* Blinded by the Sun
Talk of the City

Collected works

POLIAKOFF PLAYS: 1
(Clever Soldiers, Hitting Town, City Sugar, Shout Across the River,
American Days, Strawberry Fields)

POLIAKOFF PLAYS: 2
(Breaking the Silence, Playing with Trains, She's Been Away, Century)

POLIAKOFF PLAYS: 3
(Caught on a Train, Coming in to Land, Close My Eyes)

The Methuen Drama Guide to Contemporary Irish Playwrights

Edited by Martin Middeke and Peter Paul Schnierer

Includes studies of twenty-five writers whose work during the last fifty years has helped to shape and define Irish theatre:

Sebastian Barry, Dermot Bolger, Marina Carr, Anne Devlin, Emma Donoghue, Brian Friel, Marie Jones, John B. Keane, Thomas Kilroy, Hugh Leonard, Martin Lynch, Owen McCafferty, Martin McDonagh, Frank McGuinness, Tom Mac Intyre, Conor McPherson, Gary Mitchell, Tom Murphy, Donal O'Kelly, Mark O'Rowe, Stewart Parker, Christina Reid, J. Graham Reid, Billy Roche and Enda Walsh

The Methuen Drama Guide to Contemporary British Playwrights

Edited by Martin Middeke, Peter Paul Schnierer and Aleks Sierz

An authoritative guide to the work of twenty-five British playwrights who have risen to prominence since the 1980s:

Richard Bean, Gregory Burke, Jez Butterworth, Jim Cartwright, Martin Crimp, Sarah Daniels, April De Angelis, David Eldridge, Kevin Elyot, debbie tucker green, David Greig, Tanika Gupta, David Harrower, Jonathan Harvey, Terry Johnson, Sarah Kane, Kwame Kwei-Armah, Anthony Neilson, Joe Penhall, Winsome Pinnock, Mark Ravenhill, Philip Ridley, Simon Stephens, Shelagh Stephenson and Roy Williams

Decades of Modern British Playwriting
Voices, Documents, New Interpretations

Essential for students of theatre studies, this series of six decadal volumes provides a critical survey and study of the theatre produced in each decade from the 1950s to the first decade of the twenty-first century. Each volume features a critical analysis of the work of four or five key playwrights from that decade, together with an extensive commentary on the period as a whole.

Modern British Playwriting: the 50s
(T. S. Eliot, Terence Rattigan, John Osborne, Arnold Wesker)
David Pattie

Modern British Playwriting: the 60s
(John Arden, Edward Bond, Harold Pinter, Alan Ayckbourn)
Steve Nicholson

Modern British Playwriting: the 70s
(Caryl Churchill, David Edgar, Howard Brenton, David Hare)
Chris Megson

Modern British Playwriting: the 80s
(Howard Barker, Jim Cartwright, Sarah Daniels, Timberlake Wertenbaker)
Jane Milling

Modern British Playwriting: the 90s
(Philip Ridley, Anthony Neilson, Sarah Kane, Mark Ravenhill)
Aleks Sierz

Modern British Playwriting: 2000–2009
(David Greig, Simon Stephens, Tim Crouch, Roy Williams,
debbie tucker green)
Dan Rebellato

Other guides to the work of dramatists available from Methuen Drama

At the Sharp End
Uncovering the Work of Five Leading Dramatists: David Edgar,
Tim Etchells and Forced Entertainment, David Greig,
Tanika Gupta and Mark Ravenhill
Peter Billingham

Ten Ways of Thinking About Samuel Beckett:
The Falsetto of Reason
Enoch Brater

Pinter the Playwright
Martin Esslin

Dario Fo: People's Court Jester
Tony Mitchell

Edgar the Playwright
Susan Painter

The Theatre of Martin Crimp
Aleks Sierz

Rewriting the Nation: British Theatre Today
Aleks Sierz

Rage and Reason:
Women Playwrights on Playwriting
Heidi Stephenson and Natasha Langridge

A Guide to the Plays of Bertolt Brecht
Stephen Unwin

The Theatre Of Bertolt Brecht
John Willett

For a complete catalogue
of Methuen Drama titles
write to:

Methuen Drama
Bloomsbury Publishing Plc
36 Soho Square
London W1D 3QY

or you can visit our website at:

www.methuendrama.com